XSL-FO

XSL-FO

Dave Pawson

O'REILLY®

Beijing · Cambridge · Farnham · Köln · Paris · Sebastopol · Taipei · Tokyo

XSL-FO
by Dave Pawson

Editor:	Simon St.Laurent
Production Editor:	Linley Dolby
Cover Designer:	Hanna Dyer
Interior Designer:	David Futato

Printing History:

August 2002:	First Edition.

ISBN: 0-596-00355-2

[M]

To my parents, Emily and John, and Henry,
all of whom I lost in 2000.

Table of Contents

Preface

This book is an introduction to Extensible Stylesheet Language Formatting Objects (XSL-FO). The Extensible Stylesheet Language (XSL) provides a means of producing high-quality print output from your XML documents. XSL describes how to use XSL Transformations (XSLT) to generate XSL-FO documents that represent page layouts. Using XSL, you can create standard print representations of XML documents using XSL-FO to specify how information should appear on pages.

Who Should Read This Book?

This book is for people who want to create print versions of their XML documents. It provides an introduction to the XSL as specified by the World Wide Web Consortium (W3C) at *http://www.w3.org/Style/XSL*. It focuses, in particular, on the XSL-FO aspect of XSL, an XML vocabulary targeted at expressing how source content should be laid out and paginated for presentation.

This book should be useful to everyone from technical authors who have moved into stylesheet design to software developers engaged in media design to those exploring the developing XML family of standards. If you are curious about XSL-FO or want to produce print output from XML, read on. When you stop enjoying the chase, stop reading. When you reach an "Aha!" moment, smile with me. I'm not saying it's easy, but this avenue of learning can be fun. You'll be rewarded quickly by the feedback of visual output, although there are a few dead ends.

I make few assumptions about the audience other than a familiarity with basic XML and an awareness of XSLT processing. You won't enjoy this book until you can process XML with an XSLT processor. With that in mind, my recommendation for a companion volume is Mike Kay's *XSLT Programmer's Reference* (Wrox Press). It's an excellent reference book that has never failed to explain to me how to use the W3C recommendation.

The intended audience of this book is users of the recommendation, not implementors. If you want to implement the specification then the specification is your primary reading matter, though this book may be of some assistance.

What Does This Book Cover?

This book covers the same content found in the published recommendation. The focus throughout this book is to help users of XSL-FO. It is not a theoretical discourse on the recommendation, but a complement to the recommendation. I have tried to write something that bridges the gap between implementor and user, with a bias towards the user.

Motivation

A large part of my motivation for writing this book was my experience with Document Style Semantics and Specification Language (DSSSL), an SGML style language. I had approached DSSSL within weeks of learning that SGML existed and that it was supported by accessible tools. The tools were not well explained, however. My struggles with DSSSL, SGML, Scheme, and Emacs, all in one go, were very nearly too much. Very few technologies can gain support without sufficient explanatory material available to the end user. So with that in mind, and my reaction to XSL-FO similar to what I had with DSSSL, I decided to do something about it.

Organization of This Book

Chapter 1, *Planning for XSL-FO*, provides a brief explanation of what XSL-FO is good for and how it can fit into your XML print production processes.

Chapter 2, *A First Look at XSL-FO*, introduces the big picture of XSL-FO, its foundations, and its capabilities.

Chapter 3, *Pagination*, explores XSL-FO's notions of pages, page masters, and page sequences.

Chapter 4, *Areas*, explains how to define areas, which hold content within pages.

Chapter 5, *Blocks*, introduces blocks, the units of the document that fill areas, which may be split across areas and pages, and reflect document components such as paragraphs, tables, and figures.

Chapter 6, *Inline Elements*, explains the special inline formatting that may occur inside block elements.

Chapter 7, *Graphics and Color*, explores XSL-FO's facilities for presenting information using graphics and color.

Chapter 8, *Styling at the Character Level*, explores XSL-FO's text-specific capabilities.

Chapter 9, *Cross-Document Links*, examines how XSL-FO lets you create links for use with chapters, cross-references, indexes, and similar structures so you may present documents that feel complete.

Chapter 10, *Putting It All Together*, examines how all the different pieces interact and combine when XSLT and XSL-FO are used to produce formatted renderings.

Chapter 11, *Stylesheet Organization*, examines different types of stylesheets and issues of inclusion and reuse.

Appendix A, *How Do I Do That?*, provides a quick reference for common formatting tasks and the best ways to support them in XSL-FO.

Appendix B, *Finding Your Way Around the Specification*, provides you with a basic framework for reading the W3C's XSL Recommendation in detail, as it isn't exactly light reading.

Appendix C, *Today's Tools*, lists a variety of XSL-FO tools available at the time of writing.

Appendix D, *Objects, Properties, and Compliance Levels*, explains the compliance levels that XSL-FO permits processors to support. This appendix should help you determine which implementation is appropriate to your needs.

Appendix E, *Inheritance Characteristics*, provides a quick guide to which properties are inherited among formatting objects.

Appendix F, *Examples for Chapter 10*, provides a full listing of the XSLT stylesheet created in Chapter 10.

Appendix G, *Elements and Valid Properties*, helps you pick the property or trait you need for a given task.

Appendix H, *GNU Free Documentation License (GFDL)*, provides the most updated version of the license at the time of this printing.

The Glossary lists terms you'll need to use XSL-FO effectively.

What Else Do You Need?

As mentioned earlier, you'll need some level of understanding of how to obtain an XML document compliant to the XSL-FO vocabulary from an XML document. Plenty of examples are provided, but use of XSLT is necessary, because I do not believe that authoring directly in XSL-FO is either viable or especially worthwhile. I always assume your starting point is an XML instance and that the resultant XSL-FO is a temporary intermediary file that will be thrown away once the final form document is available.

Next, you'll want a processor to convert the XSL-FO into its final form, either a printed document on paper or a PDF document for web delivery. Appendix C addresses the options, covering tools available from the Web as part of the open source movement through to commercial offerings and embedded tools.

Conventions Used in This Book

The following font conventions have been used in this book:

Italic
Is used to introduce new terms, as well as for email addresses and URLs.

`Constant width`
Is used for code examples and fragments, as well as for functions and properties.

`Constant width bold`
Is used to highlight a section of code being discussed in the text.

`Constant width italic`
Is used for replaceable elements in code examples.

Theis icon indicates a tip, suggestion, or general note.

This icon indicates a warning or caution.

I have, when discussing the elements and attributes of XSL-FO, frequently omitted the namespace prefix, as it should be clear from the context. Where examples are included inline, I have attempted to keep them reasonably short. Most examples are accompanied by images taken from the final output to show their actual appearance. If your processor does not produce identical output, there are two possibilities: you've created your code slightly differently than the example or your processor is interpreting the specification differently than the one I've used. The latter case will happen until a far wider experience is fed back to the Working Group for resolution. Even then, there are places where implementations will differ and both will be correct in the strictest terms. Implementation dependencies are, for now, a fact of life.

How to Contact Us

Please address comments and questions concerning this book to the publisher:

O'Reilly & Associates, Inc.
1005 Gravenstein Highway North
Sebastopol, CA 95472
(800) 998-9938 (in the United States or Canada)
(707) 829-0515 (international/local)
(707) 829-0104 (fax)

There is a web page for this book, which lists errata, examples, or any additional information. You can access this page at:

> *http://www.oreilly.com/catalog/xslfo/*

To comment or ask technical questions about this book, send email to:

> *bookquestions@oreilly.com*

For more information about books, conferences, Resource Centers, and the O'Reilly Network, see the O'Reilly web site at:

> *http://www.oreilly.com*

Acknowledgments

First, I'd like to thank Norman Walsh (*http://nwalsh.com*) and predecessors for docbook, without whom this book would have been written in Word. For his stylesheets, now gaining even wider adoption, and his support over the last four years.

To Nikolai Grigoriev of RenderX and Arved Sandstrom of e-plicity and FOP, and Karen Lease, also a member of the FOP team, for their contributions, and also for their early support of the belief that we could write a book.

To the reviewers for their valuable contributions: Paul Grosso, Norman Walsh, Jeni Tennison, and David Eisenberg. It's far better for their input.

To Sue, my wife, for her patience and understanding when I'm on the computer instead of doing other things on my to-do list.

To my current employer, Royal National Institute of the Blind in the United Kingdom, who gave me the opportunity to get some way along the path to understanding the XML family, thank you Keith.

Last but not least to Simon and Len at O'Reilly, who made it a real treat to deal with a publisher, thank you.

CHAPTER 1

Planning for XSL-FO

XSL-FO is a terrific technology for creating paginated print versions of information contained in XML documents, but it is only one ingredient in the overall information-publishing recipe. Deciding whether XSL-FO suits your needs and choosing which XSL-FO tools to use are first steps toward implementing applications of XSL-FO.

 If you already have information stored in XML that you need to publish and an XSL-FO toolkit you're comfortable with, you might want to go on to the next chapter.

XML and Document Processing

Individuals and organizations who need print output from computer-based content have many choices. Typically, these range from basic text editors through to high-end word processors available to most, via office suites. The high end of non-specialist tools is probably a desktop publishing package available for a few hundred dollars. This stretches the capabilities of the casual user, introducing concepts not available to word processor users. Within this toolset, the quality of output is generally sufficient for a large percentage of the documents that we see. Nevertheless, these tools have several important drawbacks.

The limits appear rapidly as the importance of volume, print quality, layout options, repeatability, and document organization increases. Within each of these areas, the effort needed to attain a desired output increases as more features are sought. When these limits are reached, organizations either outsource the work to professional printers or bring skills and an appropriate toolset in-house. The deciding factors vary between documents, users, financial limitations, the frequency of need, and accurate growth forecasts.

One key aspect of this decision—perhaps a sign that XSL-FO is appropriate—is whether repeatability is an issue. When a document is produced regularly, it becomes familiar in certain ways; its look and feel become recognizable. We may not be able to say exactly what those elements are, but if the magazine, report, or manual fails to align with style expectations, it is noticed. The content changes with each new issue, but the *house style* becomes established. In some cases, the house style is dictated by simple description: "The editorial cannot be more than 200 words." "We always have Anne's piece here." This repeatability and regularity form a key to processing and begin to drive input needs.

If you regularly read a report or newspaper, you begin to know what to expect where. This is one aspect of style as it applies to document preparation.

Styles need to be flexible, however. A common example of necessary flexibility is media creep. Someone may want to add another medium. A print document is no longer adequate, and the toolset that has been good enough for a print media is suddenly required to produce a web version, a version on compact disk, or an alternative media accessible to nonprint users. This brings a critical question. Do we ask our present toolkit to produce this? Often, the answer should be no, though it may take a long time to come to this realization. Tools designed for one media show their heritage when applied to other media.

XSL-FO fits in with types of document preparation in-house. Eventually, old-fashioned preparation of documents will no longer be satisfactory and the tools being used will no longer fit the bill. There are many options for improved document preparation. Among the many options is XSL-FO.

The starting point for XSL-FO is the availability of source material marked up in XML. So one of the fundamental questions is why bother with XML? Let's consider the alternatives, making the assumption that the information will be available electronically. Data sources of interest (electronic text, either derived or originally authored) tend to reside in one of two forms: on a database or as a document derived from direct human effort. The former is just as easy to extract into XML as it is in any other format. A typical waste of effort, time, and money is to deliver information from a database in print form, then to retype it for presentation in another format.

Information sourced from a contributor is a difficult task for the system administrator because of its format. The author naturally prefers to see what she is giving, thus, the use of the What You See Is What You Get (WYSIWYG) word processor. Why should she change? What are the benefits? To answer this, I ask you to consider the costs of document preparation and manipulation. The critical costs lie in document transformation from WYSIWYG to the separation of content and style.

There is a substantial psychological barrier in any move away from direct preparation of visually styled material to the separation of content from style. This is often harder to overcome than many technical barriers. Any shift to XML-based processing at the author level will be at least as disruptive as changing between word processors, although some XML editors are emerging that appear to the user as a conventional word processor while producing XML. The business case for using XML is hard to make without case histories, few of which are openly documented. There are also tools that attempt to transform word processor formats to XML, with mixed success.

Choosing when to use XML can be difficult, but there are some rough guidelines. My organization, the Royal National Institute for the Blind, addressed this with research into the issue of multimedia production, concluding that XML is cost-beneficial for cases where more than one media is involved (statistically for greater than 1.6 media). Single-media production (just print, web, or audio) has a greater overhead when XML is used. Extrapolating from that, it may be reasonable that single-purpose documents should be produced for the target media. The only factor countering this is the lifespan of a document. For documents that may have alternate uses in the future (you define an appropriate lifespan for your use), can you risk using a proprietary format? Again, ask what is the value of the information contained within the document to your organization and if it will be used again.

Choosing Your Print Production Approach

When you create selection criteria, you should address the following questions. Is XML input available? What access do you have to expertise in any of these areas? What access do you have to other organizations that have chosen that particular path, and how well do their needs match yours? Is expertise available locally, or can you afford to import it? What are the timescales of the investment: are you expecting to use this toolset for a significant period or simply to meet a short term need? What payback period are you allowed for such an investment? If a particular toolset is used, how will it fit in with other tools and technology that you already use? Are your print processes isolated or part of a larger publishing process? Will you fully own the process, or will some elements be outsourced, for instance, initial markup or final printing? If so, are the interfaces known and understood? What transformations (if any) are required as part of this process? For any particular toolchain, is there a good match with the personnel involved? How readily will they accept the new tools and the associated training? Is training readily available?

Your particular answers to these questions are first steps toward addressing print production concerns.

Why XSL-FO?

So when is XSL-FO a good choice? What can it provide that other tools can't? The primary benefit is its place as an XML language that enables the use of the increasing number of XML tools. XSL-FO takes XML as its input, and delivers print, today most commonly in Adobe's Portable Document Format (PDF) or PostScript. Microsoft's Rich Text Format (RTF) is also being targeted as a final form, with two implementations available. In between XML input and print is an intermediate document in the fo namespace. Future implementations may indeed provide other delivery forms as an endpoint in an XML-based toolchain in today's organizations. The FO vocabulary is primarily for the implementors and, in the future, may even become an invisible stage (to the end user) as more graphical tools become available.

XSL-FO has natural allies in XSLT and XPath, which were developed with XSL-FO. These two are widely implemented and perform the content selection that is a part of the final form generation. The combined power of these is enormous and still underappreciated.

XSL-FO is often described as a document layout language. I am a little unsure if this is intended as a perceived limitation; I certainly don't see it this way. It is well recognized that there is a heavy investment of time and energy in the initial stylesheet design, which applies to both single-sheet output and to a full book-length document of many hundreds of pages. With careful design and good use of shared code, many documents can share the development costs.

My personal experience points to a number of variables that will support the selection of XSL-FO as a tool in the production process:

- The XML is valid to a well-understood schema (or DTD).
- The schema itself changes slowly (the stylesheets will need to keep up with those changes).
- Content selection criteria are known in advance.
- The document format is easily repeatable.
- Automation is desirable.
- Update frequency of the source document is known in advance.
- Validation can be performed prior to processing.
- Necessary character sets are available on selected processor, to avoid the surprise of producing output with missing glyphs.
- Human checking of the final form is not essential. Time spent reviewing final output is not adding process value. Once stable, the production process must be trusted.

There are also some warning signs to consider before using XSL-FO. These could include:

- Only well-formed data is available (no validation). To process this, the stylesheet author has to guess what might be coming.
- Original authors are not XML aware.
- Information comes from multiple sources (differing authoring environments that need further collation and transformation).
- Content structure is highly variable.
- Character sets of source material are highly variable.

I hope that these might help you review the options.

Alternatives

If not XSL-FO, then what? Direct competition is fairly limited. Document Style Semantics and Specification Language (DSSSL) falls into this category—it's an ISO standard, has a moderate following, and formats XML as well as SGML. XSL-FO in its very brief history already beats DSSSL in terms of number of implementations. Less direct competition includes TeX and LaTeX. These tools are more than capable of quality production and have a very active following and strong development. They satisfy many needs in the academic world, especially in the areas of mathematics formatting. More well known are desktop publishing packages ranging from packages under $100 through packages such as QuarkXPress, which is capable of producing high-quality color productions satisfying the most fastidious production needs. It is becoming more possible to get XML into and out of these systems, though it remains a considerable task.

Each alternative has its strengths and weaknesses. Solutions that hint at a combination usage are appearing slowly. An ideal would be automated processing for the majority, with "finishing" within such an environment by a professional. This is not yet generally feasible at the time of this writing. The professional printer will likely find something to complain about in all but the simplest XSL-FO document output. This is simply a realization that machines are not as good alone as with their users, which is hardly startling. Today's processors don't make it easy to adjust final output. While it is possible, it often requires that the stylesheet or content be adjusted to produce the desired result. It may take a period of tweaking to produce a stable final automated processing system.

Choosing Tools

Choosing XSL-FO processors is still difficult. Although work on some of the processors has been underway for years, the Recommendation only became final in December 2001 and there were substantial changes along the way. You'll want to inspect tools closely and try them out if possible.

Selection Criteria

If, for example, you already use the Epic editor and wish to produce output using XSL-FO, that could be the perfect choice. If your present processes leave you more room for choice, know which criteria must be met, should be met, and what are nice to have?

Next, ask yourself a few questions to further narrow the selection. What expertise do you have to apply? What level of support do you need from the supplier? What development options do you want, perhaps extending the formatter to account for your peculiar needs? Are you in a position to take what's given and use it within today's performance envelope? How simple are your needs?

The more straightforward your print requirements the wider your choice. Are you in a position to use one of the open source developments, adding to that formatter as your needs dictate? If you don't have the expertise in-house, might you buy it? The number of proficient stylesheet authors around the globe is unlikely to exceed the low hundreds and their availability for an in-house contract is questionable. Will remote support satisfy your needs? Can you negotiate a contract that includes updates for the initial period while the specification settles and interpretations are made public? These products are not necessarily complete yet. You will need someone capable of assessing each update.

The following sections discuss a couple of further issues to consider in detail.

Price

Price is always a primary determining factor. Whose money are you spending: your own, your employer's, or your clients'? There are currently three commercial implementations with support. These are the most complete implementations. More partial implementations are available in open source form.

In any event, the development of a formatter is not trivial. The people involved in that work have expended a tremendous amount of effort in developing those products, so freely available or paid for, please don't ever think of them as cheap products. On the other hand, this is not a market in which you necessarily get what you pay for. Assess the product in terms of its capability, not its price.

Compliance

Most products list each formatting object and property and state their compliance with the specification. Look on the product's web site for this compliance table and read it closely. When you encounter problems, go back to the compliance matrix and see if the features you need are implemented. If it is, what is it doing differently from the expected action? Is it clear where the difference is? Who is right and who is wrong?

The deep and dark corners of the specification will continue to hide surprises for both implementors and the Working Group for some time to come. Having said that, I'm still confident that XSL-FO has a bright future. Its timing is right, meeting a pressing need in many areas of commerce and publishing.

Usage

Fitting a formatter into a new or existing process is not easy. If your requirements are for an automated process with minimal operator intervention, this will limit your choice to a formatter that doesn't involve programming. If you are satisfied with a manual step carried out at less frequent intervals, with an operator manually creating the finished document, your needs meet with today's processors. All processors provide this, with some having hooks to drive the processor from a programmatic interface. Because this is a relatively new technology, it is worthwhile to check regularly that you have the most recent version, due to the rate of change of implemented features.

PassiveTeX and UFO require a TeX installation. If this is a present part of your process, you may be pulled in that direction. If not, then be warned: TeX is not a system that can be installed and forgotten. It has a very proud history, a wide following and is extremely capable. It's not for the faint hearted though. Watching a TeX installation makes a major office installation look trifling. What you gain, however, is wonderous to behold!

FOP and RenderX require a Java™ installation, available on most platforms. Antenna House is a standalone product, needing the least ancilliary support and system resources. Appendix C describes these tools in greater detail.

Platform and Performance

Make sure the formatter is comfortable on your target platform. Today's formatters are not of the instant variety. For a typical chapter length file, perhaps 10 to 100 kilobytes in size, expect single figure seconds or more to convert from an XML source to output format. This puts the technology into the borderline category for instant online delivery. With smaller files, this is reasonable, but for larger files it becomes embarrassing waiting for output. You shouldn't expect the sort of subsecond performance that you see with XSLT engines.

 Performance problems in FO formatters are a situational problem. The processing of XML source documents to final form is inadvisable for online processing. Typically a three-page document can take up to 10 seconds or more depending on content, which is perceived (rightly) as an unacceptable delay for direct download. This limitation may change as experience is gained in engine design, but is likely to remain for some time. This mandates pre-preprocessing content and web updating, which is worth some serious consideration. Error handling raises the stakes.

Future developments are likely to extend the range of the final-form output of XSL-FO processors. Likely output formats include:

- PDF (currently available)
- PostScript (currently available)
- Microsoft Rich Text Format
- PCL and/or PostScript

I hope that this list will fill out over time. For more details on particular tools currently available, see Appendix C. Remember that your situation may matter as much as the particular features of any given tool.

The Future for XSL-FO

Like all other technologies, the success or failure of XSL-FO will be determined by user uptake and demand, implementation response to that demand, and so on. A recent development that I found hopeful was the start of work on more than one implementation of XSL-FO with RTF format being the target. Because Microsoft Word is so widely in use, the availability of that specific format has potential importance in terms of numbers and interest—perhaps not in the commercial sphere, but more in the home or office environment. I have no idea what will be the make or break points in the development of XSL-FO, but the option to produce Word documents for the office environment could be one of those.

The present focus of using PDF as the deliverable format is pragmatic. PDF is one of a small number of formats that has been widely deployed, is readily available, is well known and has the capability of browser integration for web delivery. Whether future implementations will maintain that pragmatic focus, I don't know, but alternatives are not abundant. Few, if any, typesetting languages have been opened up to exploitation in this field, perhaps with the exception of TeX, with its target of electronic typesetting. Perhaps the advent of electronic paper (rewritable sheets of a plastic) will be a natural media for XSL-FO.

The need for paper-based delivery is, today, not in question. How that will be achieved in a multimedia-capable organization in a few years is still open to debate. Will XSL-FO be a preferred part of the delivery chain? What will help and hinder in making that choice? Tool availability, yes. Familiarity or access to the skills to develop the stylesheets? Yes, or maybe not. If the sort of visual tool that allows me to paint styles onto content becomes available, it should be possible to autogenerate the bulk of a stylesheet. Whether the impetus will be felt to develop such a tool depends on whether there's a market for it. One of the fascinating developments in the history of XSL is transformation. Once it became known that XSLT and XPath could produce HTML from XML, that swiftly overtook the original intention. Such a twist of fate has surprising impact. What other factors are likely to move XSL-FO into widespread use? Support networks? XSLT is extremely well supported via the Mulberrytech mailing list. One of the XML Usenet groups just about splits evenly between XML and XSLT. XSL-FO has a single, quiet list. Newsworthiness? XSL-FO is nowhere near as sexy as XML (either that or it doesn't have the support of people who are good at hyping a technology), which could influence its fate. We are unlikely to see XSL-FO streams in the mainstream conferences unless someone does some serious marketing.

Still, XSL-FO solves the problem of converting XML to print quite nicely.

CHAPTER 2

A First Look at XSL-FO

This chapter introduces the details of XSL-FO, including a look at XSL-FO markup and an explanation of how to produce print documents with XSLT and XSL-FO. You should have a basic understanding of XSL-FO processing by the end of the chapter, which will provide a foundation for learning the rest of XSL-FO.

An XSL-FO Overview

This section provides a high level view of XSL-FO and its major parts, describes the process of getting from source to finished output, and describes some of the available tools. It introduces some of the necessary concepts (which will be expanded on later) and some of the jargon.

The production process starts with an XML document that you have been given or that you have created: the source XML. You take that document and apply an XSLT transformation (using an XSLT stylesheet) to select parts or all of the document content, and it produces an output XML document that uses the XSL-FO vocabulary. Let's call this output document the XSL-FO stylesheet. The XSL-FO stylesheet formatting instructions describe how the content of the document should be laid out for presentation to the end user. The formatting engine interprets the XSL-FO stylesheet to produce formatted output, often PDF, TeX, or some other print-ready form. This formatted document is then ready for use. This end-to-end process is shown in Figure 2-1.

Making this work requires some means of creating XML documents, an XSLT processor, and an XSL-FO formatter to produce the printer ready output. This may be a command-line tool, part of an editing suite, or a graphical user interface–based tool. This formatter needs the XSL-FO document as its input and produces some form of printable output. The only other tool you will need is a printer (or similar output device) if you want paper-based output.

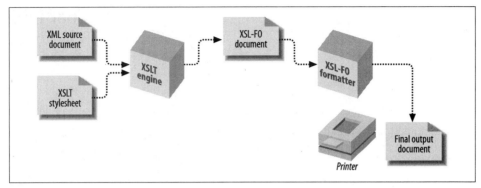

Figure 2-1. The end-to-end process

You should use XSLT to generate your XSL-FO from source documents (described later in this chapter). To do that, however, you need to have some idea of what XSL-FO documents look like, so we'll start by looking at the result XSL-FO documents.

The XSL-FO document specifies page layout, page size, any headers and footers, margins and page numbers, etc. For example, the page specifications may be for A4 pages (or U.S. letter pages) of a certain height and width. The title page may be specified separately from the main content. Other pages may need separate specification. The bulk of the content of the document is likely to have a common layout. Any appendixes may need page numbers with letter prefixes, for instance, page A1 for the first page of Appendix A. You can do all this using the page specifications.

The XSL-FO document also specifies in detail how each piece of content should be formatted, for example, titles should be big, bold, and centered. This second aspect is the bulk of the work of the XSL-FO document author.

There are also some key supplementary tasks, including generating tables of contents, lists of figures, and perhaps an index. Building these features will require a combination of XSLT processing to extract the information and XSL-FO to format it.

Page specification is a two-part task. First, pages are defined in terms of size, margins, etc. These are called `simple-page-masters`. Then they are called up in a sequence, referred to as a `page-sequence`. The sequence might tell the formatter in which order to use the title page specification, the main page specification, and the rear matter page specification. Standard XML techniques relate one to another. Example 2-1 shows a very simple page specification, first defining a `simple-page-master` and then applying it to a small `flow` of text.

Example 2-1. A basic page specification

```
    <?xml version="1.0" encoding="utf-8"?>
❶    <fo:root xmlns:fo="http://www.w3.org/1999/XSL/Format">
❷    <fo:layout-master-set>
        <fo:simple-page-master
```

Example 2-1. A basic page specification (continued)

```
          page-height="11in"
          page-width="8.5in"
❸        master-name="only">
             <fo:region-body
❹        region-name="xsl-region-body"
               margin="0.7in" />
❺           <fo:region-before
                region-name="xsl-region-before"
                extent="0.7in" />
             <fo:region-after
❻        region-name="xsl-region-after"
               extent="0.7in" />
          </fo:simple-page-master>
     </fo:layout-master-set>

❼     <fo:page-sequence master-reference="only" format="A">
          <fo:flow flow-name="xsl-region-body">
❽           <fo:block >Some base content, containing an inline warning,
                <fo:inline >Warning: </fo:inline>Do not touch blue paper,
                a fairly straightforward piece requiring emphasis
               <fo:inline font-weight="bold">TEXT</fo:inline>, and
                some instructions which  require presenting in a different
                way, such as <fo:inline font-style="italic">Now light
                the blue paper</fo:inline>.
             </fo:block>
          </fo:flow>
     </fo:page-sequence>
</fo:root>
```

❶ The document element in the fo namespace

❷ The layout master, which wraps the page specification

❸ The page specification with name only

❹ The main body area of the page

❺ The header area

❻ The footer area

❼ The page-sequence, which refers to the page specification

❽ Some content, wrapped in blocks and inlines, which will appear in the output

As you can see, this isn't quite straightforward, but once mastered, any page specification can be reused. Twenty lines of XML can specify a page that is good enough to provide quality print output. The formatted output is shown in Figure 2-2.

Some base content, containing an inline warning, Warning: Do not touch blue paper, a fairly straightforward piece requiring emphasis **TEXT**, and some instructions which require presenting in a different way, such as *Now light the blue paper*.

Figure 2-2. Resulting output

In this example, note the use of *regions*. Three are used: xsl-region-before, xsl-region-after, and xsl-region-body. You can read these as header, footer, and page content. These regions separate these areas of a page. Once you have specified what you want in the header and footer, the focus will normally be on the body area.

Areas, blocks, and inlines are the basic building blocks of a page layout. As you look at a page, you could probably draw rectangles around the page boundary, each paragraph's boundary, a figure's boundary, and so on. Each provides what is termed an area (of the page), with lesser areas nesting inside greater ones. This nesting of areas is how the formatter lays out each page in turn, following your instructions in the XSL-FO document. The contents of each area are either blocks or inlines. Blocks are formed from paragraphs, lists, titles, images, examples, tables, etc. Within a block, inlines lay out the lines of text, with attributes specifying how the inline should be formatted, for example in bold or italics. In this way, the inlines build into blocks, which are built into areas, which form the pages you produce.

If you have ever used a desktop publishing tool, you may be familiar with the term *text flowing*. Conceptually, text is poured into areas, which form the pages. The text originates from your XML source document and the formatter does the pouring for you. When an inline area is filled, the formatter seeks the next piece of content (the next paragraph perhaps). A new area is created for the next piece of content. Similar transitions occur at the block level and page level. Any block can have margins, padding around it, and color and backgrounds applied to it, but all within the framework of these areas of the page through which text and images pour, flow, and fill.

The XSL-FO element set provides the stylesheet author with the tools of her trade. From the small example given earlier, you can see a few of these tools. Each is identified by the fo prefix, which is the namespace used for XSL-FO. This tells the formatter that they are instructions to be followed. Content within such an element is used by the formatter according to those instructions.

The fo:root element wraps the entire XSL-FO document. The fo:layout-master-set element specifies the page layout the formatter will use for your document. Each is identified by fo:simple-page-master and its attribute, master-name. The element fo:page-sequence tells the formatter when to start using a particular page master, when to stop using it, and when to change to another. The element fo:flow contains your content, primarily in the body region mentioned earlier. This relates back to the ideas of text flowing into areas. It is within this element that most of your time will be spent if you are writing XSL-FO or generating it with XSLT.

You'll need to be aware of the writing mode and what is termed progression direction (block-progression-direction and inline-progression-direction). Had the specification been designed for Western use only, these would probably not be necessary. However, it is an international specification, thus, these terms are relative rather than absolute. The writing mode uses acronyms to specify the sequence of inline-progression-direction then block-progression-direction. It might be left to right, then top to bottom. I personally write lines of text across the page (inline progression), then lines continue down the page, top to bottom. This is abbreviated lr-tb (left-to-right, top-to-bottom). In this way, all combinations of directions can be specified for all languages.

The `fo:block` element performs a multitude of roles, from providing 36pt titles that are centered and bold, right down to holding the single bullet character used to visually identify a list item. Blocks build up into areas, adding to one another in the block-progression-direction. Other block-like elements include tables, lists, and images, which all act similarly.

Within a block, the `fo:inline` element specifies the formatting requirements when a line break is not needed, such as for a section of bold or italic text, or when a font change is needed.

Finally, at the atomic level, the `fo:character` element is available. Each character in this book takes up its own tiny area on the page; hence, chapters, paragraphs, and lines can all be broken down to this element when laying out a book.

When talking about blocks having a multitude of uses, it is appropriate to know just how each of these is provided by the single element. Attributes are used heavily to specify the formatting needed. In some cases, the number of attributes can make the element hard to find. How and when to use these attributes is the subject of much of the rest of this book.

Related Stylesheet Specifications

While XSL is a powerful set of formatting tools, it is far from the only option. XSL comes from a rich heritage of stylesheet development, and can be used with or in place of these technologies.

XSL and DSSSL

One of the originators of the W3C submission was James Clark, the initial editor of the W3C document. He worked on the Document Style Semantics and Specification Language (DSSSL) standard. The ISO/IEC 10179 document states that DSSSL provides the specification of document processing for two purposes:

1. The transformation language for transforming SGML documents marked up in accordance with one or more DTDs into other SGML documents marked up in accordance with other DTDs....

2. The style language, where the result is achieved by applying a set of formatting characteristics to portions of the data, and the specification is, therefore, as precise as the application requires, leaving some formatting decisions, such as line-end and column-end decisions, to the composition and layout process.

From this, it's quite clear that XSL-FO falls into the second group, that of specifying the formatting of documents. DSSSL was designed with SGML in mind, whereas XSL-FO had XML in mind. The experience of DSSSL was a key input to XSL-FO.

You may be asking the obvious by now. Why not DSSSL? Why XSL-FO? Two very clear reasons are implementation and support. DSSSL has a small following for its single open source implementation, OpenJade, produced by a group of faithfuls who took up the development of Jade when James Clark ceased its development. The one commercial implementation is from Nextsolution (*http://www.nextsolution.co.jp/English/index.html*). They recently announced the release of Version 2.0. Their initial release followed Jade in 1998.

The one key advantage DSSSL has over the XSLT/XSL-FO combination is its full programming language support, often a complaint about XSLT. The Jade implementation is based on Scheme, one of the Lisp family of languages. (While it provides all the functionality of a full programming language, Scheme is not an especially popular language with the users of XML.) Another plus on the DSSSL side is that can produce Rich Text Format (RTF) as an output, as used in Microsoft Word. The downside to DSSSL is its limited implementation. OpenJade has not added sufficiently to the original product to make it comprehensive in its capabilities. A series of limitations, combined with a steep learning curve, have deterred many people. DSSSL has very few tutorials and a specification written for implementors rather than users.

With these issues holding it back, the future for DSSSL may be viewed as restricted. I may be wrong; I like Jade, and it has an active support list of perhaps 30 to 50 regular users who are always very helpful. I just can't see its adoption by a wider audience. One quote that amused me was, "If you put the world's DSSSL experts into one room, it would still leave room for the toilet."

The lessons of DSSSL have been learned. XSL-FO uses an XML vocabulary. It has taken three years to get where it is at the time of this writing (currently, Recommendation status). It fits beautifully with XSLT and XPath. Together, these three will be complete, will have multiple implementations, will initially satisfy early adoptors, and will have the potential to meet the needs of business-to-business transactions involving human access to XML-based information, as well as to meet the needs of the publishing industry.

XSL and CSS

High-quality print output may be just one modality that integrates with others to provide the *write once, deliver anywhere* promise of XML. The print document may have several siblings: some are delivered over the Web, some are summarized in a WAP message, and others are converted to synthetic speech. This maze of information is possible to navigate using the tools that adapt XML.

Remember that XSL-FO is compatible with W3C technologies for other media. There are many similarities to the properties that form a part of Cascading Style Sheets (CSS) and XSL-FO. This is deliberatly done by the W3C. The rationale for this, when looking from the stylesheet writer's perspective, is clear. Although the syntax is different, the terms and terminology are similar. When you read the recommendation, you will see many cross-references to CSS Version 2, along with direct quotes and nominal variations from it. The advances in CSS from basic web page styling through to the complexities of Versions 2 and 3 use many of the formatting statements of DSSSL adapted for CSS. This alignment of semantics helps the stylesheet author, reduces confusion, and reduces the effort in the transition. Those used to the strengths of CSS will only have to respond to the shift in syntax when moving to XSL-FO. XSL-FO has borrowed much of the semantics of CSS Level 2, adding to it and modifying it a little, as necessary.

The variation in syntax is significant. XSL-FO uses a regular XML vocabulary, whereas CSS has its own syntax. Consider the following bit of CSS in XML:

```
<element style="font-size:12pt;font-weight:bold">content</element>
```

XSL-FO would have this as:

```
<fo:element font-size="12pt"
            font-weight="bold">content</element>
```

The similarities are clear. The shift to the syntax of XSL-FO will depend on the writer's familiarity with XML syntax. XSL-FO goes beyond CSS in many areas, adding features that are page based as opposed to screen based. One often-raised question is whether the major browser providers will ever have the capability of XSL-FO styling. This remains to be seen, although, there are some indications that client side XSL-FO styling may become a feature in browsers at some stage in the future. The specification does address screen output, so there is potential. Considering that the W3C recommendation is now published, XSL-FO has three open developments ongoing, and two commercial developments that are nearly feature complete provide some indication of its potential, even before it's widely known.

I see XSL-FO as an exciting technology, providing much-needed functionality that can connect the staid office users with the newer uses of XML. If Tim Berners-Lee is right, and the Semantic Web becomes a reality, slowly intruding more into daily life, the need for automated print production from web-based information will increase exponentially.

Using XSL-FO as Part of XSL

This section looks at the integration of XSLT and XSL-FO. The two recommendations started out as one and, rightly, have a close relationship. I make the assumption that the reader has some background in XSLT.

An XSLT transformation defines a mapping from the source document structures to XSL-FO formatting. When run, the XSLT transformation produces an XSL-FO document that is then run through a formatter. Tools can combine these two steps either overtly or behind the scenes, but it's worth understanding what happens under the hood. The advantage of this two-stage approach is that content selection can take place in the first stage. Certain parts of the source XML document may not be wanted in the final printed form. These can be ignored by this first stage. In the same way, literal content can be added by the stylesheet (to save the XML source document author having to retype a long company name, for instance), that is then output into the XSL-FO document, along with content from the source document, and that becomes a part of the final presentation.

History

XSL and XSL-FO have suffered from some naming confusion, largely because of history in the W3C. Initially, what we are calling XSL-FO was simply XSL, the Extensible Stylesheet Language. It became apparent that two-stage processing of SGML or XML into a print format was necessary. The prevailing view was that these two stages should be combined into a single W3C recommendation. This was proposed to the W3C, and XSL was born. When James Clark first released a product based on the working draft of this recommendation, its immediate use was for a slightly different purpose.

Remember I said that the transformation from XML into XSL-FO was done by XSLT? Initially, it was done by what was then called XSL. It soon became obvious that XSL had a very clear and quite large market using the transformation aspect to take one XML document through to another XML (or XHTML) format. This usage was well received, as people began using XSLT to transform XML into web-viewable HTML, XHTML, or WML (for mobile phones). Indeed, having realized that this general transformation capability was extremely useful, many people simply started to ignore the original purpose of XSL and demanded more features in this transformation area. User demand to speed up the delivery of the transformation side, at the expense of the formatting side, increased to the point where the Working Group accepted the inevitable and split out what are now XSLT and XPath from what remained XSL. (Some people still refer to XSLT as XSL.)

This is the reason we refer to what is XSL as XSL-FO; the FO appendage refers to the formatting objects, which are central to the life of XSL-FO and also are the only part of the original XSL that discriminates it from XSLT, the transformation language. fo also happens to be the most common namespace prefix used for XSL-FO. This intimate bond between the two still remains. XSLT provides the necessary tools in the first stage of transforming XML into a paper-based deliverable of selection, combination, reorganization, and so on. XSLT can generate the table of contents and all the cross links, while XSL-FO generates the page and paper-based outputs.

Before we move on, I would like to clarify, from the stylesheet author's perspective, how XSLT and XPath relate to XSL-FO.

First, let's make it clear that the stylesheet author and the source XML document author may not be the same people. As tools are produced to introduce XML into the office, generating valid XML will become easier. Styling that source document is not a task for the office administrator coming directly from Microsoft Word. I have in mind a job description that might equate to that of the analyst: taking the styling requirements of the originator and turning them into a formatting specification that results in an XSL-FO stylesheet.

In an XML document, there are many ways different users may want information content presented. Take a company report, for example. The company CEO may only want the executive summary. Others may want all the financial information stripped out. This selection and reordering is the job of the combination of XSLT and XPath. XPath provides the means to select content, XSLT, the means to transform it into the vocabulary of XSL-FO. XPath specifies the parts of the source document on which to operate; XSLT specifies how the output vocabulary will be used. It's this powerful combination that makes it easy to select all chapter titles (XPath) and specify that they be indented, with dot-leaders prepending the page-number-citation (XSLT). The formatter (a part of an XSL-FO implementation) then takes the markers placed there by the transformation and works out the actual page numbers to replace the page-number-citation object.

The stylesheet author, therefore, needs a number of skills:

- An understanding of the source XML document
- An appreciation of page layout, which used to be the domain of the print industry
- An understanding of the ways in which XPath and XSLT can be used to select and reorganize source content
- A good understanding of how to turn a layout idea into XSL-FO (which this book will provide)
- An understanding of the capabilities of the formatter that will be used
- On the less technical side, the ability to translate the needs of the person who wants the high-quality output into the desired formatting specification

Only when the final document is completed will the average recipient understand the difference between what he requested verbally and what it actually looks like. That's the diplomatic aspect of the stylesheet author's job.

Page Layout, Blocks, and Inline Content

One stylesheet design aspect I found strange at first is worth explaining before we create our first stylesheet. The three fundamental aspects of styling are understanding the functions of page layout, blocks, and inline content.

Page layout is fairly straightforward. Any page has a physical size, margins on all four sides, perhaps some header content, maybe marginalia, page numbers, etc.

Blocks are a little less obvious. A single word could be a block, as could the title of a chapter. Any area of a page (regardless of its content) that is set apart from other content may be laid out as a block. This applies to paragraphs, titles, figures, tables, captions, and many other items. XSL-FO generalizes blocks to a high degree, providing flexibility to specify how they are formatted to meet user requirements.

Within blocks we often see lines of content, usually source document content. Some items within blocks are styled using inline formatting objects. A typical example might be the page number citation that we often see at the end of a line in the table of contents. Here, a number of items are wrapped in a block, each as an inline object. The chapter title, for instance, followed by a line connecting the content to the actual page number. The page number citation itself should not be split out onto a separate line, so it is marked as an inline object and, thus, is displayed in the same line as the title. This may sound odd to the HTML author accustomed to using the br element to break lines.

The lesson here is to get used to identifying and realizing the difference between true inlines and blocks. Figure 2-3 shows an interaction between a long inline in a set of blocks. Whether to use a block formatting object or an inline formatting object is a decision made early on.

Table of Contents
```
one ............................................................................................................... 1
    one one ..................................................................................................... 1
    one two ..................................................................................................... 1
    one three .................................................................................................. 1
two ............................................................................................................... 1
    two one...................................................................................................... 1
    two two...................................................................................................... 1
    two three, with a long title to show the effect of wrapping on long lines in this mode.
    Normal layout provides a reasonable solution ............................................... 1
    two four..................................................................................................... 1
    two five...................................................................................................... 1
    two six....................................................................................................... 1
```

Figure 2-3. A table of contents example

In stylesheet design, the appearance of a formatting object is specified by setting the properties of that object. These are specified as attributes of the XML formatting object element. There are a large number of properties from which to choose, which, can be used to determine such things as the level of indentation, the spacing around an object, the color to apply to an object's content, or whether to break a flow before or after an object. By using different properties, one block produces titles, and another produces the fine print we all love to hate!

Considering Compliance Levels

The principles of compliance discuss three levels: basic, extended, and complete. These are listed fully in Appendix D and relate to each property. No formatting engine has a complete implementation. Many implement the basic level and some, the extended level. It's easier for an implementor to implement the basics, but quite hard to implement even some of the complete! Basic elements include fo:region-body, whereas extended requires fo:region-before in addition. The former is required for any output, the latter, typically for headers, is considered an extended feature. A rule of thumb is that the shorthands are often not basic level properties, but other than that, it's necessary to look up the property.

If you are using a basic property, you will be far more likely to produce a stylesheet that is portable across implementations. If you need an extended property, fine; but if you can use basic properties, it will maximize interoperability. If non-portable stylesheets become the norm, we will be doing a great disservice to the acceptance of XSL in general. Be aware of which class of properties you are using, and the implications for portability.

The terminology of XSL-FO may seem strange at first. I will describe some of the stranger terms in plain English upon first use. Many of the terms are defined in the Glossary.

Although the XSL-FO recommendation fully specifies all the elements in the fo namespace, it doesn't show their relationship to XSLT. There are two main areas in which such an understanding is necessary: first, selecting content to format in a selected page, and second, matching XML source content markup with an appropriate element and its properties in the fo namespace. I will discuss each of these in turn.

Selecting Content for Formatting

The simplest file, perhaps of use for test purposes, is shown in Example 2-2.

Example 2-2. Minimal test file

```
❶    <fo:root xmlns:fo="http://www.w3.org/1999/XSL/Format">
❷       <fo:layout-master-set>
           <fo:simple-page-master master-name="only">
              <fo:region-body
❸                           region-name="xsl-region-body"
                            margin="0.7in"  padding="6pt" />
              <fo:region-before
                             region-name="xsl-region-before"
                             extent="0.7in"  />
              <fo:region-after
                            region-name="xsl-region-after"
                            extent="0.7in" />
           </fo:simple-page-master>
        </fo:layout-master-set>
```

Example 2-2. Minimal test file (continued)

```
      <fo:page-sequence
❹                        master-reference="only">

        <fo:flow flow-name="xsl-region-body">

❺                <fo:block>Hello World</fo:block>
        </fo:flow>
      </fo:page-sequence>
    </fo:root>
```

❶ `fo:root`, the main wrapper, stating the `fo` namespace required on all XSL-FO stylesheets

❷ Page definition

❸ The main content area of the page

❹ The page specification to use for the body

❺ The actual content to be laid out

Please don't be put off by the page specification part of this example. It's not straightforward, but it's common to simply reuse these parts of a stylesheet, because (for me at least) my paper size seldom varies, and margins, headers, etc. only rarely need modification. These parts soon become reusable boilerplates with occasional minor changes.

These elements are explained more in Chapter 3, so for now it is sufficient to say that the content should be matched at the:

```
      <fo:flow flow-name="xsl-region-body">
```

element within the file.

How is this achieved using XSLT (and XPath, of course)? I'm presuming that the XSLT stylesheet is using a push model rather than the simpler pull model, so templates will be used to match content rather than simply selecting required content from a root template. The push model is rule based, where the output structure depends on the input structure and is typically used for transforming documents. The pull model, has an output structure independent of the input structure that uses the same approach as server pages. For this example, I'll take a very simple source document as shown in Example 2-3. This is no more than an outer wrapper of `doc` with `section` wrappers and simple `para` content.

Example 2-3. Source XML for the examples

```
<doc>
<section><head> Simple sectioned title </head>
<para>Some base content, containing an inline warning,
  <emphasis role="warning">Do not touch blue paper</emphasis>,
  a fairly straightforward piece requiring emphasis
  <emphasis>TEXT</emphasis>, and some instructions which
```

Example 2-3. Source XML for the examples (continued)

```
  require presenting in a different way, such as
  <instruction>Now light the blue paper</instruction>.
</para>

</section>

....

</doc>
```

The stylesheet to produce the basic outline of Example 2-3 is shown in Example 2-4.

Example 2-4. Basic stylesheet

```
      <?xml version="1.0"?>
      <xsl:stylesheet version="1.0"
❶           xmlns:xsl="http://www.w3.org/1999/XSL/Transform"
        xmlns:fo="http://www.w3.org/1999/XSL/Format">

      <xsl:output method="xml"/>
❷     <xsl:template match="/">
         <fo:root>
           <fo:layout-master-set>
           <fo:simple-page-master
             master-name="only">
             <fo:region-body
                region-name="xsl-region-body"
                margin="0.7in"
                />
             <fo:region-before
                region-name="xsl-region-before"
                extent="0.7in"
                display-align="before" />

                <fo:region-after
                region-name="xsl-region-after"
                display-align="after"
                extent="0.7in"
                />
           </fo:simple-page-master>
           </fo:layout-master-set>


           <fo:page-sequence master-reference="only">
             <fo:flow
                flow-name="xsl-region-body">
❸             <xsl:apply-templates />
             </fo:flow>
           </fo:page-sequence>

         </fo:root>
❹     </xsl:template>
      </xsl:stylesheet>
```

❶ Note the namespace usage, for both xslt and xsl-fo

❷ The root template

❸ Apply templates to the children of the document root

❹ End of the root template

This is similar to an XSLT stylesheet targeted at (X)HTML output. The root template produces the basic outline, then makes use of `apply-templates` to process the children of the root of the source document. This is no different than processing XML through to (X)HTML, where within the root template, the elements `html`, `head`, and `body` are output. So this is a simple use of XSLT to start processing a source document.

Further processing takes place within other templates, processing more source content to produce output in the `fo` namespace. Example 2-5 shows two of these templates.

Example 2-5. Other templates

```
❶    <xsl:template match="section">
❷        <fo:block  id="{generate-id}">
              <xsl:apply-templates/>
          </fo:block>
      </xsl:template>


❸    <xsl:template match="head">
          <fo:block
            font-family="Times"
            font-size="18pt"
            font-weight="bold"
            space-before="18pt"
            space-after="12pt"
            text-align="center">
              <xsl:apply-templates/>
          </fo:block>
      </xsl:template>

❹    <xsl:template match="para">
          <fo:block
            font-family="Times"
            font-size="12pt"
            space-before="12pt"
            space-after="12pt"
            text-align="justify">
              <xsl:apply-templates/>
          </fo:block>
      </xsl:template>

❺    <xsl:template match="emphasis[@role='warning']">
          <fo:inline
              color="red">Warning: </fo:inline>
              <xsl:apply-templates/>
      </xsl:template>
```

- ❶ Template for the section element
- ❷ An id that may be required for cross-referencing
- ❸ Template for a heading
- ❹ Template for a basic paragraph
- ❺ Template for a warning notice

These templates (for a section that simply outputs a wrapper with an id value, a basic block for a paragraph, and a simple inline that outputs red text) are all simple examples showing how each template must produce well-formed XML. In the fo namespace, it might mean wrapping content or further processing content using XSLT's apply-templates, in the xsl namespace. These principles provide the basis of processing XML through to print.

Matching Source to Content

Now to look at matching content with elements in the fo namespace. For any element in the source document, it's necessary to decide what processing is needed to format it to the appearance needed in the print version.

Example 2-4 shows the processing for the root template, which contains mostly literals in the fo namespace, with a single application of further processing. Other candidates for this class of processing might include boilerplate warnings and cautions where the output is content not available in the source document.

Another class of processing is the feedthrough type of element. In Example 2-5, the processing of a section could simply amount to an apply-templates instruction, to process the children of the element. The section tag might require this. Typical applications for this class of processing are wrappers for content that provide structural integrity.

Finally, there are those elements that are wrappers for actual content, such as the para and emphasis elements in the example. Here, the decision is to select an appropriate element from a limited range of either block or inline containers. This is basically restricted to one from the following list:

- Block
- Inline
- List
- Table
- Graphic

So, for example, you would use a block for paragraphs, titles, and any other elements from the source document that require the construction of separated content in the block progression direction (down the page for Western output). These will be discussed in Chapter 3. Inlines are selected—for emphasis, a font change, a change of color—where the content is laid out in the `inline-progression-direction` at right angles to the `block-progression-direction` (along the line for Western output). Lists are a subclass of the block, as are tables. Graphics can be either inlines or blocks.

With these selections made, the remaining task is to specify the appropriate property set for that element, which is what the bulk of this book discusses.

Another class of processing is put to use by the index, table of contents, or cross-document links. Here, the problem domain is cross-referencing one piece of source document with another, repetitively selecting content to format with respect to its formatted position within the printed document. This is a repeat of its counterpart in the production of (X)HTML.

For the table of contents, the basic processing model is to select the point in the output at which the table of contents is required and call an appropriate template. The basis of the processing is shown next. I'll assume this processing is done early in the document. Having output any frontmatter, and before processing further children, a call is made to a named template that produces the table of contents as shown in Example 2-6.

Example 2-6. Out-of-line processing for a table of contents

```
     <xsl:template match="/">
      <fo:root>
        <fo:page-sequence master-reference="only">
           <fo:flow flow-name="xsl-region-body">
           <!-- Produce the frontmatter here -->
❶            <xsl:call-template name="toc"/>
             <xsl:apply-templates />
             </fo:flow>
         </fo:page-sequence>

      </fo:root>
     </xsl:template>

❷    <xsl:template name="toc">
❸     <xsl:for-each select="section">
         <fo:block text-align-last="justify"><xsl:value-of
           select="head"/> <fo:leader
              leader-pattern="dots"/> <fo:page-number/>
❹       <xsl:for-each select="section">
           <fo:block text-align-last="justify"> <xsl:value-of
             select="head"/> <fo:leader
                leader-pattern="dots"/> <fo:page-number />
           </fo:block>
         </xsl:for-each>
       </fo:block>
      </xsl:for-each>
     </xsl:template>
```

❶ Produce the table of contents prior to processing the majority of the document

❷ The out-of-line processing template

❸ Process each section by formatting the head contents

❹ Recursively process each section child to an appropriate depth

A more complete example of this is shown in Chapter 9. The principle is to select content from the source document and wrap it in elements in the fo namespace. This aspect demonstrates the real strength of mixing XSLT and XSL-FO. XPath selects the appropriate content from the source document, and XSL-FO provides the cross-references within the formatted document, in this case, page references.

I hope this has given you an idea of the strengths of this combination. Remember that together, these three recommendations provide a toolset that has the strength to re-order, select, and present source content in the way that the stylesheet designer wants.

Shorthand, Short Form, and Inheritance

The word *shorthand* in XSL is reserved for the CSS-compatibility shorthands in the complete conformance level (it's described in section 7.29 of the specification, Shorthand Properties). Setting all components of a compound property by omitting the component specification is termed a *short form*; it is not a shorthand and is part of the basic conformance level. More on compound properties is discussed in Chapter 4. As an example, the background property (except for a specification of border width, color, and style for all four borders) is derived from and aligned with a similar CSS property.

By whatever name we choose to call it, a shorthand is a time-saving device for specifying more than one property with a single statement. For example, section 7.29.3 in the specification defines the single property, border. The border property is a shorthand property for setting the same width, color, and style for all four borders—top, bottom, left, and right—of a box. Section 7.29 of the specification lists them all. The visual ones are shown here:

```
background                border-bottom
background-position       border-color
border                    border-left
border-bottom             border-right
border-color              border-style
background                border-spacing
background-position       border-top
border                    border-width
```

Note that each shorthand expands to specify other related properties. Also note that it will save you typing at a potential cost of not being implemented in your customer's formatter. Shorthand properties do not inherit from the shorthand on the parent. Instead, the individual properties that the shorthand expands into may inherit. For example, border is not inherited, but border-before and border-start are.

In XSL-FO, most properties are inherited from an area to the areas that it contains. For example, if the color property says that a block's text should be red, all the text in that block and other contained blocks will be red, unless a child area overrides that color property.

XSL defines a precedence order when multiple interrelated shorthand properties, or a shorthand property and an interrelated individual property, are specified. They are processed in increasing precision (for example, border is less precise than border-top, which is less precise than border-top-color). The individual properties are always more precise than any shorthand.

In general, you should stay away from shorthands that are only in the complete conformance level, because these can always be replaced with corresponding basic properties, are mostly there just for CSS compatibility, and will not always be supported by all implementations. If portability is an issue for you, this is important.

Inheritance

Using *inheritance*, I place common properties as high up in the FO tree as possible. Specification of common properties can be made once, rather than repeated throughout the document. This promotes correctness, maintenance, and legibility of the stylesheet and of the FO. This is both good practice and a good way to avoid errors.

Some of the properties applicable to formatting objects are *inheritable*. Those properties are identified as such in the property description in the specification. The inheritable properties can be placed on any formatting object. They are propagated down the formatting object tree from parent to child. (These properties are given their initial values at the root of the result tree.) If a given inheritable property is present on a child, the value of the property is used for that child and its descendants until explicitly reset. Hence, there is always a specified value defined for every inheritable property for each formatting object.

If all properties were explicit on all elements, the description would become too verbose even by XML standards. To constrain the amount of markup, the following expedient is introduced: certain properties may take their default values from the closest ancestor in the tree where the property is specified. For example, to specify a font family for a whole document, you can put a respective attribute on the root element. Any element with no explicit font-family will pick their values from there. This is common in typography and styling, which have similar mechanisms.

To make inheritance work, you must break the coupling between properties and elements that consume them. In XSL-FO, inheritable properties can be specified almost anywhere on the tree, not necessarily on elements whose formatting is influenced by them. For instance, `leader-pattern` is inheritable: therefore, specifying it on a `fo:table` will influence any and all `fo:leaders` inside cells of that table (unless a lower element redefines it to some other value).

Inheritance breaks the standard scheme of getting default values for attributes from a DTD or schema, a property used by an element may appear on any of its ancestors. Common sense and programming style are needed to avoid confusion. A DTD for XSL-FO has been provided. Its authors admit it is not 100% accurate, but it is useful.

Later in the book, I will use inheritance occasionally to reduce the amount of typing. I will note examples when they occur.

In summary, be aware of inheritance. It can be very useful to achieve a common style; on the other hand, if you ignore inheritance, it can trip you up with unwanted effects.

Tips on Using Inheritance

It is common practice to specify inherited values on flows and block-level elements. There is also a special `fo:wrapper` element that serves as a host to inherited properties. It is neither block-level nor inline-level, we can define it as a *transparent* property carrier. Use it to specify properties on a group of consecutive elements without introducing a fake extra area.

Don't abuse inheritance. When your stylesheets become complex, it may become hard to debug. Don't neglect another mechanism to assign identical properties to many objects—for example, `xsl:use-attribute-sets` may be more appropriate than relying on inheritance.

Inherited properties are propagated down the object tree regardless of the respective area placement. This may sometimes lead to difficulties in styling your documents properly.

Out-of-lines (e.g., `fo:footnote-body` and `fo:float`) inherit properties from the content in which they occur. So, if a footnote happens to be located in an indented paragraph, it takes inherited values of all indents; if the text was red, the default color will also be red; if the text was a formula, the footnote may appear in Symbol font. Take care to explicitly predefine as many inheritable properties as possible at the top of your `fo:footnote` or `fo:float` element. There is no way in XSL-FO to assign a common set of properties to all footnotes; `xsl:use-attribute-sets` remains the only plausible alternative.

Indents are inherited universally. For instance, indents from `fo:flow` will carry to all cells in all tables, to all block and inline containers (even absolutely-positioned ones), despite the fact that these elements define a reference-area of their own that is different from the page-reference-area. In practice, this often leads to unwanted effects. When you try to adjust the position of a table by increasing its `start-indent`, the contents of each cell are shifted by the same amount inside the cell. Don't forget to reset indents to zero somewhere in the middle between fo:table and fo:table-cell; it is a good idea to add zero indents to fo:table-body, fo:table-header, and fo:table-footer.

There are more delicate things about inheritance, e.g., peculiarities of line-height behavior or font shorthand that silently resets a whole bunch of properties to their default values, which will be discussed later in their particular contexts. As a further observation, I'd also like to point out that markers take their properties from where they end up, not from where they started. These are discussed further in Chapter 9.

Before moving on, we need to understand compound datatypes. Certain property values are described in terms of compound datatypes. Every property has a datatype, which is the kind of information that it can hold, such as a color or a number. Some properties have compound datatypes, such as length or keep. The compound datatypes are represented in the XSL-FO result tree as multiple attributes. The names of these attributes consist of the property name, followed by a period, followed by the component name.

For example, a space-before property may be specified as:

```
space-before.minimum="2.0pt"
space-before.optimum="3.0pt"
space-before.maximum="4.0pt"
space-before.precedence="0"
space-before.conditionality="discard"
```

This notation may be familiar to those who have experience with object-oriented systems. It simply means that the space-before property has separate components that specify the optimum, minimum, and maximum values, and so on.

A short form of a compound value specification may be used in cases where the datatype has some length components and for the keep datatype. In the first case, the specification consists of giving a length value to an attribute with a name matching a property name. Such a specification gives that value to each of the length components and the initial value to all the non-length components.

For example:

```
space-before="4.0pt"
```

is equivalent to a specification of:

```
space-before.minimum="4.0pt"
space-before.optimum="4.0pt"
space-before.maximum="4.0pt"
space-before.precedence="0"
space-before.conditionality="discard"
```

It's a way of reducing typing (unless you want to explicitly specify limits). Note that short forms may be used together with complete forms; the complete forms have precedence over the expansion of a short form.

Compound values of properties are inherited as a unit and not as individual components. After inheritance, any complete form specification for a component is used to set its value.

Layout-Driven and Content-Driven Layout Types

The XSL 1.0 specification has a number of limitations that we will encounter throughout this book (and I will diligently strive to point them out). One of these pertains to the classes of document that are best suited for this version of XSL. It is possible to draw a fairly clean line between two primary categories of document: those that are *layout-driven* and those that are *content-driven*.

In the layout-driven case, a container searches the content flow to find matching content to put inside itself. In other words, the layout comes first. (A container is, loosely speaking, a region on a page that can accept content. Refer to Chapter 4 for more detail.) Typical documents in this category include magazines, newspapers, web pages, brochures, newsletters, catalogs, and presentations (slides and overheads). Content is often adjusted to satisfy the constraints of the layout.

In the content-driven case, the content itself identifies a model (think template), which, in turn, specifies the creation of suitable containers. As many containers (layout areas on pages) are produced as required to consume all the content of the document. Page layouts are usually relatively uncomplicated, and their selection is based on simple rules. Examples of this category of documents include books, manuals, technical documentation, articles, and documents driven by data. Content flows are sequential and unbroken. I find that XSL 1.0 is best suited for content-driven documents (page layout, blocks, and inlines).

These concepts and terms—the three main divisions of any abstract document, and the distinction between layout-driven and content-driven layout—are useful to keep in mind as we begin to discuss the highest-level structures in FO documents.

CHAPTER 3

Pagination

Practical publishing projects start with a number of constraints. Unless you are experimenting, you will already know if your XML source is targeted at a book, an article, a business form, or a newsletter. In other words, the final product will be a concrete instance of what I will informally call *document categories* or *document classes*.

Decades and centuries of usage have established publishing conventions for many document classes. Many readers who have experience with at least one desktop publishing system or formatting software application will be familiar with standard document classes. These conventions suggest rules to be followed at all levels of the formatting process. It is at the pagination level, however, where the effect of these rules is most strongly felt. This chapter discusses XSL pagination—how to design pages and how to put them together.

Document Classes

The rules and conventions that apply to a given document class will determine the presence and structure of the three major divisions of any single document: the *front matter*, the *main matter* (probably most commonly known as the body), and the *back matter*. (These terms are generally used in connection with only certain types of documents. Because the concepts have more general utility, they will be extended to all documents.) The front matter obtains its fullest form in books and typically contains most of the following: a title page, a copyright page, a preface, a table of contents, and lists of figures or other illustrations. Dedications and similar material also belong to the front matter of a document.

The main matter of a document consists of the actual content: everything from the introduction to the appendixes. The back matter may contain an index, more acknowledgments, a glossary, a bibliography, a colophon, and so forth. It is worth pointing out at this stage of the discussion (and I will repeat this point often) that these are *logical* structures. They may be present and identifiable in your source XML, but will not be the same in the FO document. Equally, items like a table of contents will not exist in the source but will be generated when transforming to the fo namespace.

Depending on the specific type of document, the front matter may be greatly abbreviated, may be missing altogether, or may be combined with the main matter. This is typical of articles and reports. Letters and business forms may have only main matter. Books have all three, and these contain nearly all of the listed sections.

The Main Parts of an XSL-FO Document

XML instances in the fo namespace, or XSL-FO stylesheets, consist of two major parts. The first part describes the general layout of all possible pages and provides instructions to the formatter regarding which page templates to use. The second part assigns the actual content of the document to the pages and describes the formatting of the content. The general *pagination* problem consists of properly and fully constructing the first part and in making the proper assignment of content *flows*. This chapter will cover all of this in detail. The formatting of content remains for subsequent chapters.

The top-level element of an FO document is the fo:root element.*

One important attribute on the fo:root element is the source-document, which has been added such that the source document may be accessed from the XSL-FO document. It's a good habit to pass this to the XSLT stylesheet as a parameter for inclusion.

The children of the fo:root element consist of:

- One layout-master-set
- An optional declarations
- One or more page-sequence

Figure 3-1 shows a very useful diagram from the XSL specification that illustrates the pagination formatting objects.

The declarations element, if used, contains one or more color-profile children. declarations are a wrapper for formatting objects whose content is to be used as a resource to the formatting process. This element groups global declarations for the FO file. See Chapter 7 for a discussion on color profiles.

The layout-master-set corresponds to the first major part of an FO file that I mentioned earlier. Its function is to fully specify the pages to be used in the document. The children of this element consist of simple-page-master elements and page-sequence-master elements. You must have at least one simple-page-master defined. It is good practice to organize your simple-page-masters and page-sequence-masters in

---

* I will adhere to the convention of using an fo: prefix to refer to elements in the FO, or *http://www.w3.org/ 1999/XSL/Format* namespace. You may use anything you like in place of fo:. For sake of simplicity, I will not generally use prefixes in the main narrative, except where necessary to avoid confusion (as when referring to the fo:flow element as a *flow*).

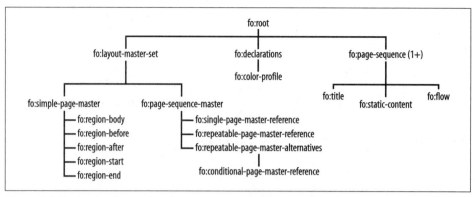

Figure 3-1. Pagination formatting objects

a way that suggests how they will be used. This will make more sense once you see some examples.

The `simple-page-master` has a `master-name` attribute by which it is referenced, and the page-sequence element has a `master-reference` attribute that refers back to one of the `simple-page-master` elements. Similarly, the page-sequence-master has a `master-name` attribute. This is how content is assigned to one or another layout within the formatting operation. The significance of the `master-name` attribute is that this is how masters are referenced by content flows.

The value of the `master-name` attribute must be unique across all the content of the `layout-master-set`. The formatter will treat an empty or conflicting `master-name` attribute as an error, and may or may not continue to process the FO file.

The `page-sequence-master` is simply a way of sequencing the use of `simple-page-master` elements as more content is added. A typical use of this element is to specify that left- and righthand page layouts (properly, verso and recto) are to be used alternately throughout the pages of a book. More on this later.

Let us make one more connection. As can be seen from Example 3-3, the selection of content for a particular type of page layout (the `simple-page-master` elements) is achieved by either the use of one or more page-sequence elements that follow the layout-master-set, or, indirectly, from references within the page-sequence-master element's repeatable-page-master-reference element (see the section "Conditional Selection of Page Masters" for more detail). Each page-sequence has a master-reference attribute, and the value of this attribute for a given page-sequence designates the `simple-page-master` or page-sequence-master that will paginate the content contained in that page-sequence. I think of this as the base relationship between *this* piece of content and *that* particular type of page, so I might want to put all chapter elements into a standard page layout, where standard is the `master-name` attribute of the `simple-page-master`. This attribute names this particular page specification, which may be one of many such specifications. This attribute uniquely identifies the associated page specification.

 The formatter will treat an empty or conflicting `master-reference` attribute as an error, and may or may not continue to process the FO file.

 There is no requirement for `master-references` to be unique across page-sequence elements. Several page-sequence elements may point at the same `simple-page-master` or page-sequence-master. (The state of page-sequence-master elements is not shared across page-sequence elements. We will see what this means when we examine the use of multiple page-sequence elements.)

Simple Page Master

XSL 1.0 specifies just one way of laying out a page: the page description. We use the `simple-page-master` element for this page description. Any discussion of page masters presupposes the concept of a page. It may seem self-evident at this point that we *do* have a page, but there is actually more to this concept in XSL than immediately meets the eye.

The CSS and XSL specifications overlap, and this is reflected in shared models at various levels. CSS originally approached pagination from the web point of view—a single unlimited canvas, effectively restricted in the horizontal, but not in the vertical, direction. XSL is heavily weighted towards *paged* media; this distinction operates primarily at the level of page master selection, not in the description of single pages. However, CSS is actively embracing paper media (in CSS2), and XSL from the start has acknowledged formats other than print—namely, HTML.

This means in XSL, we must deal with the idea of non-paged media and viewports. *Non-paged* effectively means *one* page with flexible boundaries, which is obviously not the case with print. Hence, if you are reading this on a web browser, you are effectively viewing it in a non-paged form. Viewports introduce the ideas of clipping and scrolling, again, not things we will encounter in print. Fortunately, these are XSL capabilities that may be ignored by readers interested in print; implementors are not so lucky. I will sufficiently explain viewport concepts so you will be able to read the spec without confusion.

In XSL under normal (meaning print) circumstances, we use the `page-width` and `page-height` attributes on the `simple-page-master` element. In a production context, these attributes are obvious candidates for XSL parameterization. A simple model of the page is illustrated in Figure 3-2. Note that the labeling of the outer regions supposes a left-to-right, top-to-bottom (lr-tb) writing mode.

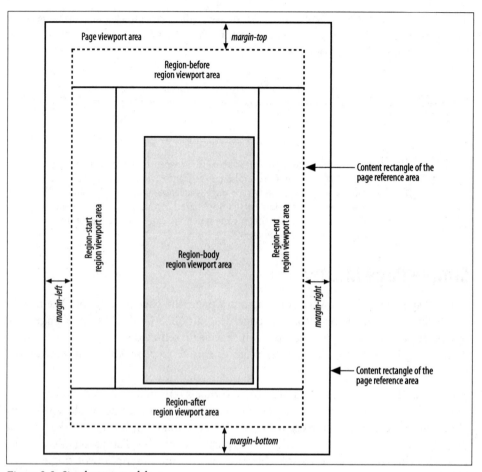

Figure 3-2. Simple page model

The page-viewport-area content rectangle is the outermost rectangle, and for any media, this represents the physical bounds of the output medium, e.g., the edges of the sheet of paper.

These might typically be set, for an A4 sheet, using:

```
<fo:simple-page-master
  master-name="simple"
  page-height="29.7cm"
  page-width="21cm"
  ...
```

For U.S. letter or other, substitute appropriate dimensions. The page-height would be "11in", and the page-width would be "8.5in".

The margin properties on the `simple-page-master` (see "Margin Properties for Blocks") determine the size and position of the page-reference-area content rectangle relative to the content rectangle of the page-viewport-area. For page-masters, there is no ambiguity about the meaning of `top`, `bottom`, `left`, or `right` when discussing the page-viewport-area edges, and therefore no ambiguity with respect to the corresponding margins (see "Country and Language").

These might be set using:

```
<fo:simple-page-master
    master-name="simple"
    page-height="29.7cm"
    page-width="21cm"
    margin-top="1cm"
    margin-bottom="2cm"
    margin-left="2.5cm"
    margin-right="2.5cm">
```

Note the `height` and `width` properties here. One simple way of obtaining a landscape page is to shift vertical and horizontal properties, providing a greater width than height.

Margin Properties for Blocks

XSL-FO defines what are called *common margin properties—block*. These are also applicable in the page context. The common margin properties consist of `margin-top`, `margin-bottom`, `margin-left`, `margin-right`, `space-before`, `space-after`, `start-indent`, and `end-indent`. Note that how these properties map on the actual page depends on the writing mode and reference orientation selected.

The value of each property may be either an absolute length or a percentage of the applicable dimension of the containing block or page.

In other words for the page-reference-area content rectangle, we have that:

1. `content-rectangle width = page-width - margin-left - margin-right`
2. `content-rectangle height = page-height - margin-top - margin-bottom`

The `page-height` is the distance from top to bottom, and the `page-width` is the distance from left to right.

Two other attributes that may be set on `simple-page-master` are `writing-mode` and `reference-orientation`. We will shortly examine their impact on the placement of regions.

 Be aware that the page-reference-area may not have borders or padding. This is an XSL 1.0 limitation.

The following is a rough description of simple-page-master and its contents:

Element
    `simple-page-master`

Purpose
    Defines the basic page master used in XSL 1.0

Properties

- Common margin properties—block
- `master-name`
- `page-height`
- `page-width`
- `reference-orientation`
- `writing-mode`

Content model
    `(region-body,region-before?,region-after?,region-start?,region-end?)`

Regions

Figure 3-2 indicates the five regions that make up any page that can be created by using simple-page-master. All four outer regions, which correspond to the header, footer, left side-bar, and right side-bar, are optional. These elements are children of the simple-page-master element. Example 3-1 provides a simple-page-master that includes all five regions.

Example 3-1. Region example

```
<fo:simple-page-master
    master-name="simple"
    page-height="29.7cm"
    page-width="21cm"
    margin-top="1cm"
    margin-bottom="2cm"
    margin-left="2.5cm"
    margin-right="2.5cm">
    <fo:region-body
        margin-top="1cm"/>
    <fo:region-before
        extent="3cm"/>
    <fo:region-after
        extent="1.5cm"/>
    <fo:region-start
        extent="2cm"/>
    <fo:region-end
        extent="2cm"/>
</fo:simple-page-master>
```

Absolute and Relative Directions

Directions and how they are specified are key concepts in XSL. They figure prominently throughout. To understand some aspects of pagination, we must begin to discuss them here.

A number of formatting objects, including simple-page-master, define so-called *reference areas*. The important characteristic of such elements is that they may have reference-orientation and writing-mode attributes. That is, they can define coordinate systems.

reference-orientation defines the top for the content-rectangle of the reference area in question, with respect to the containing reference area. Permitted values are 0, ±90, ±180, and ±270, and these specify counter-clockwise (CCW) rotations in degrees. Thus, 90 is the same as 9 o'clock, and −90 is the same as 3 o'clock. The default, or initial, value of reference-orientation is 0, so that if you do not explicitly set any other value, the top of all areas will be the same as the top of the sheet of paper, which is the normal requirement for Western usage. The only valid values are −270 , −180, −90, 0, 90, 180, and 270.

Writing Mode

A clear understanding of writing-mode is necessary both for background and to facilitate the insertion of content that does not use the default.

Loosely speaking, writing-mode specifies the progression direction of blocks (lines and paragraphs, for example) as they are laid out on a page and the progression direction of characters and words within a line. For our purposes, it is sufficient to know that we must use writing-mode to fix both progression directions; this can then be used to determine before, after, start, and end, and we can then map these relative directions to some permutation of top, bottom, left, and right. The specific permitted values for writing-mode are lr-tb (left to right, top to bottom), rl-tb, and tb-rl. The relative directions, as determined by writing-mode, are shown in Figure 3-3.

There are other possibilities for writing modes, but these are the three that can be currently specified. It should be clear that the writing-mode uniquely determines the two progression directions, one for blocks and one for inlines; and this, in turn, uniquely fixes the four relative directions.

I don't find these terms particularly intuitive and, hence, keep a small diagram in front of me that shows (for Western use) the before direction at 12 o'clock, the after direction at 6 o'clock, the end direction at 3 o'clock, and the start direction at 9 o'clock. This equates with the first diagram in Figure 3-3. If I ever change the writing-mode, all I need to do is rotate the diagram to maintain my orientation. When I want to specify a border at the left edge of my page, I translate this as being

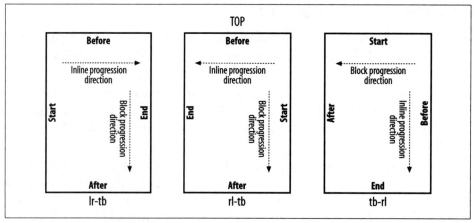

Figure 3-3. Writing mode and relative directions

at 9 o'clock for my usage. Further examples of orientation of writing-mode can be found in Chapter 8.

The writing-mode property also determines the four edges of an area. Specification of writing-mode on the simple-page-master identifies the before, after, start, and end edges of the page-reference-area content-rectangle, *relative* to the top of that content-rectangle, as determined by the reference-orientation we have specified on the simple-page-master. This is illustrated in Figure 3-4.

Rule of thumb: the direction of top is specified by reference-orientation. This is determined first, whether by explicit specification on the formatting object, by inheritance, or by using an initial value. Only then is the writing-mode used to figure out the meaning of before, after, start, and end. When reading writing-modes, bear in mind that lr, rl, and tb are short forms, and correspond to lr-tb, rl-tb, and tb-rl, respectively. These are all related to your manner of writing; for instance, English uses lr-tb, that is, left to right, top to bottom. Other languages have different writing directions. The first part of the writing-mode is the inline-progression-direction, which determines start and end. Similarly, the second part of the writing-mode is the block-progression-direction, which determines before and after.

To illustrate, if you lay out text with blocks (paragraphs) stacking from right to left, and words and characters stacking from bottom to top, this would be a bt-rl writing-mode. If the current absolute orientation of the area in question had top at the (real-world) left (at 90), then bottom-to-top (the inline-progression-direction) runs from −90 (start) to 90 (end), and right-to-left runs from 0 (before) to 180 (after).

Now you will understand exactly how we placed the regions for the diagram in Figure 3-2. The writing-mode is taken as lr-tb, and the reference-orientation on the simple-page-master is assumed to be 0 degrees. Hence, region-before is at 12

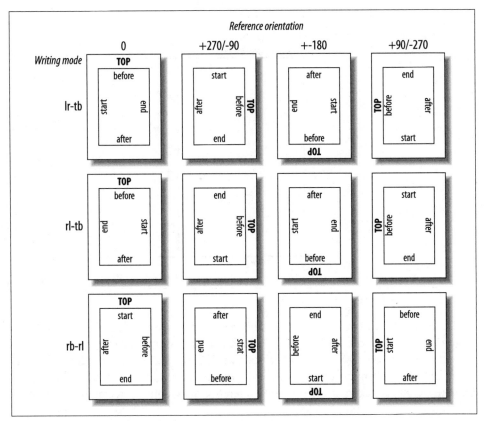

Figure 3-4. The regions of a page

o'clock, or the top; region-after is at 6 o'clock, or the bottom; region-start is at 9 o'clock, or the left; and region-end is at 3 o'clock, or the right.

Each of the four outside optional regions is flush with the edge of the page-reference-area content-rectangle of the same name. That is, the before edge of region-before is flush with the before edge of the page-reference-area content-rectangle. The same is true for the other three regions.

The single dimension that can be specified on any of the four optional regions is the extent. This is the value of the extent attribute. The extent is the size of the region measured perpendicularly from the flush edge. It is specified either as an explicit length or as a percentage of the corresponding height or width of the page; the default is 0.0pt. Figure 3-5 illustrates this for Example 3-1. The region-body is not displayed, for clarity's sake.

The region-body is sized differently. This formatting object has margins, just as does the simple-page-master. For example, let us assume that we have specified a reference-orientation of 90 on the simple-page-master. top for the simple-page-

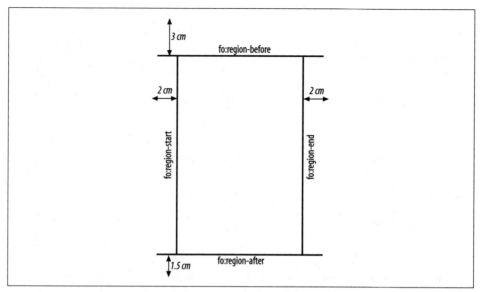

Figure 3-5. Region extents

`master` points to real-world 9 o'clock. This means that the absolute directions for the page-reference-area content-rectangle, which contains all the regions, are `top` at 90 (9 o'clock), `bottom` at –90 (3 o'clock), `left` at 180 (6 o'clock), and `right` at 0 (12 o'clock). Margins on the `region-body` use *these* directions; `margin-top` on the `region-body` therefore is taken from the page-reference-area content-rectangle edge at an absolute direction of 90 (9 o'clock).

Specifying a `reference-orientation` on the `region-body` does *not* affect the determination of margin directions for the region. The `reference-orientation` on the region establishes a coordinate system for *its* descendant areas.

The four margins—`margin-top`, `margin-bottom`, `margin-right`, and `margin-left`—on the `region-body` are used to size *and* position that region, relative to the edges of the content rectangle of the page-reference-area. It is important to understand that the positioning and size of the `region-body` are therefore *independent* of the extents of any of the four optional outer regions, present or not.

It is up to you to ensure that the margins for the `region-body` are equal to or exceed the extent of the outer region on each corresponding edge. If you do not explicitly specify any margin properties, they will be set to 0. If percentages are used, the containing block is the page-reference-area content-rectangle. The percentages are therefore mismatched between the region extents and the margin of the `region-body`. On `region-left`, 10% extent is 10% of the page width; on `region-body`, 10% `margin-left` is 10% of the page-reference-area (that is, less than the extent!).

Each region establishes a viewport-area/reference-area pair, as does the simple-page-master. The reference-orientation of the reference-area, which receives the actual content, is 0, so it has the same top as the corresponding viewport. The overflow property controls behavior when the content "overflows" the viewport. This has relevance to printed media: the default value of auto allows for user-agent–dependent behavior, and none of the other choices—hidden, visible, scroll, or error-if-overflow—can be translated into well-defined behavior in a print environment. If this is of concern, refer to Section 7.20.2 in the XSL specification and the formatter documentation.

 None of the region reference-areas may have any borders or padding. This is an XSL-FO 1.0 limitation. When combined with the similar injunction placed on the simple-page-master, it means that if you want page borders, you will have to do fairly convoluted things with block formatting objects.

You may also need to control the along-edge dimension of the four outer regions. The degree of control is limited, but you can specify how the regions overlap at the corners. You may specify a value of true or false for the precedence property on the region-before or region-after. The default, or initial, value is false. The block-progression-direction of the region-start or region-end extends to the page margins (to the start or end edge of the content-rectangle of the page-reference-area) if the value of the precedence on the adjacent region-before or region-after is false; otherwise, if the precedence of the region-before or region-after is true, then *those* regions float into the area that would be otherwise occupied by region-start or region-end. In other words, if you specify true for the precedence on the header (region-start), it will cover the top left and right corners; if you specify false, the left and right areas will cover the corners.

Let us work up a fairly complex simple-page-master and depict the resulting regions:

```
        <fo:simple-page-master
❶           master-name="recto"
            page-height="11in"
            page-width="8.5in"
            margin-top="1in"
            margin-bottom="1in"
            margin-left="0.75in"
            margin-right="0.5in"
❷               reference-orientation="90"
❸               writing-mode="tb-rl">
        <fo:region-body
            reference-orientation="90"
            margin-top="3in"
            margin-bottom="1in"
            margin-left="1.5in"
            margin-right="1.25in"/>
```

```
        <fo:region-before
            precedence="true"
            extent="2in"/>
              <fo:region-start
❹                   extent="1in"/>
              <fo:region-end
❺                   extent="1in"/>
      </fo:simple-page-master>
```

❶ Page sequence references the simple-page-master using the master-name recto.

❷ The reference-orientation of 90 and the writing-mode of tb-rl mean that top for the page-reference-area content-rectangle is at 9 o'clock; with an inline-progression-direction of tb, start is at 9 o'clock, and end is at 3 o'clock. Similarly, blocks are stacked rl, so before is at 12 o'clock, and after is at 6 o'clock.

❸ The extent of the region-start and region-end are set to 1 inch to be the same as the margins.

To associate content with regions of a page, each region must have a region-name property. The defaults are listed in Table 3-1.

Table 3-1. Default region-names

Region	Default region-name
region-body	xsl-region-body
region-before	xsl-region-before
region-after	xsl-region-after
region-start	xsl-region-start
region-end	xsl-region-end

The default values are reserved for the specific regions mentioned in the table. For example, you may not assign a value of xsl-region-before to the region-start.

The region-name property may be assigned a value of your choice, other than the default for that region. region-names must be unique within a single simple-page-master. Finally, you may reuse your own names across page-masters, but they must refer to the same region class. For example, Example 3-2 shows a full document with these areas, using the names correctly.

Example 3-2. Correct region names

```
<fo:root xmlns:fo="http://www.w3.org/1999/XSL/Format">
<fo:layout-master-set>
<fo:simple-page-master
        master-name="odd"
        page-height="11in"
        page-width="8.5in"
        margin-top="1in"
```

Example 3-2. Correct region names (continued)

```
        margin-bottom="1in"
        margin-left="1.25in"
        margin-right="0.75in">

    <fo:region-body
        region-name="xsl-region-body"
        margin-top="0.6in"
        margin-bottom="0.6in"
        margin-left="0.6in"
        margin-right="0.6in"/>

    <fo:region-before
      precedence="true"
      border="thin black solid"
      region-name="xsl-region-before"
      extent="0.5in"/>

    <fo:region-after
      border="thin black solid"
      region-name="xsl-region-after"
      extent="0.5in"
      precedence="true"/>

    <fo:region-start
      region-name="xsl-region-start"
      border="thin black solid"
      extent="0.5in"/>

    <fo:region-end
      border="thin black solid"
      region-name="xsl-region-end"
      extent="0.5in"/>

</fo:simple-page-master>

</fo:layout-master-set>

  <fo:page-sequence master-reference="odd" format="A">
    <fo:static-content
      flow-name="xsl-region-start">
      <fo:block> <fo:page-number/>
       <fo:block>Ch 1 </fo:block>
      </fo:block>
    </fo:static-content>

    <fo:static-content
      flow-name="xsl-region-end">
      <fo:block>Page <fo:page-number/>

      </fo:block>
    </fo:static-content>
```

Example 3-2. Correct region names (continued)

```
<fo:static-content flow-name="xsl-region-before" >
  <fo:block display-align="before">Part 1

  </fo:block>
</fo:static-content>

<fo:static-content
  flow-name="xsl-region-after"
  display-align="after">

  <fo:block
   text-align="center">Page <fo:page-number/>
       </fo:block>
</fo:static-content>

<fo:flow flow-name="xsl-region-body">

  <fo:block>

The quick brown fox jumps over the lazy dog.
(fill out with further content to show the full page)

  </fo:block>


  </fo:flow>
</fo:page-sequence>

</fo:root>
```

The following summary provides a rough description of region-body and its contents:

Element
    region-body

Purpose
    Region containing the body content for a page

Properties

- Common border, padding, and background properties
- Common margin properties: block
- clip
- column-count
- column-gap
- display-align
- overflow
- region-name

- reference-orientation
- writing-mode

Content model
    EMPTY

The region-body can be specified to be multicolumn. Although I will not discuss the complex structure of the resulting areas in a region-body in this chapter, suffice it to say that the column-count property indicates the number of columns on every page instance formatted using the simple-page-master to which this region-body belongs. The column-count must be a positive integer greater than or equal to 1. The default is 1.

If a column-count of greater than 1 is specified, a value may be specified for the column-gap property; the default is 12.0pt. The value is either an explicit length or a percentage of the inline-progression-dimension of the content rectangle of the region-body.

The following summary provides a rough description of the region elements and their contents:

Elements
    region-before, region-after, region-start, region-end

Purpose
    Regions serving as the header, footer, left sidebar, and right sidebar for a page

Properties
- Common border, padding, and background properties
- clip
- display-align
- extent
- overflow
- precedence (region-before and region-after only)
- region-name
- reference-orientation
- writing-mode

Content model
    EMPTY

Each region also has a display-align property. This has the default value of auto, and may be assigned the values auto, before, center, and after. The display-align property controls the alignment of the child areas of the region in the block-progression-direction (top to bottom for a lr-tb page). A detailed explanation of the nuances of this property requires concepts not yet discussed; just be content knowing you can, in fact, influence the vertical placement of content on a page.

Because display-align defaults to before, its default value works well in region-before to keep the content *away from* the content of the region-body, but unless you explicitly set display-align to after for region-after, the footer content will meet the contents of the region-body, which is generally not desired. In footers, display-align is generally better set to after to separate the footers from the main page content.

Content Flows

The page-sequence element contains the content to fill a sequence of pages. This element is a wrapper for content; the semantics of it derive entirely from its association with either a single simple-page-master or a page-sequence-master. A single page-sequence-master can adequately describe the pagination requirements for one chapter of a book; hence, we consider a page-sequence to be the vehicle for encapsulating the content for a chapter.

A page sequence consists of one primary stream of content, contained within the flow. It may also contain as many content chunks, described by static-content elements, as are required by the header, footer, and sidebar regions of the simple-page-masters ultimately referenced by the page-sequence.

Both fo:flow and fo:static-content are referred to as *flows*. The terminology is confusing because of the existence of the element of that name, but it is hard to devise anything better. Both *are* flows in the sense that they provide content to be laid out into regions of pages. A fo:flow is intended to supply content for the region-body and, as content is consumed, it will not be reused. Static-content elements, on the other hand, are reuseable content *chunks*, capable of customization, which is normally derivative of the specific page that they are currently addressing to provide content for the region-start and region-end (also known as left and right sidebars),* for headers and for footers. Page numbering and running headers and footers are examples of content that depends either on the current page or on the content delivered by the fo:flow that has been placed on the current page. This is *derivative* content.

A Basic Example

Example 3-3 demonstrates the most basic concepts that we have discussed so far.

Example 3-3. A Hello World example

```
<?xml version="1.0" encoding="utf-8"?>

<fo:root xmlns:fo="http://www.w3.org/1999/XSL/Format">

  <fo:layout-master-set>
```

---

* In this context, a *sidebar* refers to the content placed into region-start or region-end. Be aware that sidebars, in a more general sense, are blocks of explanatory text taken out of the normal narrative flow and visually set apart.

Example 3-3. A Hello World example (continued)

```
❶        <fo:simple-page-master
              master-name="simple"
              page-height="29.7cm"
              page-width="21cm"
              margin-left="2.5cm"
              margin-right="2.5cm">
        <fo:region-body margin-top="3cm"/>
      </fo:simple-page-master>

    </fo:layout-master-set>

    <fo:page-sequence
          master-reference="simple">

            <fo:flow
❷              flow-name="xsl-region-body">

        <fo:block>Hello, World</fo:block>

      </fo:flow>
    </fo:page-sequence>
  </fo:root>
```

❶ page-sequence references the `simple-page-master` using the reference to the simple element.

❷ The `flow-name` on `fo:flow` specifies the `fo:region-body` using its default (implicit) region-name.

An A4 sized page is used (again, use your own dimensions if needed), with reasonable margins and the single content that is the block within the flow. This amounts to the smallest XSL-FO document without using default values and having content meet the edges of the page.

Complex Pagination

We have, so far, developed a reasonably complete understanding of simple-page-masters, but now it is time to examine complex pagination. What mechanism is available to us to specify the sequence of simple-page-masters that will be used to format a given page-sequence and the flows contained within it? For this purpose, XSL 1.0 provides the page-sequence-master element.

This section will look at how the children of a page-sequence-master may be used to vary the selection of page masters.

A page-sequence may select a simple-page-master directly, using the master-name attribute. This simple-page-master then generates every page required by the flows contained in that page-sequence. In other words, the page master is referenced as many times as is needed. This is shown in Figure 3-6.

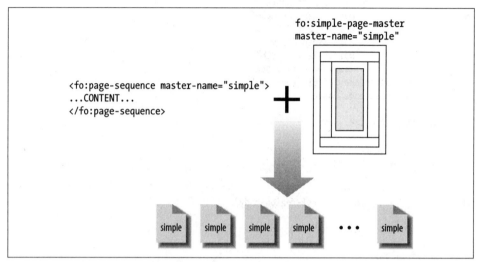

Figure 3-6. Single simple-page-master

A page-sequence may alternatively select a page-sequence-master, also through use of the master-reference attribute. The master-reference on the page-sequence matches the master-name on the page-sequence-master. This is most often useful when the layout goes beyond the simple, single layout needs, requiring varying simple-page-master usage, as is the case when recto and verso pages differ.

 A page-sequence is not constrained to use a page-sequence-master that has not been used already. page-sequence-masters are not stateful, in this sense, and effectively "reset" themselves when called upon to supply page-masters to a new page-sequence.

The page-sequence-master is a container for so-called sub-sequence-specifiers, which, by definition, are children of the page-sequence-master. Each of the sub-sequence-specifiers defines a subsequence of the page-sequence in question; the sum of all subsequences is the sequence of pages that results from completely formatting the flow in that page-sequence.

The following summary provides a rough description of page-sequence-master and its contents:

Element
    page-sequence-master

Purpose
    Specifies the constraints on, and the order in which, a certain set of page-masters generates a sequence of pages

Property
    master-name

Content model
    (single-page-master-reference|repeatable-page-master-reference|repeatable-page-master-alternatives)+

The XSL specification requires that sufficient virtual page-master capacity be available in the page-sequence-master, as provided through its children, to accommodate the needs of the page-sequence. In other words, if the last subsequence runs out of page-masters and the fo:flow is not exhausted, it is an error. A formatter may recover by using the last page-master.

The mapping of sub-sequence-specifiers to the subsequences that comprise the page-sequence is *ordered*, and there must be at least as many sub-sequence-specifiers as there are subsequences of pages that are satisfied by the specifiers. In plain English, this means it is acceptable for the flow to finish and leave a number of unused sub-sequence-specifiers. The general idea is depicted in Figure 3-7.

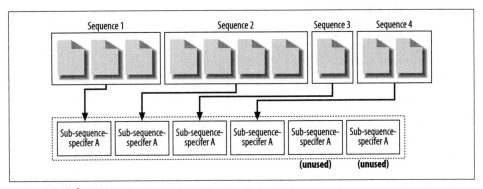

Figure 3-7. Subsequences

During the processing of one page-sequence, once a page-sequence-master is selected, the sub-sequence-specifiers are used, in order, starting with the first, and without breaks,* until the flow is completely processed. Sub-sequence-specifiers may *not* be reused within the context of formatting a single page-sequence.

Single-page-masters

The single-page-master-reference causes exactly one page to be generated. The subsequence that corresponds to this specifier consists of one page. The simple-page-master that is to be used is identified using the master-reference attribute on the page-sequence that corresponds to the single-page-master-reference.

---

* It is possible for a sub-sequence-specifier to match a subsequence containing zero pages.

This sub-sequence-specifier is especially useful for front matter and back matter. It is most commonly found at the beginning of page-sequence-masters. Example 3-4 shows a single-page-master-reference.

Example 3-4. A single-page-master-reference

```
<fo:root>
<fo:layout-master-set>
<fo:simple-page-master
        master-name="single"
        page-height="11in"
        page-width="8.5in"
        margin-top="1in"
        margin-bottom="1in"
        margin-left="0.5in"
        margin-right="0.5in">
    <fo:region-body
        margin-top="0.5in"
        margin-bottom="0.5in"/>
</fo:simple-page-master>
<fo:page-sequence-master
        master-name="single-page">
    <fo:single-page-master-reference
        master-name="single"/>
</fo:page-sequence-master>
</fo:layout-master-set>

<fo:page-sequence
        master-reference="single-page">
    ... CONTENT ...
</fo:page-sequence>
</fo:root>
```

Note the difference between using a single-page-master-reference and using a simple-page-master *directly*. In the latter case, the number of instances of pages that are generated is potentially unbounded. In the former case, the renderer will produce an error or warning if the page-sequence contains more than one page of content.

Note also the required link-back from the page-sequence back to the page-sequence-master, which in turn links back to the simple-page-master. This is the basic mechanism by which a page layout is selected for any content.

Constructing Runs of Identical Pages

The repeatable-page-master-reference causes a bounded or unbounded sequence of pages to be generated using the same page-master. The simple-page-master is referenced using the master-reference attribute on repeatable-page-master-reference. The maximum-repeats attribute can be used to set an upper limit on the number of pages that may be generated using this specifier.

The `maximum-repeats` attribute is typically used to restrict a flow to a fixed number of pages. Use this if, for example, you require a particular content to be limited to 10 pages.

The initial, or default, value of `maximum-repeats` is `no-limit`, meaning it will generate a subsequence of pages that consume the rest of the current `fo:flow`. Other permitted values are integers, from 0 to N. A value of 0 indicates that this `sub-sequence-specifier` maps to a page subsequence of zero length. Negative values are rounded to 0; positive fractions are rounded up to the nearest integer. Example 3-5 shows the use of a `repeatable-page-master-reference`.

Example 3-5. A repeatable-page-master-reference

```
<fo:root>
<fo:layout-master-set>
<fo:simple-page-master
        master-name="many"
        page-height="11in"
        page-width="8.5in"
        margin-top="1in"
        margin-bottom="1in"
        margin-left="0.5in"
        margin-right="0.5in">
    <fo:region-body
        margin-top="0.5in"
        margin-bottom="0.5in"/>
</fo:simple-page-master>
<fo:page-sequence-master
        master-name="many-pages">
    <fo:repeatable-page-master-reference
        master-name="many"
        maximum-repeats="10"/>
</fo:page-sequence-master>
</fo:layout-master-set>

<fo:page-sequence
    master-reference="many-pages">
    ... CONTENT ...
</fo:page-sequence>
</fo:root>
```

Conditional Selection of Page Masters

The most powerful and challenging `sub-sequence-specifier` is the `repeatable-page-master-alternatives` formatting object. Some of the nuances will become more clear when we discuss page-breaking in Chapter 5. This element does *not* have a `master-reference` attribute, because it doesn't reference page masters directly—its children do.

Use this element to select one from a number of alternatives for content. A number of conditions may be tested, related to a page's position within a sequence, the page number, or whether or not a particular page is blank.

The children of the repeatable-page-master-alternatives element are known as *alternatives*. Each alternative is represented using the conditional-page-master-reference formatting object. Each one refers to a specific simple-page-master by name, using the master-reference attribute. It considers each alternative in order. The first condition for which all of the subconditions are *true* causes its corresponding conditional-page-master-reference to be selected, and the simple-page-master referenced by that alternative generates the current page. The repeatable-page-master-alternatives element may contain one or more of alternatives, although in practice, there are rarely more than three or four. The alternatives have *traits*, specified using properties on each conditional-page-master-reference, that specify the conditions that must be satisifed for this particular page layout to become active. Example 3-6 uses odd, even, blank, or last pages. If all the conditions for a particular alternative are satisfied, the simple-page-master referenced is used.

The primary use of this class of sequence is to organize content layout such that page layout is grouped according to the formatted output page position or content.

It is considered good practice to supply a final conditional-page-master-reference that has a condition that must always be true. This is akin to a default: statement inside a C or Java switch block. If, at some point during use of a repeatable-page-master-alternative, no condition is true, use of this sub-sequence-specifier will terminate.

Three properties may be used to specify the conditions upon which the selection of the alternative is made:

- page-position
- odd-or-even
- blank-or-not-blank

The page-position trait may take the values first, last, rest, or any. The default is any. The values are interpreted as follows:

first
> The subcondition is true if the current page is the first page in the page-sequence.

last
> The subcondition is true if the current page is the last page in the page-sequence.

rest
> The subcondition is true if the current page is neither the first nor the last page in the page-sequence.

any
> Always true.

---

first or last relates to the formatted output of the flow. Think of it as pouring text into containers. The first piece of content poured has the value of first; the last piece of content has the value of last, in this sense. This might be the first or last piece of content of a chapter or article, as templates are applied to produce the content within the flow.

The odd-or-even trait may have the values odd, even, or any. The default is any. The parity of the page-number is determined with respect to the page-number trait for the current page; see "Page Sequences."

The values are interpreted as follows:

odd
    The subcondition is true if the current page number is odd.

even
    The subcondition is true if the current page number is even.

any
    Always true.

This property is used to select the formatting required for odd or even pages, for example, a page layout with left and right margins appropriate for the layout of a book such that the margins nearer the gutter are larger than the opposite margins; this provides a more even appearance when the book is laid open.

The blank-or-not-blank trait may have the values blank, not-blank, or any. The default is any. It may not be immediately obvious that a blank page would be generated; one possibility is to use force-page-count, mentioned in "Page Sequences"; a discussion of other possibilities will have to wait for the examination of page breaks. The values of this property are interpreted as follows:

blank
    The subcondition is true if the current page contains no areas generated from the fo:flow.

not-blank
    The subcondition is true if the current page contains areas from the fo:flow.

any
    Always true.

Note that we are concerned with areas generated by the fo:flow, not by fo:static-content. So-called "blank" pages will often *end up* with headers or footers. If you do not yet know what page-master you will use, how can you make a determination of what, if any, the applicable static-contents are? But you can always determine whether the current page will contain areas from the fo:flow. So this condition concerns itself only with fo:flow, not all content on the page.

Static content (as it is referred to in the specification) isn't exactly static. The idea is that, compared to page body content, the headers and footers change relatively little, hence, they are said to be "static." I find this confusing because the most common content for a header or footer is the page number, which changes every page! However, the specification calls it static content, so that's that. It is also static in that it is the same size and location for each page layout, so perhaps we might sway towards agreeing with the spec writers. For simplicity's sake, where you see static content, think headers and footers.

The repeatable-page-master-alternatives formatting object has a maximum-repeats property, which has the same meaning and default value as it does for the repeatable-page-master-reference formatting object. In effect, the number of times we test the conditions supplied by the repeatable-page-master-alternatives to select appropriate page masters may be bounded.

Let us construct an example and use it to clarify everything we have learned so far about repeatable-page-master-alternatives, conditional-page-master-reference, conditions, and subconditions.

Page Conditions

I have already mentioned that a fo:page-sequence is often used to model a chapter of a book or a complete article. In this capacity, let us surmise that we wish to prepare a page-sequence-master that can handle chapters with the following structure:

- First page
- The rest of the pages, except for the last
- Last page

Let us also consider that the chapters have some internal structure that might result in blank pages (page break conditions, which are mentioned later, could cause this). We are also using the force-page-count property on the page-sequence. Note that this is an extended property that should probably be avoided in favor of initial-page-number="auto-odd". We are using the force-page-count property on the page-sequence to ensure that the total page count is even. (A portable alternative is to use the initial-page-number attribute on the following page-sequence). We also want to handle internal blank pages and blank last pages differently. Because we want new chapters to start on an odd page, we set force-page-count to even. Separate page masters will be employed for the first page, for the last page, for blank pages, and for even and odd pages.

The comments prior to each block of code in Example 3-6 explain the purpose of that block.

Example 3-6. Conditional page selection

```
<?xml version="1.0" encoding="utf-8"?>

<fo:root xmlns:fo="http://www.w3.org/1999/XSL/Format">

    <fo:layout-master-set>

        <!-- layout for the first page -->
        <fo:simple-page-master
            master-name="first"
            page-height="29.7cm"
            page-width="21.0cm"
            margin-top="2cm"
            margin-bottom="2cm"
            margin-left="2.5cm" margin-right="2.5cm">
                        <fo:region-body
                            margin-top="10cm"
                            margin-bottom="2cm"/>
                        <fo:region-after
                            region-name="non-blank-after"
                            extent="2cm"/>
        </fo:simple-page-master>

        <!-- layout for odd pages -->
        <fo:simple-page-master
            master-name="odd"
            page-height="29.7cm"
            page-width="21.0cm"
            margin-top="2cm"
            margin-bottom="2cm"
            margin-left="3.5cm"
            margin-right="1.5cm">
                        <fo:region-body
                            margin-top="2cm"
                            margin-bottom="2cm"/>
                        <fo:region-before
                            region-name="odd-before"
                            extent="2cm"/>
                        <fo:region-after
                            region-name="non-blank-after"
                            extent="2cm"/>
        </fo:simple-page-master>

        <!-- layout for even pages -->
        <fo:simple-page-master
            master-name="even"
            page-height="29.7cm"
            page-width="21.0cm"
            margin-top="2cm"
            margin-bottom="2cm"
                margin-left="1.5cm"
                margin-right="3.5cm">
```

Example 3-6. Conditional page selection (continued)

```
                        <fo:region-body
                            margin-top="2cm"
                            margin-bottom="2cm"/>
                        <fo:region-before
                            region-name="even-before"
                            extent="2cm"/>
                        <fo:region-after
                            region-name="non-blank-after"
                            extent="2cm"/>
        </fo:simple-page-master>

        <!-- layout for odd last page, blank or not-blank -->
        <!-- Note that this is redundant in the example -->

        <!-- layout for even last page, blank or not-blank -->
        <fo:simple-page-master master-name="last_even"
            page-height="29.7cm"
            page-width="21.0cm"
            margin-top="2cm"
            margin-bottom="2cm"
            margin-left="1.5cm"
            margin-right="3.5cm">
                        <fo:region-body
                            margin-top="2cm"
                            margin-bottom="2cm"/>
                        <fo:region-before
                            region-name="even-last-before"
                            extent="2cm"/>
                        <fo:region-after
                            region-name="last-after"
                            extent="2cm"/>
        </fo:simple-page-master>

        <!-- layout for blank pages (non-last) -->
        <fo:simple-page-master
            master-name="blank"
            page-height="29.7cm"
            page-width="21.0cm"
            margin-top="2cm"
            margin-bottom="2cm"
                margin-left="2.5cm"
                margin-right="2.5cm">
                        <fo:region-body
                            margin-top="2cm"
                            margin-bottom="2cm"/>
                        <fo:region-before
                            region-name="blank-before"
                            extent="2cm"/>
                        <fo:region-after
                            region-name="blank-after"
                            extent="2cm"/>
        </fo:simple-page-master>
```

Example 3-6. Conditional page selection (continued)

```
            <fo:page-sequence-master
                master-name="chapter">
                    <fo:repeatable-page-master-alternatives>
                        <fo:conditional-page-master-reference
                            master-reference="odd"
                            page-position="rest"
                            odd-or-even="odd" />
                        <fo:conditional-page-master-reference
                            master-reference="even"
                            page-position="rest"
                            odd-or-even="even" />
                        <fo:conditional-page-master-reference
                            master-reference="first"
                            page-position="first" />
                        <fo:conditional-page-master-reference
                            master-reference="last_even"
                            odd-or-even="even"
                            page-position="last" />

                        <fo:conditional-page-master-reference
                            master-reference="blank"
                            blank-or-not-blank="blank" />
                    </fo:repeatable-page-master-alternatives>
            </fo:page-sequence-master>
    </fo:layout-master-set>
    <!-- end: defines page layout -->

    <!-- actual layout -->
    <fo:page-sequence
     master-reference="chapter"
     force-page-count="even"
     initial-page-number="1">

    <fo:static-content
         flow-name="non-blank-after">
         <fo:block> <fo:page-number/>
<!-- content for non-blank page footers --></fo:block>
    </fo:static-content>

    <fo:static-content
        flow-name="blank-before">
        <fo:block> <fo:page-number/>
           <!-- content for blank page headers -->
        </fo:block>
    </fo:static-content>

    <fo:static-content
        flow-name="blank-after">
        <fo:block> <fo:page-number/>
            <!-- content for blank page footers -->
        </fo:block>
    </fo:static-content>
```

Example 3-6. Conditional page selection (continued)

```
        <fo:static-content flow-name="odd-before">
            <fo:block> <fo:page-number/>
               <!-- content for odd page headers -->
            </fo:block>
        </fo:static-content>

        <fo:static-content flow-name="even-before">
            <fo:block> <fo:page-number/>
           <!-- content for even page headers -->
            </fo:block>
        </fo:static-content>



        <fo:static-content flow-name="even-last-before">
            <fo:block> <fo:page-number/>
             <!-- content for even last page headers -->
            </fo:block>
        </fo:static-content>

        <fo:static-content flow-name="last-after">
            <fo:block> <fo:page-number/>
              content for last page footers --- >
            </fo:block>    </fo:static-content>
        <fo:flow flow-name="xsl-region-body">

            <fo:block>
              Insert sufficient content for 35 pages to complete
              this example
            </fo:block>
            <fo:block break-before="page"/>
        </fo:flow>
    </fo:page-sequence>
<fo:page-sequence
        master-reference="chapter"
        force-page-count="even"
            initial-page-number="39">

        <fo:static-content
            flow-name="non-blank-after">
            <fo:block> <fo:page-number/>
             content for non-blank page footers --- >
            </fo:block>
        </fo:static-content>

        <fo:static-content flow-name="blank-before">
            <fo:block> <fo:page-number/>
            content for blank page headers --- >
            </fo:block>
        </fo:static-content>

        <fo:static-content flow-name="blank-after">
            <fo:block> <fo:page-number/>
```

Example 3-6. Conditional page selection (continued)

```
                content for blank page footers --- >
                </fo:block>
        </fo:static-content>

        <fo:static-content
           flow-name="odd-before">
            <fo:block> <fo:page-number/>
             content for odd page headers --- >
            </fo:block>
        </fo:static-content>

        <fo:static-content flow-name="even-before">
            <fo:block> <fo:page-number/>
            content for even page headers --- >
            </fo:block>
        </fo:static-content>



        <fo:static-content flow-name="even-last-before">
            <fo:block> <fo:page-number/>
             content for even last page headers --- >
            </fo:block>
        </fo:static-content>

        <fo:static-content flow-name="last-after">
            <fo:block> <fo:page-number/>
             content for last page footers --- >
            </fo:block>
        </fo:static-content>

        <fo:flow flow-name="xsl-region-body">

            <fo:block> Insert sufficient content for some
             more  pages to complete this example
            </fo:block>

        </fo:flow>
    </fo:page-sequence>
</fo:root>
```

The repeatable-page-master-alternatives formatting object has a maximum-repeats attribute, which is used in exactly the same fashion as described for repeatable-page-master-alternatives, except that the individual pages are instances of simple-page-masters that are chosen according to conditions. Figure 3-8 demonstrates how these alternatives may work.

Page Sequences

So far, I have talked about aspects of fo:page-sequence—its children, the page-masters to which it points in one fashion or another—that pertain to how sequences

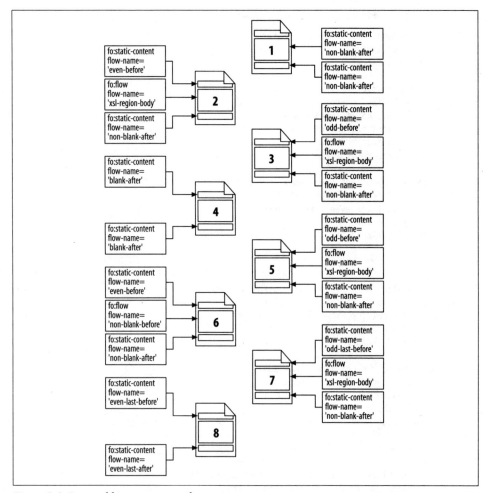

Figure 3-8. Repeatable-page-master-alternatives

of pages are married with their page-masters. I have also talked at length about the structure of a page. I have left out several properties that deal with page numbering, but I'll introduce them soon. There are also two other properties that I will talk about that introduce elements of internationalization.

Page Numbering

The initial-page-number property fixes the page number for the first page of the page-sequence to which it applies. The values of the property and its interpretation are listed as follows:

auto

If this is the first page-sequence, the initial page number becomes 1. If it is not the first page-sequence, the initial page number of the current page-sequence becomes the page number of the last page of the preceding page-sequence, plus 1. That is, it simply continues numbering pages sequentially.

auto-odd

As for auto. If the resulting value is even, add 1.

auto-even

As for auto. If the resulting value is odd, add 1.

[number]

A positive integer, that is, 1 or greater. If a non-positive integer is supplied, this number is rounded to the nearest positive integer.

To force content to be numbered starting at, say, page 51, simply use this property, as in Example 3-7.

Example 3-7. Forced page numbering

```
<fo:page-sequence
 master-reference="chapter"
 initial-page-number="51"
...
```

If the first page-sequence has no value specified for initial-page-number, the default of auto is used, and hence, the first page is numbered as 1.

The force-page-count property imposes a condition on the number of pages in a page-sequence. This number may be an absolute count or a parity condition. For each condition, if the condition is not satisfied, one page is added to the current page-sequence. The values of the property and its interpretation are listed as follows:

auto

The action taken depends on the existence of a succeeding page-sequence and the value of its initial-page-number property. If there is a succeeding page-sequence and an even initial-page-number is explicitly specified on it, the current page-sequence must adapt.

even

Force an even page count for the page-sequence.

odd

Force an odd page count for the page sequence.

end-on-even

Force the last page to have an even page number.

end-on-odd

Force the last page to have an odd page number.

no-force

Do not force any page count.

Note that the default value is auto, which is mostly what is wanted, resulting in alignment in the before direction. As a starting point, try the initial-page-number property, which is the easier option here.

Consider what will happen if we set various values for the force-page-count property on the first page-sequence, and modify the second page-sequence to have an explicit initial-page-number value of 39. Let us also assume that the first page-sequence now formats out to less than 39 pages, say 37. If the first section actually formats out to 15 pages, by default, the renderer will add an even page, so that the next page-sequence can start on an odd page, but it won't add the extra pages that are needed to fill in the numeric gaps.

If the default, auto, is in effect, then because the next page-sequence is required to start with a page number of 39, the last page of this one must be even. Currently, it is 37, so a page must be added.

If we set force-page-count to even, a page must be added, bringing the page count up to 38. The last page is numbered 38. Again, note that this could be achieved more portably using simply the initial-page-number property. If we set force-page-count to odd, no action needs be taken. If we set force-page-count to end-on-even, a page must be added, so that the last page is numbered as 38. If we set force-page-count to end-on-odd, no action needs be taken.

If you use initial-page-number attribute and a value of auto (the default) on the page count, this should normally result in the output needed. It is simple and reliable.

Do not assume that an actual formatter will follow a particular method of forcing the page count, as in adding blank pages. An implementation may elect to use a different strategy to satisfy this constraint; and this may result in an unexpected blank page or no blank page where you would expect one.

If you are concerned with this class of problem, it may well be worth experimenting with content and these properties to fully come to terms with them. It is also wise to ensure which of these properties are supported by the formatter of your choice.

Four properties that influence the formatting of the page number if it is requested are format, letter-value, grouping-separator, and grouping-size. These properties are defined in Section 7.7.1, "Number to String Conversion," of the XSLT specification.* Read that W3C Recommendation for a full exposition; here's a short synopsis.

---

* You can find this at *http://www.w3.org/TR/xslt*.

The common values that the format property may include are 1, which results in a sequence of the form 1, 2, 3, ..., 10, 11, 12, ..., 100, 101, 102, ..., or variants such as 001, which results in a sequence of the form 001, 002, 003, ..., 010, 011, 012, ..., 100, 101, 102, ... A generates an uppercase sequence of the form A, B, C, ..., AA, AB, AC, ... a generates a lowercase sequence of the form a, b, c, ..., aa, ab, ac, ... i generates a sequence of lowercase Roman numerals, and I, a sequence of uppercase Roman numerals. There are other possibilities. Be advised that numbering is influenced by language (see the next section) and that these examples are true for Western scripts, not necessarily others.

The letter-value property disambiguates between an alphabetic letter sequence, such as that realized in English by the format token a and some other assignment of numbers to letters, such as the Roman numeral system in English. The first is obtained by specifying the value of alphabetic, and the other is obtained by specifying a value of traditional. The property is used when the format token would be the same; in other words, the first member of the alphabetic sequence is the same as the first member of the traditional sequence. This is not an issue in English.

For readability, long numbers are frequently grouped, e.g., 10000 becomes 10,000. The grouping-separator property specifies the separator, in this example, a comma; and the grouping-size property specifies the size of the grouping, in this example, 3. For a grouping-separator of . and a grouping-size of 2, 10000 would become 1.00. 00, which may or may not be meaningful to you.

Country and Language

The page-sequence country property is specified either as the value none, which is the default, or as an ISO-3166 country specifier; for example, United States is us, United Kingdom is gb, Canada is ca, and Estonia is ee. See *http://www.ietf.org/rfc/rfc3066.txt* for more information.

The page-sequence language property is specified either as the value none (the default), or as an ISO-639 language code, listed at *http://xml.coverpages.org/ languageIdentifiers.html*. This is a two-letter tag. Again, if you have programmed for web services to any extent, you will be somewhat familiar with such codes as en for English, fr for French, and et for Estonian.

The values of the language and country properties affect the formatting of the fo: block and fo:character elements, which you'll learn about in upcoming chapters. Both of the properties in combination influence hyphenation, line justification, and line breaking.

CHAPTER 4

Areas

In Chapter 3, I discussed how pages are organized into sequences, how page masters are selected for processing, and how the page area is divided into regions. In this chapter, we will delve deeper into what happens on a page. We will go into some detail about page layout. After this, you should appreciate why the formatter produces output as it does, and perhaps have some sympathy with implementors.

Informal Definition of an Area

As you have seen in Chapter 3, formatting objects contain data that should be rendered as a series of marks on the canvas—text, images, lines, etc. The formatter turns objects into series of imaginary rectangles on the page, called *areas*. One object may produce more than one area: e.g., an fo:block element produces two areas if split by a page break, as shown in Figure 4-1.

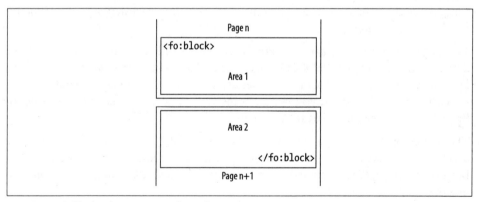

Figure 4-1. A block split over a page boundary

FOs have properties that specify constraints on the appearance and placement of areas generated by them. These constraints are used to calculate *area traits*, which are attributes of areas that uniquely identify their placement, appearance, and contents. Most properties and traits have one-to-one correspondence: e.g., the color property unambiguously defines a trait with the same name. But there are several cases where relations between properties and traits are more complicated; they will be considered later.

 Traits are actual attributes of an area as calculated by the formatter, whereas properties are a set of constraints imposed on the traits.

Areas form a tree structure: a larger area can contain smaller subareas. Typically, the area tree closely resembles the source FO tree: an area generated by formatting object A contains subareas generated by descendant elements of A. Important exceptions are out-of-line elements, such as floats and footnotes.

Area Types

Areas created by formatting objects can be of two principal types:

Inline-areas
   These areas correspond to text chunks, inline images, etc. Areas of this type are stacked on a line in the inline-progression-direction (see Chapter 6). Inline-areas are placed inside other inline-areas or inside line areas. The following objects create only inline-areas: fo:character, fo:inline, fo:inline-container, fo:bidi-override, fo:leader, fo:external-graphic, fo:instream-foreign-object, fo:page-number, and fo:page-number-citation.

Block-areas
   These areas correspond to text paragraphs, tables, lists, etc. Areas of this type are stacked on a page in the block-progression-direction (see Chapter 5). The following objects create only block-areas: fo:block, fo:block-container, fo:table, fo:table-and-caption, and fo:list-block.

Each area has a set of font traits, derived from font properties of the respective formatting object. These traits uniquely define a *nominal font* associated with the area. The area need not actually contain glyphs from this font; parameters of the nominal font may be used in calculating area position. Two such traits are text-altitude and text-depth: they specify the inline-progression-dimension of glyph-areas and are used in line-stacking calculations. These are the low-level items that determine the area sizes.

Two more area types are useful for defining the area model:

Glyph-area

These areas can be viewed as an extreme case of an inline-area, corresponding to a single glyph. Every printable character of the text data in the source FO tree generates a glyph area. A glyph-area has two important traits that other areas don't have:

`text-altitude`
> The height of the nominal ascender of the font to which the glyph belongs

`text-depth`
> The depth of the nominal descender of the font

These are illustrated in Figure 4-2.

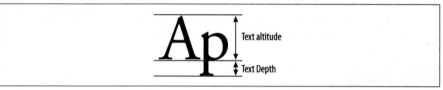

Figure 4-2. Text-altitude and -depth

Note that `text-altitude` and `text-depth` are *font* properties, common to all glyphs in a given font, rather than glyph properties: two glyph-areas containing glyphs from the same font will get identical values for these traits. The specification says conforming implementations may choose as any value in the range of text-altitudes used by fonts of the same script and font-size, instead of the values from the font data.

These two traits determine the size of the content-rectangle for the glyph-area in the `block-progression-dimension`: from the top of `text-altitude` to the bottom of `text-depth`.

 The height of the content-rectangle of a glyph-area is different from the font-size (the latter is greater by the amount of the default *leading* for the font).

In the `inline-progression-dimension`, glyph-area size is determined by the glyph itself (for Western fonts, this would be the glyph width inclusive of left and right bearings). This is worth being aware of, even though the stylesheet author has no control over them.

Line-area

This is a special kind of a block-area, corresponding to a single line of text. It has no corresponding formatting object; its traits are derived from properties of the embracing block-level object, such as `line-height`, `line-height-shift-adjustment`, and `line-stacking-strategy`. It is a useful abstraction to describe the switch between inline-level and block-level areas: inlines are stacked inside line-areas, which are packaged into the surrounding block-area. Line-areas cannot have borders or padding, and their stacking in the `block-progression-direction` is controlled by special rules (see "Stacking Block-Areas and Spaces" for line stacking strategies). Figure 4-3 shows a line-area containing an inline.

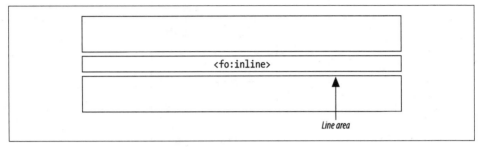

Figure 4-3. Line-areas

There are other area types, used in constructing upper levels of the area tree, which also have no formatting objects directly corresponding to them:

Region-reference-areas

Each region into which a page is divided (region-before, region-after, region-start, region-end, and region-body) forms an area. The dimensions of the regions are defined by the respective region descriptors in the `fo:simple-page-master` currently selected.

Main-reference-area

This implicit area is created inside the region area that accepts the contents of the `fo:flow` (typically, region-body) and differs from it by the adjustments necessary to allocate conditional subregions: xsl-float-before, xsl-footnote, and xsl-footnote-separator. When there are no out-of-line elements on the page, the page-reference-area coincides with the region-reference-area. It contains one or more span-reference-areas.

Span-reference-area

In a multicolumn layout, a block-level element may have an attribute span="all" making it span all columns on the page; others have span="none", meaning that areas produced by these elements lay within one column. When laying out the page, a formatter partitions the flow into chunks such that all blocks in a chunk have the same value of the span attribute. Each chunk creates a span-reference-area. This enables common column areas to be laid out together.

Column-area

A span-reference-area is further subdivided into areas for single columns. For span-reference-areas with span="all", there will be only one such area, coinciding with the span-reference-area itself. For span="none", the number of areas is defined by the column-count property, and their separation by the column-gap property of the fo:region-body element in the current simple-page-master element.

Figure 4-4 shows the main areas of a normal page.

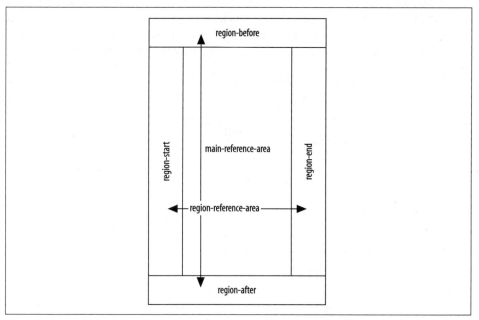

Figure 4-4. Pagelevel areas

Components of an Area

An area may have a border around it, with or without a background inside it (which may be an image or a color fill). The following are terms for rectangles that constitute an area:

Content rectangle
This is the innermost part of an area. It represents the space actually available to host area contents, such as children areas, glyphs, and graphics.

Padding rectangle
This rectangle extends up to the inner boundary of the border. It includes the content rectangle plus padding offsets from all the four sides. This rectangle delimits the zones covered by the background of the area.

Border rectangle
This rectangle is delimited by the external edge of the border frame. It includes the padding rectangle, plus border widths of all the four sides. Except for special cases (absolute/relative positioning, overflow, out-of-line elements, etc.), no marks are produced by a formatting object outside the border rectangle of its generated area(s)—the rectangle is surrounded by spaces transparent to marks left by other areas.

All these rectangles should be present in CSS2 box model. There is one more rectangle defined in CSS: a *margin rectangle* that incorporates margins around the border. In XSL, margins are not used for area positioning (they are replaced by spaces); so it does not make sense to include the respective rectangle in the model. Figure 4-5 shows the content, padding, and border rectangles.

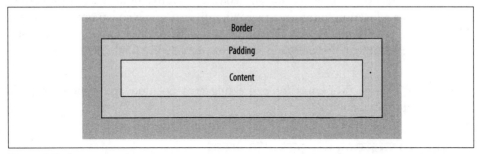

Figure 4-5. Area nomenclature

Reference Areas

In CSS2, normally positioned blocks have properties that determine their placement with respect to the content rectangle of their parent box. All boxes are equivalent: children inside a box are always stacked in the same manner.

XSL takes a different approach: it designates some areas for use as reference for defining inline-progression-dimension and orientation of their descendant areas. Such areas are called *reference areas*; I will refer to other areas as *normal*.

Reference areas have the following distinctive features:

- They define starting points for start-indent and end-indent traits of all descendant normal block-areas.
- They can set new writing-mode and reference-orientation (normal areas can change inline-progression-direction only via the direction property or bidi mechanism).
- Their dimension is always bound in both directions, and the display-align trait can be set to align their contents in the block-progression-dimension.

All *region* and *column areas* are reference areas; areas produced by fo:block elements are normal. table-cell is a reference area; label and body of a list item are normal. Only three formatting objects can explicitly generate reference areas:

- fo:table-cell
- fo:block-container
- fo:inline-container

Area Positioning

The XSL specification defines a large variety of properties to express constraints over the appearance of areas on a page. The formatter tries to choose an optimal location for the area. This is not a straightforward process: properties may clash with each other, giving rise to an *overconstrained* geometry specification. It's the formatter's task to choose a location for an area that will satisfy as many constraints as possible. The XSL spec is flexible about rule conflicts: it defines rules for prioritizing some constraints over others, but delegates the right to make the final decision to the formatter engine.

Next, I will analyze properties for expressing area position and dimensions, and describe their interaction rules.

Turning Formatting Objects into Areas

It is not uncommon that a single formatting object produces two or more areas. A single block of text may be split by a page break; an inline element may be scattered into several lines. Traits of the resulting areas are controlled by properties of their source formatting object.

Borders and padding can be applied conditionally, using the extended property, `border-after-width.conditionality`, for instance. The values are either `retain` or `discard`, and affect the border or padding when it is at the beginning or the end of a reference area. This can cause problems when you actually want the border or padding at the before or start side, and the conditionality is set to `discard` (the default). It is explained further when I discuss space resolution in "Stacking Block-Areas and Spaces."

This is another case where a *trailing* area (here, a border) may be discarded if it is the last in a reference area. Roughly, this means if a sequence of areas has a border specified, the final one may be discarded, because its area is lost in the parent area. For example, if you have specified `border-after` on six successive areas, with the final one ending a chapter, this may be discarded (default) by the formatter, because its area will be lost in the break before the start of the next chapter. Similar logic works in the `inline-progression-direction`. Again, this is controlled by the spaces and conditionality logic. If the conditionality is set to `retain`, the normal logic is overridden.

There are also a number of constraints that don't directly assign traits to the areas; rather, they control the number and the appearance of the areas produced by the formatting object that bears them. They are expressed by the following properties:

`break-before`
> The first area generated by a formatting object with `break-before` set to something other than `auto` should be placed first in the area-tree inside some reference-area.

The stylesheet author specifies the condition, and the formatter determines the placements. The type of this reference-area depends on the value of the property:

auto
> No constraint is present; the property is discarded.

column
> The object starts a column-reference-area.

page
> The object starts a page-reference-area.

odd-page
> The object starts an odd-numbered page-reference-area.

even-page
> The object starts an even-numbered page-reference-area.

This property triggers a break immediately before the first area generated by the current object, starting a new column, page, odd-page, or even-page. Note, however, that this property is not like a *form-feed* command for a printer; if the constraint on area placement had been generated without this property, no additional pages would be generated. In plain words, consecutive break constraints separated by objects that create no areas are merged.

Break-after
> An inversion of the preceding property, with the same set of values. It generates a break after the object: the last area generated by the object should be last in its column-area, and the next area should start a new column, page, odd-page, or even-page.

Keep-with-previous
> The opposite of break-before: the first area generated by the object *should not* be the first in the area. This property is compound, with the following components:

.within-line
> The object should not start a new line.

.within-column
> The object should not start a column.

.within-page
> The object should not start a page.

Each component may assume the following values:

auto
> Constraint disabled.

Integer value
> Specifies the strength of the constraint.

always
> Specifies a strength value greater than any integer.

The strength of the constraint is used to arbitrate its conflicts with other constraints.

keep-with-next

Inhibits break after the last area produced by the object. It has the same component structure and the same choice of values.

keep-together

This property prescribes that the formatting object should generate only one area—in other terms, it inhibits respective breaks *between* areas generated by the formatting object. The components and the set of values are the same as for the preceding two values.

Like space specifiers, keep and break constraints can lead to overconstrained specification, when it is impossible to satisfy them all simultaneously. In these cases, the following rules of constraint relaxation apply:

- All break constraints are satisfied first.
- Keep constraints with lower strength are relaxed first.
- The resulting set should satisfy the maximum number of constraints with the highest strength possible.

There are two more properties that constrain area placement inside reference areas: orphans and widows. They specify the minimum number of line-areas that can be left at the end of the page (orphans) or carried over to the next page (widows). The spec does not define how these properties should interact with other keep constraints.

Area Dimensions

Each area has two traits that define its dimension: inline-progression-dimension and block-progression-dimension. These traits define the width and height of the content rectangle of the area; which one is horizontal and which is vertical depends on the current writing-mode and reference-orientation. However, not all formatting objects may have properties that directly map to these traits; they are permitted only on objects that create reference areas or images:

- fo:simple-page-master gets page-width and page-height properties, and margins. There is a size shorthand, too.
- fo:region-body has margins to specify its offsets from the page-reference-area content rectangle (defined in its parent fo:simple-page-master). While there are no traits for direct settings of dimensions, it is still possible to fix the size because the dimensions of page-reference-area are known.
- fo:region-before, fo:region-after, fo:region-start, and fo:region-end cannot control their dimension in the direction parallel to the sheet edge to which they are attached. In the other direction, their size is given by the extent property.

- `fo:block-container` and `fo:inline-container` may have explicit attributes of `inline-progression-dimension` and `block-progression-dimension`, specified either as a percentage, range, or length. `width` and `height` may be also specified for these two elements. In addition, when an `fo:block-container` is absolutely positioned, it may get its dimensions from top, bottom, right, or left.
- `fo:external-graphic` and `fo:instream-foreign-object` have the same size-related properties as the containers above.
- `fo:table` and `fo:table-cell` have `width` and `height`.

 Note that there is no link between extent and margins on `fo:region-body`. It is the stylesheet writer's responsibility to ensure that side regions fit into the place left free by `fo:region-body`.

All other elements can only specify their dimensions in terms of distance from the edges of a reference area. (This is more a feature than a limitation; to set any dimension explicitly, you always have an option of wrapping the desired element into a block- or an inline-container).

Positioning a Block-Area: Margins and Indents

Each block-area has two traits that specify its position and size in the inline-progression-dimension: start-indent and end-indent. They specify the distance from an edge of the content rectangle of the area (start-edge for start-indent, end-edge for end-indent) to the respective edge of the content-rectangle of its closest ancestor reference area. Each formatting object that produces areas may have properties that map directly to these traits (and are named the same). See Figure 4-6.

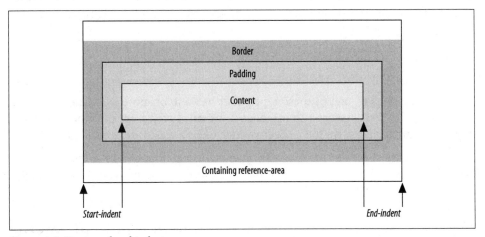

Figure 4-6. Start- and end-indents

XSL has an alternative mechanism for setting indent traits: an area can be positioned using margin properties. There are four margin properties: `margin-top`, `margin-bottom`, `margin-left`, and `margin-right`. A margin property specifies the distance from the respective edge of the content-rectangle of the closest ancestor reference-area to the edge of the border-rectangle of the current area. Margin properties can only be absolutely oriented: no `writing-mode` relative equivalents are provided. There is also a short form* property `margin` that sets all the four margins simultaneously, using standard CSS2 rules.†

In XSL, indents are inheritable. Unless you set them explicitly (in either of the two ways described previously), the content-rectangle of a nested area gets the same `inline-progression-dimension` as that of an embracing area. Inheritance is discussed further in Appendix E. If you add padding and/or border to the nested area, its border-rectangle will extend outside the content-rectangle of its parent. Note that this differs from CSS2 habits: there, the border-rectangle of a contained box always fits inside the content-rectangle of the container one. If you want to enforce CSS2-style box nesting, you have to specify `margin="0pt"` explicitly on every contained block.

For the sake of completeness, let's now mention the effects that side floats have on the placement of block-areas. These are areas specified to *float* in the start or end direction, as might be found in an explanatory note. A side float F is said to *intrude* into a block-area B if:

- B and F have the same nearest ancestor reference-area.
- There is a line parallel to the `inline-progression-direction` that intersects border rectangles of both B and F. Think of this as the float stealing space from the block.

Intruding floats make no impact on the placement of normal block-areas. However, they do influence the `inline-progression-dimension` of the following types of areas:

- line-areas
- reference-areas (generated by a `fo:block-container` element)
- Areas generated by `list-item-body`

If an area belongs to one of these types, and has one or more side-floats intruding into it, then its `start-indent` and `end-indent` are calculated from the inner side of the float box, rather than from the respective edge of an ancestor-reference-area.

In a typical case, a paragraph of text with an intruding float will have lines shortened to make room for the float. Note that the block itself is not influenced by the float; if

---

* Setting all components of a compound property by omitting the component specification is termed a *short form*.

† In fact, margins are tolerated in XSL as a secondary mechanism to ensure CSS2 compatibility, but they don't integrate well with XSL layout model based on constrained spaces. We strongly advise using indents instead of margins.

it has a border around it, the float will be pasted inside the border. On the other hand, a block-container with an automatically determined width will shrink as a whole, leaving the float outside.*

Stacking Block-Areas and Spaces

Let's now consider how block-areas are stacked one after another in the block-progression-dimension. We have already seen that the XSL model is based on spaces; now we will see which properties can be used to constrain spaces between areas, and how they interact.

What is a space? Informally speaking, a space is a distance between the area's border-rectangle and *the closest visible mark* left on the page by any normally positioned area. This mark may be left by a nonzero border, by padding (because padding may contain background), or by a nonempty content-rectangle of any area. Border and padding need not belong to the next or previous area: they may be left by an embracing block that happens to start or end just before or after the current area. Note also that for two consecutive areas, the space-before of the first area is equal to the space-after of the second area. See Figure 4-7.

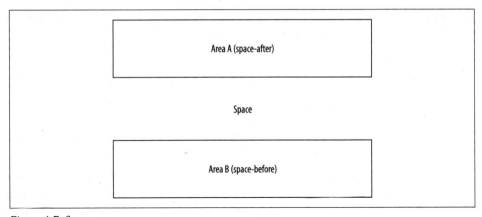

Figure 4-7. *Space*

Spaces before and after a block-area are controlled by space-before and space-after properties. These two properties are *compound*, with the following components:

.minimum
> A length. Default is 0pt.

.optimum
> A length. Default is 0pt.

---

* This is expected to change significantly in the next version of the XSL spec.

`.maximum`

A length. Default is 0pt.

`precedence`

A number or a special token, `force`. Default is 0.

`conditionality`

Either `discard` or `retain`. Default is `discard`.

There is also a shorthand notation: by specifying `space-before="X"` you set all numerical components (`.minimum`, `.optimum`, and `.maximum`) to the same value of X.

These compound properties represent a very versatile mechanism: you can constrain a range for the space (from `minimum` to `maximum`), indicate the preferred value (`optimum`), set the relative strength for the constraints (`precedence`), or define space behavior when there is no adjacent area in the same reference-area (`conditionality`).

This complexity is due to the fact that space constraints are not independent. When two consecutive areas meet, there may be several space constraints applicable: a single space value should be chosen to satisfy them all (or rather, to satisfy them to the best extent). In this situation, it is desirable to give a stylesheet writer the maximum control over the selection of the correct space.

As I mentioned earlier, a space constraint between two consecutive areas A and B can be specified in any of the following ways (see Figure 4-8):

- As a `space-after` of A
- As a `space-before` of B
- As a `space-after` of any block-area A1 descendant of A such that there is no other content, padding, or border between A1 and B
- As a `space-before` of any block-area B1 descendant of B such that there is no other content, padding, or border between A and B1

All these constraints are considered together and merged into a single value, or better, a single range specifier with `.minimum`, `.maximum`, and `.optimum` components. The final decision is delegated to the XSL formatter; it should stick to the resolved `.optimum` value whenever possible, and choose another value within the `.minimum` to `.maximum` range if there are other constraints to satisfy.

The merged space specifier is calculated by the following algorithm:

- If any space property has `.precedence="force"` (forcing spaces), all space specifiers but forcing ones are discarded. The resulting space specifier should have the sum of `.minimum` components as its `.minimum`, the sum of `.optimums` as `.optimum`, and the sum of `.maximums` as `.maximum`. In other words, forcing spaces are additive: they suppress all other spaces but don't merge with each other.

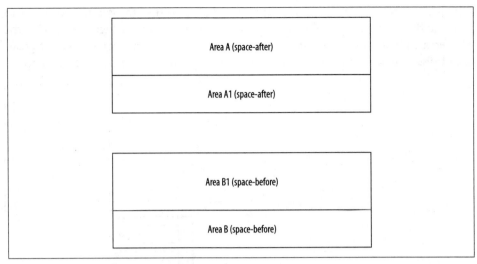

Inside figure:
Area A (space-after)

Area A1 (space-after)

Area B1 (space-before)

Area B (space-before)

Figure 4-8. Space resolution

- Otherwise, spaces with the maximum value of .precedence are selected, and others are discarded. If there is more than one space specifier with the same precedence, the one with the higher .optimum value is selected. If there are two or more specifiers with the same .precedence and .optimum values, the resulting space specifier will be equal to the intersection of their ranges; that is, the .minimum will be equal to the greatest of all .minimums, and the .maximum will be set to the smallest of all .maximums.

If an area happens to be the first on the page with no preceding marks from which to count space-before, space-before is counted from the before-edge of the content-rectangle of the closest ancestor reference-area. Remember that in this case, only specifiers with .conditionality="retain" are taken into consideration.

Now let's see an example of how all this works. Figure 4-9 represents a typical configuration. Two blocks, each specifies a space: the first specifies a space-after and the second specifies a space-before. Example 4-1 demonstrates how to achieve this.

Example 4-1. Space resolution

```
<fo:block space-after.minimum="3pt">
         space-after.maximum="24pt"
           space-after.optimum="12pt">
  .....

</fo:block>
<fo:block space-before.minimum="6pt"
           space-before.maximum="18pt"
           space-before.optimum="12pt">
 ....
</fo:block>
```

The resolution is for the resultant minimum to be set to 6pt, the maximum to be set to 18pt, and the computed value, set to 12pt. This is shown in Figure 4-9, with the shaded area indicating the extents. When the optimum values are equal, take the greatest minimum and least maximum, so the resolved space in this case has a minimum of 6pt.

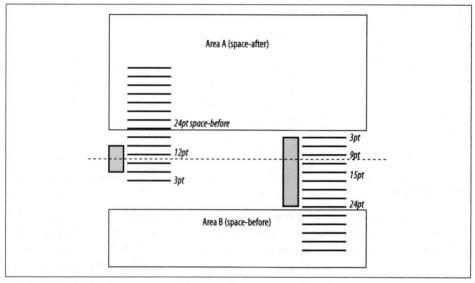

Figure 4-9. Space resolution (2)

It is easy to create a contradictory set of space constraints. In such a case, formatter behavior is not described by the specification and remains application-specific. The stylesheet writer is responsible for the consistency of the constraint system. The space mechanism is powerful and versatile, but not fool proof.

This differs drastically from the CSS box model where top- and bottom-margins are a single value. Margins in CSS are self-contained and additive in most cases, and the margin merging algorithm is rudimentary—the widest margin is selected. XSL supports margin properties on before-edge and after-edge, too; they are converted into space-specifiers as follows:

```
margin-{correspondent}="X":
    .minimum = .optimum = .maximum = X
    .conditionality="retain"
    .precedence="force"
```

This permits you to simulate CSS-style box stacking in XSL. Note that CSS-style margins won't merge with each other and will overcome every non-forcing space specifier.

Stacking Inline-Areas

Stacking inline-areas inside a line-area is perfectly parallel to stacking block-areas inside a reference-area. An inline-area has traits to control free space left before and after it in the `inline-progression-direction`:

space-start
> Controls how much space is left before the start-edge of the inline-area; it is set by the space-start compound property;

space-end
> Controls how much space is left after the end-edge of the inline-area; it is set by the space-end compound property.

space-start and space-end for inline-areas are calculated by the same rules as space-before and space-after for block-areas (accounting for possible change of direction). Any conditionality components control constraint suppression at the start or end of a line-area.

Alignment of inline-areas in the `block-progression-direction` is controlled by the baseline mechanism (see Chapter 6).

Stacking Line-Areas

Stacking line-areas inside a block-area is less trivial. The distance between lines is controlled by the compound property `line-height`, with the same components as other space specifiers. Its interpretation depends on the algorithm selected for line-stacking. There are three algorithms available, switched by the `line-stacking-strategy` property on the parent block-area: `font-height`, `max-height`, and `line-height`.

To describe the placement of lines in terms of stacked areas, here are some terms. A line-area can be logically divided into three parts (see Figure 4-10):

- The *allocation-rectangle* is the central part of the line-area around the baseline. It roughly corresponds to the content-rectangle, but doesn't necessarily coincide with it. Its size in the `block-progression-dimension` is determined differently depending on the `line-stacking-strategy` selected.

- There are two spaces around the allocation-rectangle, which are both equal to *half-leading*. Half-leading spaces get .conditionality and .precedence attributes from the `line-height` property and can be merged with other spaces and suppressed in the beginning or at the end of a reference area—just like other spaces. However, half-leading spaces never get merged with their likes.

Line-areas are stacked one after another inside a block-area, leaving no other space before or after them but the half-leadings from both sides. The gap between allocation rectangles of two adjacent line-areas consists of the half-leading-after of the first line *plus* the half-leading-before of the second line. (Note that these two spaces aren't merged.)

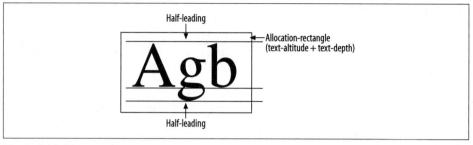

Figure 4-10. Line area layout

The available line-stacking strategies are line-height, font-height, and max-height.

Note that for lines built entirely of text using a nominal font, all three line-stacking strategies give the same value of base line separation (equal to the line-height). They differ only in the treatment of large elements that go outside the nominal-requested-line-rectangle: the simplest strategy is font-height: separation between baselines of adjacent line areas is constant throughout the whole block and does not depend on the actual contents of any line. Inter-line distance should equal line-height.optimum, unless the formatter chooses another value in the range .minimum to .maximum to satisfy other constraints on block placement. Sizes of line-area elements are determined as follows:

- Allocation-rectangle for line-stacking-strategy="font-height" depends solely on the nominal font for the block. Its before-edge is offset by text-altitude from the baseline, and its after-edge is placed at text-depth from the baseline in the block-progression-direction. In the XSL spec, this is called nominal-requested-line-rectangle, and is likely to be the most common one used.

- Half-leading is half the difference between the line-height chosen and the height of the allocation rectangle:

```
half-leading = (line-height - text-altitude - text-depth) / 2
```

In other words, this strategy stacks lines as if the whole block consisted entirely of plain text, with text-altitude and text-depth remaining constant across the block. Eventual inclusions of other font glyphs or large images don't influence the distance between the baselines. Using font-height will certainly make a mess of things if you include, for instance, graphics in your document. In such a case, use max-height.

max-height is a more complicated strategy. The half-leading is calculated by the same formula as with font-height and remains constant for all lines in the block. The allocation-rectangle, instead, is calculated in a more complex way: its dimension in the block-progression-dimension is determined by the elements whose before-edge and after-edge are the most distant from the baseline (for Western scripts these are determined by the tallest/deepest elements; that's why the strategy is called max-height).

With this strategy, the gaps between the lines remain constant across the block; if the line has elements bigger than glyphs of nominal font, its separation from its neighboring lines will be increased so as to leave the gap between lines equal to the constant value (two half-leadings). However, if the line consists only of small elements, the baseline separation is not stretched: the allocation-rectangle will always contain the nominal-requested-line-rectangle.

One more trait influences line placement with this strategy: line-height-shift-adjustment. It controls processing of areas whose baselines are shifted from the common baseline of the line-area. There can be two values for this trait:

consider-shifts

> When calculating the allocation-rectangle, baseline shift elements are taken into account. For instance, if a line contains a subscript, the next line will be placed lower because the allocation-rectangle will extend to reach the after-edge of the subscript glyph.

disregard-shifts

> Baseline shifts are disregarded. If a line contains subscripts or superscripts, its placement is not influenced by their presence.

The last strategy is line-height. This way of stacking lines comes from CSS and differs greatly from the preceding two. In this method, the line-height trait is considered a property of each inline-area, rather than the whole block-area, and may vary across the block: it is even possible that areas within the same line have different values of line-height. There is no common half-leading defined for the block; instead, every single area gets margins before and after it, depending on the local value of the line-height trait. The allocation-rectangle of the line-area is defined to be the least rectangle to include both the nominal-requested-line-rectangle and all inline-areas with their margins. Allocation-rectangles defined this way are stacked one after another, with no additional gap between them.

The algorithm to determine margins on inline-areas is similar to the method of calculating line separation in the max-height strategy:

- For inline images and reference-areas (containers), margins are set by normal space-specifiers that are treated as CSS margins: conditionality and precedence are neglected, and no merging ever occurs.

- For other types of areas, the half-leading is calculated as a function of line-height, text-altitude, and text-depth. The formula is the same as earlier for font-height and max-height, but trait values are taken from the inline-area. This half-leading is added before and after the content-rectangle (determined by text-altitude/text-depth traits). Note that the block-progression-dimension of the resulting margin-rectangle will be always equal to the line-height.

Within this strategy, `line-height-shift-adjustment` is also applicable and has the same meaning: when `line-height-shift-adjustment="disregard-shifts"` is set, all calculations are performed as if all inline-areas were aligned along the same baseline. This permits exclusion of inter-line gap widening due to subscripts and superscripts.

- `font-height` neglects big elements—line separation is always fixed. This strategy gives the tightest line placement. Other strategies can only increase inter-line spaces.

- `max-height` adjusts separation in such a way that visible gap between lines remains constant.

- `line-height` permits variation of the treatment of outstanding elements on a case-by-case basis.

CHAPTER 5

Blocks

Blocks represent smaller parts of a document, familiar as features such as paragraphs, lists, and tables. Using these pieces, you can structure your documents and present them within the page contexts you've established.

Block Basics

Think of the last document you styled. Each major space-separated block of contiguous text, graphic, table, or list is most likely to be a block when styled with XSL-FO. fo:block could be called the basic building block of page content. Simply inserting content into an fo:block element produces a simple paragraph style with all the default properties. Blocks are most commonly used within the page layout you have specified, specifically within the fo:flow element.

To appreciate the flexibility of blocks, it's necessary first to select the right type of block, then to select from its list of available properties.

The top-level blocks include:

- fo:block
- fo:block-container
- fo:list
- fo:table

These are the major divisions, each producing an area within the block-progression-direction, visually separated by a new line. I'll cover each of these in turn.

The Basic Block

The content model for a block consists of other blocks, inlines, or textual content. The simple block, acting as a paragraph, is likely to be your most used element in the fo namespace, for normal text-heavy documents. Note that the same fo:block may be used for any content that requires whitespace separation in the block-progression-direction. This ranges from the title of a document on a page by itself to list item contents. The block is a versatile element.

The stylesheet snippet in Example 5-1 picks out the para elements in an XML source document, styles them as blocks with no start indent, has fairly typical spacing between its predecessor and successor, uses the Times font, and has simple content. The border around the block is simply to outline its area, as I'll be referring to this again.

Example 5-1. A simple block

```
<xsl:template match="para">
    <fo:block
      border-style="solid"
      border-width=".1mm"
      font-family="Times"
      font-size="12pt"
      space-before="12pt"
      space-after="12pt"
      text-align="justify">
          <xsl:apply-templates/>
    </fo:block>
  </xsl:template>
```

This delivers a fairly standard paragraph, as shown in Figure 5-1.

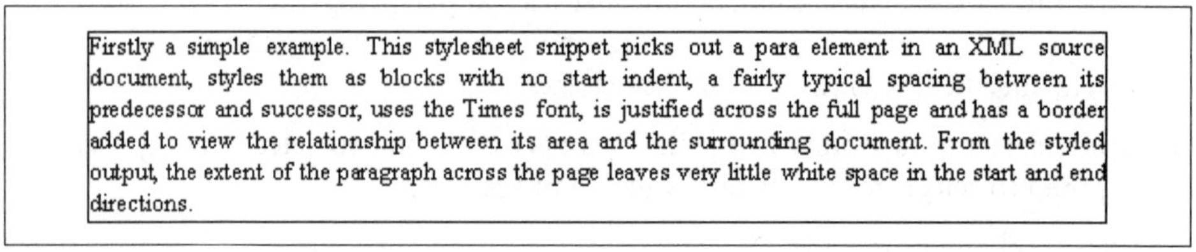

Firstly a simple example. This stylesheet snippet picks out a para element in an XML source document, styles them as blocks with no start indent, a fairly typical spacing between its predecessor and successor, uses the Times font, is justified across the full page and has a border added to view the relationship between its area and the surrounding document. From the styled output, the extent of the paragraph across the page leaves very little white space in the start and end directions.

Figure 5-1. Basic paragraph layout

The basic syntax is simple, but choosing the correct suite of attributes for any particular context is not quite so simple. I've selected the font-family, font-size, and text-align (basic alignment) properties, a minimal set of properties for consistent display. I've set the space-before and space-after properties, rather than using the default (which places almost no space between succeeding paragraphs). Without the borders, spacing the same size as the font (or slightly bigger) is a reasonable choice.

Now back to that border. It should show up as black, but I'm cheating here, relying on an inherited attribute to make the color. To ensure that it is, I normally add color='black' to the fo:flow element containing the region-body. The example specifies a border of 0.1mm width. I could have followed older HTML principles and specified 1px (1 pixel), but there is a downside to this. The specification, in Section 5.19, warns about the pixel as a unit of measure: stylesheet authors should understand a pixel's actual size may vary between devices. Stylesheets using pixels may not produce consistent results across different implementations or different output devices from a single implementation.

The text alignment specified by the text-align attribute can be start, center, end, justify, inside, outside, left, right, or inherit. The more common choices are start (the lefthand side in a left-to-right layout), which provides what is sometimes called "ragged right" layout; center, which centers text; end, which provides right justification; and justify, which provides both left and right justification, creating the simplest of paragraphs, without any special features. inside and outside are peculiar to bound documents. When documents are bound, particularly with stitched bindings, the text can be aligned relative to the binding. For example, where the binding is toward the start side, the text is aligned to that side.

Indentation is provided by the two properties: start-indent and end-indent. Each takes a length specification as its value and has an initial value of 0pt, or no indentation. This is not the same as text-indent, which indents only the first line of text within the block. A negative value of text-indent will produce the hanging indent. With start-indent, indentation is applied to the whole block. Possible uses are to indent a quotation, perhaps similar to Example 5-2.

Example 5-2. Indentation

```
<xsl:template match="quote">
    <fo:block
       start-indent="6em"
       end-indent="6em"
       font-family="Times"
       font-size="12pt"
       space-before="12pt"
       space-after="12pt"
       text-align="start">
          "<xsl:apply-templates/>"
    </fo:block>
  </xsl:template>
```

This creates an indented block (indented at the start and end directions), offset by 6em from its nearest ancestor. I've added the quote characters around content as decoration. Perhaps if the quotation is attributed to a specific author, it could be offset to the right, in its own block, using text-align="end".

An alternate use for this form of indentation is to create a wrapper block element, with the indentation set to whatever offset is needed from the edge of the printed area of the body, then to nest all other blocks within it, which reduces the need to specify it for all the children of this block.

First line indentation, a common style in some texts, is achieved by using the text-indent attribute. To keep it proportional to the font size in use, the em length specification is again useful. Example 5-3 and its result, Figure 5-2, illustrate this.

Example 5-3. First line indentation

```
<xsl:template match="para">
   <fo:block
     space-before="12pt"
     space-after="12pt"
     text-indent="3em"
     text-align="justify">
        <xsl:apply-templates/>
   </fo:block>
</xsl:template>
```

> This paragraph uses the property text-indent to require that the first line be indented by a
> fixed distance. This paragraph has the property set to a value of 3em

Figure 5-2. First line indentation

A variation on this is the hanging indent, using a combination of the text-indent and start-indent properties as in Example 5-4.

Example 5-4. Hanging indents

```
<fo:block
       text-indent='-4em'
       start-indent='4em'>

An example of a hanging indent, a paragraph with the first
line left aligned, and the remainder of the paragraph
indented by a fixed amount. Set by using the start indent
and text-indent properties on a block. The text-indent is
set to a negative value, the start indent to a positive
value.

</fo:block>
```

Similarly, the last line of a block may be given special treatment using the last-line-end-indent attribute. This assures a fixed end-space on the last line. The formatter may fit in more text than normal or may break one line to form another. Either way, your last line is guaranteed minimum whitespace as specified by this property. Due care is needed, because a positive value will indent the end-edge, and a negative value will extend it beyond the normal finish, creating an outdent.

Another line property is text-align-last, whose value may be relative, start, center, end, justify, inside, outside, left, or right. These values affect the layout in the line-progression-direction. Justified text with this property may appear strange if the content of the last line is insufficient to reasonably fill the line. The other values are self-explanatory; note that inside and outside values relate to the page binding edge. I prefer the relative value, with the majority of a paragraph set with the text-align property having the value justify, which provides start justification or a last line. Figure 5-3 shows these two options. The first option has text-align set to justify, the second has text-align-last set to start.

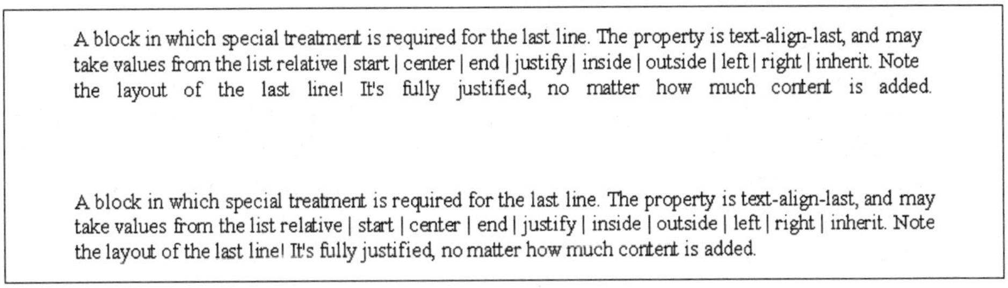

A block in which special treatment is required for the last line. The property is text-align-last, and may take values from the list relative | start | center | end | justify | inside | outside | left | right | inherit. Note the layout of the last line! It's fully justified, no matter how much content is added.

A block in which special treatment is required for the last line. The property is text-align-last, and may take values from the list relative | start | center | end | justify | inside | outside | left | right | inherit. Note the layout of the last line! It's fully justified, no matter how much content is added.

Figure 5-3. Last line alignment

A simple use of fo:block just creates a break. This is certainly not a recommended practice, because using fo:block to insert a break risks destroying the paragraph's indents, widow/orphan handling, or line-height calculations. Other alternatives would be (as in the next example) to make each line a block using nl for a new line and adjust the block separation accordingly, perhaps within a wrapper block. The problem here is that we use visual properties in the source XML; <nl/>, for a new-line, is hardly semantic markup.

Reusing this *quote* template with additional processing for the nl element produces the layout for the poem, as shown in Example 5-5 and the output, in Figure 5-4.

Example 5-5. XML source for block as a break

```
<para>This paragraph includes a quotation
<quote>The fair breeze blew, the white foam flew <nl/>
The furrow followed free; <nl/>
We were the first that ever burst<nl/>
Into that silent sea. </quote>
<author>Samuel Taylor Coleridge</author>
And continues after it. </para>
```

This paragraph includes a quotation

"The fair breeze blew, the white foam flew
The furrow followed free;
We were the first that ever burst
Into that silent sea. "

Author: Samuel Taylor Coleridge

And continues after it.

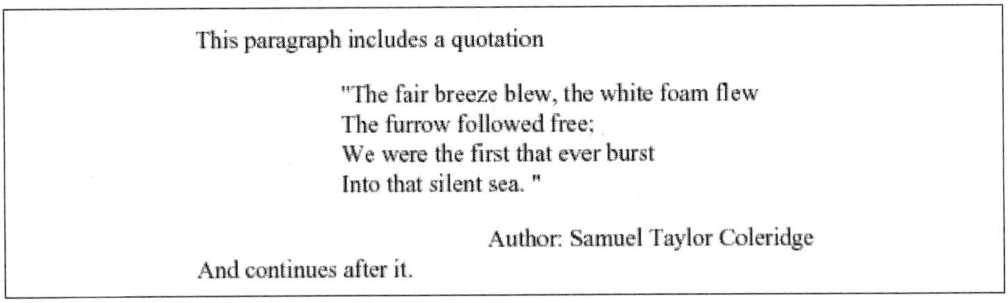

Figure 5-4. Block as a break

The associated template for the end of line element is shown in Example 5-6.

Example 5-6. The template

```
<xsl:template match="nl">
    <fo:block />
</xsl:template>
```

The nl element is used to indicate that a line break is needed. Because this is visual rather than semantic, check your output when you use this. The transformation used here is simply an empty block element, whose initial values provided the needed styling. The template for the author element uses a large start-indent value (12em) to provide the indentation for the author, because the lines themselves are short. For longer lines it may be appropriate to use the text-align attribute value of end to ensure that the block is right aligned.

Although in this release of the specification there is no special treatment for an <fo:character character='&#x0A'/> (it is treated the same as any other whitespace in content), there could be a case for using some special character (perhaps U+2028, Line Separator) for this purpose. However, until it becomes a part of the specification, I can't recommend it. The processing is shown in Example 5-7.

Example 5-7. Possible line treatment

```
<xsl:template match="nl">
    <fo:character character = '&#x2028' />
</xsl:template>
```

Block Separation

We often want to space paragraphs or other blocks of text to create the best visual effect. This is achieved by using the space-before and space-after properties of a block, each of which takes a length specification. If two succeeding paragraphs have space specified before and after, the formatter needs to combine the two specified values to obtain a final resolved value. The properties that interact here are the space-before (or space-after) precedence and conditionality. The specification is quite clear on the resolution: usually when there are two values with similar precedence, you will see the larger one. A higher precedence (or special value force) may be used to override this, if needed. To increase a value's precedence, use the value space-after.precedence="n", where n is some number larger than the default value of zero; the more you need it to increase the precedence, the higher the number. If you use a value of force, you completely change the precedence-mediated merging semantic to an additive one. Note that padding does not interact with this space resolution.

The first precedence rule may throw you: it states that if a space specifier is the first (outer) one and is conditional, it is discarded. So when you try to create a title page that is blank except for the title block, the space above it is eaten, which is quite frustrating. To invalidate this rule, use the retain value. Example 5-8 shows one way to ensure a 2-inch space prior to a block.

Example 5-8. Retaining space

```
<fo:block
 space-before="2in"
 space-before.conditionality = 'retain'>
...
```

The first of the three paragraphs has no specification of space-after; the second paragraph has a 12pt space-before specification and a space-after specification, with no precedence specified; and the third paragraph specifies a space-before with a stated precedence of 5. You can see the result in Example 5-9 and Figure 5-5.

Example 5-9. Inter-paragraph spacing

```
<fo:block  space-after="12pt"
border-style="solid"
border-width=".1mm"

>
This is the first of three blocks .</fo:block>

 <fo:block
border-style="solid"
border-width=".1mm"
 space-after="12pt">
This block has the space-after set to 12pt,
so there will be an interaction.</fo:block>


<fo:block
border-style="solid"
border-width=".1mm"
   space-before="18pt"
   space-before.precedence="5">
This block really must have the
larger (18pt) space before .</fo:block>
```

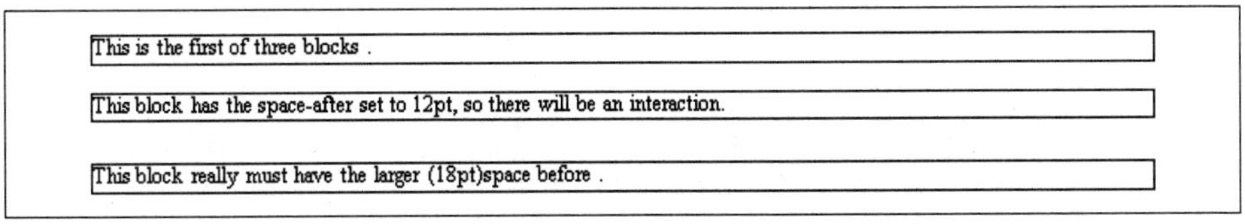

Figure 5-5. The impact of precedence on inter-paragraph spacing

Breaks Between Paragraphs

Authors often need to ensure some form of break in the flow of a document. Within blocks, two properties are used for this: break-before and break-after. Possible values are auto, column, page, even-page, and odd-page. auto is the default value, allowing the normal flow of content.

Typical use would be to ensure that a chapter starts on a new page or to start a new column in a multicolumn layout. The specification of recto or verso pages is done by stating that the break should be to a new odd or even page.

If each chapter has its own block, specifying:

```
<fo:block break-before="odd-page">
```

will, if necessary, add the blank page to ensure that the chapter starts on the new, odd-numbered page.

The Block as a Wrapper

To decorate a block of text, rather than operate at the lower level, it's often easier to wrap a series of blocks in another block to apply formatting to the outer wrapper block. This enables the styling of contained blocks within this frame. A highlighted section of a page is a case in point. If a border is applied to the wrapper block, normal blocks can be offset from this wrapper and will be presented as normal blocks within this box.

Example 5-10 shows the containing block with a border and two internal blocks, each with an indent at the start and end directions to offset them from this border. Space is allocated before and after to ensure the separation of each contained block.

Example 5-10. Wrapper blocks to offset content from the main flow

```
<fo:block
    border-style="solid"
    border-width="2mm">
  <fo:block start-indent="4em"
        space-before="2em"
        space-after="1em"
        end-indent="4em">First contained block
  </fo:block>
  <fo:block start-indent="4em"
        space-after="2em"
        end-indent="4em">Second contained block.
        The significant border together with the indents
        offsets the content,
        seperating it visually from the main flow.
  </fo:block>
</fo:block>
```

Example 5-10 uses two of the indent properties to offset the block content from its surroundings. The indent property can be applied to both the start and end directions, as shown in the example. Here, the indent property it is used to offset the content by 4em. Figure 5-6 illustrates this.

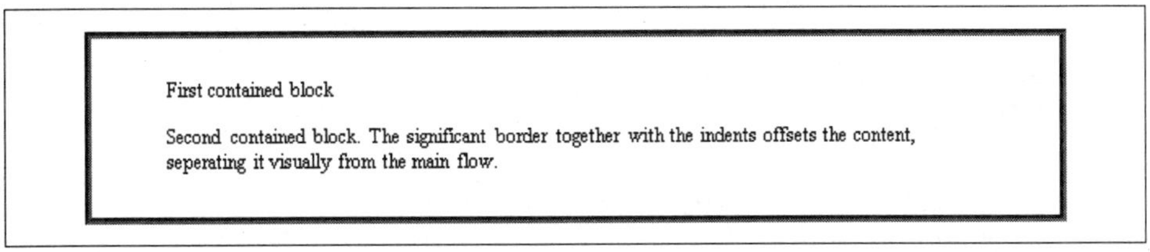

First contained block

Second contained block. The significant border together with the indents offsets the content, seperating it visually from the main flow.

Figure 5-6. Wrapper blocks to offset content from the main flow

XSL-FO also permits the use of an absolute position, fixed relative to the containing area. Note that this property is a part of complete compliance and, hence, is likely to reduce portability. In the case of paged media, the area is fixed with respect to the page. For this, there is the absolute-position property. With this property set to fixed, the top property specifies how far the content's top margin edge is offset below the top of the page. To produce content at a fixed location, such as the signature line on a letter, we might see stylesheet content like that in Example 5-11.

Example 5-11. A stylesheet snippet showing styling for a signature

```
<xsl:template match="signature">
<fo:block-container absolute-position="fixed"
                    top="240mm" left="100mm">
<fo:block xsl:use-attribute-sets="para">
  Yours Sincerely: <xsl:apply-templates/>
</fo:block>
</fo:block-container>
</xsl:template>
```

Note the use of fo:block-container here. One of the stated purposes of this formatting object is to change the writing mode or orientation. I've used it here to use the absolute-position property, to position the signature line 240mm from the top and 100mm from the left edge of the body. This achieves a regular positioning of content to ensure that (in this case) the signature line is always seen in the same place for any letter. A dot leader might be provided if the document was meant for a hand written signature.

Blocks for Special Purposes

The use of blocks for some purposes may not be readily obvious. A simple heading in a larger font may not be seen as a variant of a block, but it is. It may be used as the main heading of a document.

A title page is simply a single block that has break-before and break-after set to the value page, and the space-before.conditionality set to retain. Example 5-12 shows a specific example of this practice.

Example 5-12. A title page specification

```
<fo:block
        break-before="page"
        break-after="page"
          space-after="4in"
          space-before="3in"
          space-before.conditionality="retain"
          font="24pt Times bold"
          text-align="center">
  Document Title, using single or multiple lines.
</fo:block>
```

Note the use of the break condition in the containing block. This causes the page to appear on its own. This may also be used to create a blank page.

Other content that needs special layout might include a quotation, a heavily emphasized block, or even images, which often form the only content of a block.

Each needs consideration in terms of borders, offset spacing (using space-before, padding, or indentation), text alignment, or other decorations.

Other special uses for which the block is ideal include the indented quotation (often called the blockquote), end aligned blocks, emphasized text that is not inline, and simpler headings. Each of these is a block for which the properties are selected appropriately. When selecting how you want a block laid out, a virtual ritual is needed to choose which of the myriad properties are needed.

One possible approach is to run through the following sequence:

- Block separation: from the previous and next block vertically. Use space-before or space-after.
- Horizontal alignment within the block. Use text-align and text-align-last.
- Indentation: use text-indent for the first line, or use start-indent and end-indent for a block.
- Finally, select the font-family, font-weight, and font-size.

This sequence considers the positioning of the block vertically (relative to previous and subsequent blocks) and horizontally (in the line-progression-direction), sets up the content alignment (start, end, or justified), and then finally set the font, font weight, and size. For many blocks, this will be sufficient. Once you have selected these properties, all that remains for you to do is the decoration on the block, which I'll discuss shortly. These properties will satisfy most of your basic layout needs for simple blocks. Lists and tables also will be addressed.

Backgrounds on Blocks

A background can be specified for any block, and takes the following list of properties. Most of these properties really apply only to the use of images as a background, with the exception of color, which may be used on its own or as a fallback for the image.

- background-attachment: scroll or fixed. Not really relevant to print, but specifies what happens when an image is used as a background.
- background-color sets the color.
- background-image specifies the image to use.
- background-position-vertical (or -horizontal) specifies the position of the background image with respect to the containing rectangle.
- background-repeat specifies if, and how, the image is to be repeated in the content rectangle. This is discussed later in this chapter.

Probably the most common one is background-color, which simply specifies the color to be used for the background of the block.

Images

For figures, images, illustrations, or graphics—whatever you want to call them—XSL-FO uses a single element, fo:external-graphic ("external" simply because the actual graphics file is external to the XML source document), to add it to the flow. If it is wrapped in a block or placed inline with the content, the graphic is appropriately laid out by the formatter, as shown in Example 5-13 and illustrated in Figure 5-7.

Example 5-13. External graphics

```
<fo:block> <fo:external-graphic src='url(pig.jpg)'/> </fo:block>
   <fo:block>
     <fo:external-graphic
        src="url(pig.jpg)"/>
   </fo:block>
   <fo:block>A block containing the graphic wrapped in
             an inline container,
     <fo:inline alignment-baseline="before-edge">
       <fo:external-graphic
                          src="url(images/1.png)"/>
     </fo:inline>
   </fo:block>
```

Note the syntax of the src attribute. The url function, as shown here, simply returns the local (relative) file. It has raised some controversy in regards to its necessity, because most files will be local, although it does offer the option of a web-based image. Be aware of the display capabilities of your formatter. Common ones are JPEG and PNG.

A block containing the graphic wrapped in an inline container,

Figure 5-7. Block and inline graphics

The two images are wrapped, one in a block and one inline. Their sizes are determined automatically in this case, although sizes can be specified in applicable units using the `content-height` and `content-width` properties of the `fo:external-graphic`. The specification recommends also using `background-color`, which will fill in the rectangle outside of the actual image to the extent of the containing rectangle when the image is available and will be visible when the image is unavailable. When the image is available, it is rendered on top of the background color. (Thus, the color is visible in any transparent parts of the image.)

Figures can also use the block to create a title for the image. Nest both the title and the external graphic within a single block to keep them together (to share alignment or any other special properties), as in Example 5-14.

Example 5-14. Titled images

```
<fo:block>
      <fo:block>Title for the figure</fo:block>
      <fo:external-graphic  src="url(images/filename.ext)"/>
</fo:block>
```

Also, an image may be scaled by using the `content-height` and `scaling` properties:

```
<fo:external-graphic content-height="120%"
                     scaling="uniform"
    ...
```

The aspect ratio of the graphic is maintained using the `scaling` property with a value of `uniform`, as above. Note that uniform scaling is the default even when only the `content-height` is specified to be scaled.

Images may be used as a background for a block using the block property `background-image`. This provides the image over which the content is written. The extent of the image is controlled with the `background-repeat` property, which takes one of the following values: `repeat`, `repeat-x`, `repeat-y`, or `no-repeat`. These produce an x and y repeat, an x direction only repeat, a y direction only repeat or no repetition, respectively. Figure 5-8 shows an example using the `no-repeat` option, which produces a single image. The image may be positioned readily using the `background-position-vertical` and `background-position-horizontal` properties.

By judicious selection of the correct image and the `background-repeat` property, you will find out (probably by experimentation) which alternative provides the effect you need. This property on blocks may be used either decoratively or for a more targeted

Figure 5-8. Background images

purpose, such as indicating a property of the output to inform the reader that certain content is not valid. This is often seen with the background images on checks that say *sample only*, to avoid fraudulent use of the content.

Finally, a variant on an image, the `instream-foreign-object` element, is commonly used for SVG, but could be used for other inline approaches. It contains any markup format that isn't in the `fo` namespace and that the FO processor can invoke some other processor to handle. But the idea is that it creates a black box that is simply positioned by the FO processor, just as with `external-graphic`. SVG usage is strong in some processors as an XML-based vector graphic format. Other options are XHTML and the Synchronized Multimedia Integration Language (SMIL), both W3C recommendations. Note that this is purely a function of the renderer you are using. Ensure that your readers have that renderer prior to using this.

Identifying Blocks

Cross-references are generated at the transform stage, using perhaps the `id` and `idref` pairings from XML. The XSLT stylesheet should produce similarly identified pairs of references and identified content, as discussed in Chapter 9. The target of a cross-reference is identified by the `id` attribute on the block. This is shown in Example 5-15. A chapter element creates a block with an `id` value taken directly from the XML source document. This may then be referenced later using this `id` value.

 The `id` value from the XML source needs to be carried over to the `fo` namespace! In the XSL-FO document, the `id` value is required on the `fo:block` or whatever element is used in the `fo` namespace. Hence, when the XML source document is transformed to the `fo` namespace, the `id` value should be copied over to an appropriate element or the cross-references will not work.

Example 5-15. A cross-reference target

```
<xsl:template match="chapter">
<fo:block id="{@id}">
   .....process content
</fo:block>
</xsl:template>
```

This is discussed further in Chapter 10.

Decorating Blocks

The title of this section may seem inappropriate to some readers. What one person may view as decoration, another may view as essential content. In this section, I discuss borders, padding, color, etc., which some may view as decoration.

First, I must clarify. From outside to inside, there is a border, padding, and then content. This is illustrated in Figure 5-9.

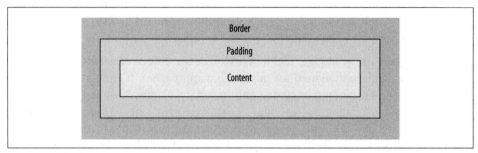

Figure 5-9. Borders, padding, and content

We can refine the breakdown of borders and padding by specifying only one side. Hence, the full list of borders is:

- `border-before`
- `border-after`
- `border-start`
- `border-end`

You should be aware that the simplest specification of a border (the form `border='black solid 1pt'`) is available only in a complete implementation. If portability is an issue, I might suggest using the basic options in combination with the inherited color, which defaults to black. The basic version is shown in Example 5-16. It might appear to be grossly inefficient, but if used as a part of your attribute sets as shown, it will not be a problem.

Example 5-16. Basic version of border specification

```
<xsl:attribute-set name='border'>
<xsl:attribute name='border-before-style'>solid</xsl:attribute>
<xsl:attribute name='border-after-style'>solid</xsl:attribute>
<xsl:attribute name='border-start-style'>solid</xsl:attribute>
<xsl:attribute name='border-end-style'>solid</xsl:attribute>

<xsl:attribute name='border-before-width'>.1mm</xsl:attribute>
<xsl:attribute name='border-after-width'>.1mm</xsl:attribute>
<xsl:attribute name='border-start-width'>.1mm</xsl:attribute>
<xsl:attribute name='border-end-width'>.1mm</xsl:attribute>
</xsl:attribute-set>
```

This is called up using:

```
<fo:block  xsl:use-attribute-sets='border'>
....
```

Padding is specified in the same way. To keep it simple, I will continue using the shorthand form, using simply border, which the formatter then expands to specify all four properties. Further alternatives are provided by border-top, border-bottom, border-left, and border-right, which are writing-mode relative. For example, border-before.length would equate to border-top.length in left-to-right, top-to-bottom writing. Feel free to interchange these if you prefer or if you are concerned about portability.

Having specified which border you want, the properties available for borders are:

color
    Specifies the color required for the border.

width
    Specifies the extent of the border.

style
    Specifies the appearance of the border. Possible values are none, hidden, dotted, dashed, solid, double, groove, ridge, inset, and outset.

Most of the border properties are self-explanatory, though the style property may be less so. Each style offers a different visual appearance. inset and outset attempt to provide a three-dimensional effect. Example 5-17 shows the basics of using the style property on a block.

Example 5-17. Using a simple border

```
<fo:block
      border-style="solid"
      border-width=".1mm"

      width="2in">
    A simple narrow  border
  </fo:block>
```

This example uses the extended option of specifying style and width, relying on the inherited color, because the basic specification requires a lot of typing.

```
border-style="solid"
border-before-style="solid"
border-after-style="solid"
border-start-style="solid"
border-end-style="solid"

border-before-width=".1mm"
border-after-width=".1mm"
border-start-width=".1mm"
border-end-width=".1mm"
```

```
            border-before-color="black"
            border-after-color="black"
            border-start-color="black"
            border-end-color="black"
```

An explicit and more comprehensive example is shown in Example 5-18; its formatted output is shown in Figure 5-10. I have added a little padding simply to separate the content from the border.

Example 5-18. A more complete border example

```
<fo:block
            border-after-color="red"
            border-after-style="outset"
            border-after-width="1em"

            border-before-color="blue"
            border-before-style="outset"
            border-before-width="1.5em"

            border-end-color="silver"
            border-end-style="outset"
            border-end-width="2em"

            border-start-color="green"
            border-start-style="outset"
            border-start-width="2em"

            padding="6pt"
            width="4in">
  A paragraph with a completely specified border.
  Style is shared as 'outset',
  color varies on each edge,
  as does width.
  </fo:block>
```

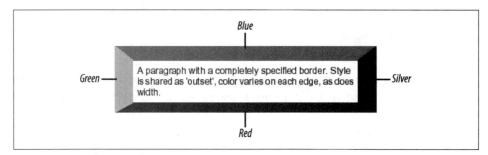

Figure 5-10. Border example

Although the simpified forms can appear complex, for most users, they will suffice. If you want to use them more fully, the specification is reasonably clear, despite the references to the Cascading Style Sheets specification.

Specifying padding is similar to borders. Its use is to offset content from its surrounding border or container if no border is specified. It could be seen as an alternative to space-before and space-after, as it has a similar visual effect, though it isn't meant for that. If padding is not specified, the default value of 0pt is used, which gives an appearance of content being placed very close to area boundaries. A more natural appearance is to provide padding on all blocks, which will be formatted in close proximity. Figure 5-11 indicates this difference clearly. The first block has no padding, and the second block has padding applied in the start and end directions, as shown in Example 5-19.

Example 5-19. Specifying padding on a block

```
<fo:block space-before="18pt">A simple block with no
    padding. Note the proximity of the content to the page
    edge (the containing area). This may be too
    close when large blocks of text are used. </fo:block>

<fo:block padding-end="6pt" padding-start="6pt">A
    simple block with padding specified as 6pt. Note the
    proximity of the content to the page edge (the
    containing area). This may be better when large
    blocks of text are used.
</fo:block>
```

> A simple block with no padding. Note the proximity of the content to the page edge (the containing area). This may be found too close when large blocks of text are used.
> A simple block with padding specified as 6pt. Note the proximity of the content to the page edge (the containing area). This may be found better when large blocks of text are used.

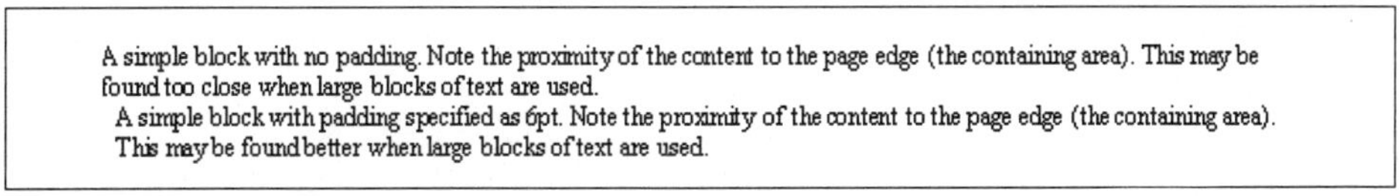

Figure 5-11. The effect of adding padding

As with borders, padding may be individually specified or used in its shortform (padding="6pt"), as in the example. The full list reads nearly the same as with borders, with the exception of the color specification.

- padding-before (padding-top)
- padding-after (padding-bottom)
- padding-start (padding-left)
- padding-end (padding-right)

The parenthesized alternatives provide the direction-oriented alternatives for left-to-right, top-to-bottom layout.

The explicit values using padding-before are:

- padding-before.length
- padding-before.conditionality (retain or discard)

The length property specifies the actual length of the padding, again using the common length specification and unit format.

The conditionality property is logically consistent with spaces, i.e., if the padding is the first in a series of spaces, and if the conditionality has the value discard, the space is discarded. If its value is set to retain, it is kept.

One property that may be of use on a block when output is not desired is the visibility property. visibility="hidden" produces no output for that block. An area is allocated for the block, but no content is inserted into it. This may be useful for a limited distribution document, where confidential data is made available only to authorized personnel.

Lists

The XSL-FO specification is reasonably clear when describing lists. It needs to be, because in XSL-FO, lists are certainly not intuitively easy. The basic syntax is shown in Example 5-20, using the Unicode symbol for the bullet, ߦ, as the label. The constituent parts of the list are the list-block containing list-item, which has both a list-item-label and list-item-body.

Example 5-20. Basic list syntax

```
<fo:list-block>
 <fo:list-item>
  <fo:list-item-label>
   <fo:block>&#x2022;</fo:block>
  </fo:list-item-label>
  <fo:list-item-body>
   <fo:block>List item contents.</fo:block>
  </fo:list-item-body>
 </fo:list-item>
</fo:list-block>
```

The list-block contains the entire list. Each list entry contains both a list-item-label and a list-item-body. The label contains the item marker or content, and the body holds the actual contents. Within both the label and body, blocks wrap actual content. This provides the hierarchy shown in this example.

Laying out the list to the required spacing uses the properties on the contained elements, which the specification demonstrates very well. Figure 5-12, which repeats the figure from the specification, illustrates the properties clearly, though the combinations can be tricky. Using default values produces a list that some may think is too close to the margins for normal use, because lists are usually indented. Indentation is achieved through the start-indent property of the list-block. The provisional-distance-between-starts property of the list-block specifies the distance between the start of the label (the bullet in Example 5-20) and the actual start of the list content. The separation between the label and the body is specified by the provisional-label-separation property. As you can see, there is interaction between them and the size of the areas produced by the formatter for whatever label you have chosen. This is less important for simple, bulleted lists than it is for glossary items, for example, where the label is actual text content. The label start-indent offsets the label from the containing area (useful for nested lists) to indent secondary lists. The final property I will mention is the body end-indent. This is useful when the extent of the list in the end direction is required to be less than the preceding content, showing the list in a narrower space than the surrounding content.

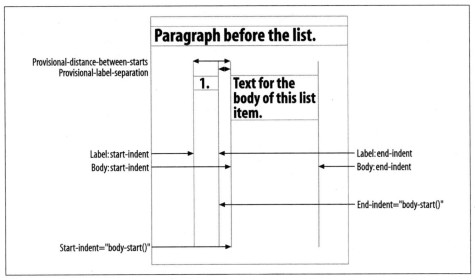

Figure 5-12. Basic list layout

Two key properties are the label end-indent and the body start-indent. For a simple list, I'd suggest for the label end-indent, using label-end( ), a function that returns a value of the end point of the label. For the body start-indent, I'd suggest using body-start( ), a function that returns the relative position of the start point of the body. These provide a reasonably successful initial positioning. This is also suitable for nested lists, as shown in Example 5-21 and Figure 5-13.

Example 5-21. A simple nested list

```
<fo:list-block
  start-indent="5mm"
  provisional-distance-between-starts="10mm">
  <fo:list-item>
    <fo:list-item-label end-indent="label-end( )">
      <fo:block>&#x2022;</fo:block>
    </fo:list-item-label>
```

Example 5-21. A simple nested list (continued)

```
      <fo:list-item-body start-indent="body-start()">
        <fo:block>List item contents.</fo:block>
```

❶
```
          <fo:list-block>
           <fo:list-item>
            <fo:list-item-label
              end-indent="label-end()">
              <fo:block font-family="ZapfDingbats">&#x2798;
              </fo:block>
               </fo:list-item-label>
               <fo:list-item-body
                 start-indent="body-start()">
                 <fo:block>List item contents of nested list.
                 </fo:block>
               </fo:list-item-body>
             </fo:list-item>
```
❷
```
           </fo:list-block>

        </fo:list-item-body>
      </fo:list-item>
    </fo:list-block>
```

❶ Start of inner list

❷ End of inner list

> •   List item contents.
> ❯   List item contents of nested list.

Figure 5-13. Figure showing a nested list

More specific layout options will use the length specifications of the list properties. These are shown quite clearly in Figure 5-12 and can fully specify list layouts, including the use of this syntax for items other than lists. Experimentation with these properties may be necessary to get the result you want. The specification, realizing how complex the syntax is, contains a few examples in Section 6.8.

Other Types of Lists

Numbered lists use the contents of the label element, during the transformation phase, to number the list item, either as a single numeric value or as part of some sequence. Often, this might use the node-set that constitutes the children of a list element. If lists are split up by intervening content, XSLT provides the facilities to continue numbering after the break by collecting the right node-set and numbering it. I refer you to Michael Kay's *XSLT Programmer's Reference* (Wrox Press) for the definitive book on such use of XSLT, particularly the sections on xsl:number and the position() function.

Display or definition lists are those often used for a glossary form, where a word or phrase is referenced in the main body of text and linked to a definition of that word or phrase. The word is placed in the list-item-label and some additional material is added as the list-item-body. Ensure that the size of the label's content is provided for when using list-item-body. The provisional-distance-between-starts property must be sufficient to fit the largest candidate if the list is to appear even. Word wrapping will take place if there is insufficient space for the label and if steps are not taken to account for it. Overflow conditions are easy to find, so ensure that each list item is given its own space and that the wrapping meets your needs. Note the wrapping in Example 5-22 and the output of Figure 5-14.

Example 5-22. Varying the label length specification

```
<fo:list-block
   start-indent="5mm"
   provisional-distance-between-starts="40mm">
 <fo:list-item space-after="1em">
  <fo:list-item-label >
   <fo:block
  font-weight="bold">A long label which wraps.</fo:block>
  </fo:list-item-label>
  <fo:list-item-body start-indent="body-start()" end-indent="5mm">
    <fo:block>List item contents. Note the text flow which takes
        place when sufficient text is placed to ensure wrapping.
        Note the text flow which takes place when sufficient text
        is placed to ensure wrapping.</fo:block>
  </fo:list-item-body>
</fo:list-item>
<fo:list-item>
  <fo:list-item-label >
    <fo:block font-weight="bold">
       Another long label which wraps.</fo:block>
  </fo:list-item-label>
  <fo:list-item-body start-indent="body-start()">
    <fo:block>Second content. </fo:block>
  </fo:list-item-body>
</fo:list-item>
</fo:list-block>
```

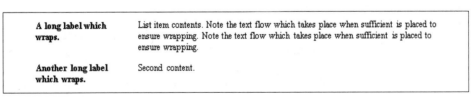

Figure 5-14. Label length variations

The example has the provisional-distance-between-starts property set to 40mm, which may still be too small for some. With care, the specification can produce very attractive lists and works for most layout options. It's even possible to use the list format in places where lists would not be considered. An example of this is in left- and right-aligned text in a header or footer, using the label as a left header and the body as the right header.

Finally, remember that the list-item-label may be empty, if it's needed to vertically align the body items without a marker or other content in the label field.

Alignment Issues

In some circumstances, you may need to consider the label-to-body alignment. This is not possible in the present version of the recommendation. You can, however, set a value of relative-align on the fo:list-item to be either before (the default) or baseline. This allows you to align either the initial lines' tops (e.g., cap-heights) or baselines. So, there is some flexibility here.

Tables

XSL-FO is not like HTML. It is mostly unnecessary to use tables for layout as has been done in HTML. The XSL-FO vocabulary provides so much more than HTML that you shouldn't fall back on tables simply to obtain an effect you have achieved on the Web. The table-formatting object is for formatting tabular data. There may be circumstances where table-based formatting is necessary, but they will be rare.

The table model used by XSL-FO is row first, which matches most—though not all—common table models in XML markup. One option is to use two properties on a table cell, starts-row and ends-row (each set to either true or false), included for use where no row wrapper is available, for example, where a particular type of content or markup indicates this change. The outline sequence is table, table-header, table-footer, table-body, table-row, table-cell. table-header keeps headings available at the top of each new page of a multipage table, and table-footer allows a "Continued on next page" message in the footer; these properties are optional.

The Basic Table

The basic table without a caption has a table-body child, which has table-row children, which have table-cell children. This provides a simple transform from a standard table with a similar model. The only caveat is that the table cells need their content wrapping in block elements. The transform shown in Example 5-23 provides this simplest of table models. Example 5-24 shows a snippet of the stylesheet.

Example 5-23. The simplest of table models

```
<table>
    <tbody>
      <row><td>R1C1</td><td>R1C2</td><td>R1C3</td></row>
      <row><td>R2C1</td><td>R2C2</td><td>R2C3</td></row>
    </tbody>
  </table>
```

Example 5-24. Stylesheet snippet

```
<xsl:template match="table">
   <fo:table width="3in">
     <xsl:apply-templates/>
   </fo:table>
 </xsl:template>
<xsl:template match="tbody">
  <fo:table-body>
     <xsl:apply-templates/>
  </fo:table-body>
</xsl:template>

  <xsl:template match="row">
   <fo:table-row>
     <xsl:apply-templates/>
   </fo:table-row>
 </xsl:template>
<xsl:template match="td">
    <fo:table-cell border="solid 1px black">
      <fo:block><xsl:apply-templates/></fo:block>
    </fo:table-cell>
 </xsl:template>
```

I have restricted the table size to 3 inches and added a border to each of the cells.

Captions

The table may be suitably captioned using the outer wrapper, table-and-caption, which holds both the table-caption and the table. This provides a bold, centered heading:

```
<fo:table-and-caption>
      <fo:table-caption text-align="center">
        <fo:block font-weight="bold" >Table Caption.</fo:block>
      </fo:table-caption>
      <fo:table>
        .....
```

The caption may be placed on any side of the table, using the caption-side property table-caption. I find the use of an appropriate block after the table quite suitable for these purposes. It is probably useful only if you need the caption to one side of the table.

Column Headings

One of the difficulties with the various table models currently available is that column headings are often not placed conveniently within the table body itself. If column headings are needed, use the transform stage to reorder the content.

The part of the model designated for column headers is the `table-header` element, the first child of the `table` element. To specify a bold, centered heading, use:

```
<fo:table-header>
    <fo:table-cell
                border="solid black 1px"
                padding="1em"
                border-collapse="collapse">
        <fo:block
                text-align="justify"
                font-weight="bold">Column 1</fo:block>
    </fo:table-cell>
    .....
```

And so on for each column. This provides the hook for repeating headers at page breaks. The `border-collapse` property is set such that the borders are merged rather than separated. The `fo:table` property `table-omit-header-at-break="false"` tells the formatter that these headings are required to be redisplayed at each new page. The treatment of footers is handled similarly. The footers use the `table-footer` element, with contained `table-cells` and follow the `table-header` element. If you have to omit the footer prior to a break, use the `table-omit-footer-at-break` property with a value of true. This improves the visual appearance and indicates that the table continues.

Fixed-Width Tables and Columns

Tables with fixed widths depend on two table properties. The first is the `inline-progression-dimension`, the second, the `table-layout`. Both of these default to `auto`. To produce a fixed-width table, set `table-layout` to either a length specification, such as `100mm`, or to a percentage, then set the `table-layout` property to a value of `fixed`. So, to get a 3 inch–wide table, specify:

```
<fo:table inline-progression-dimension="3in" table-layout="fixed">
```

Similarly, to obtain a table half the width of the page, use:

```
<fo:table inline-progression-dimension="50%" table-layout="fixed">
```

To specify the column widths separately, use the element `fo:table-column` set to a value of, say, 50, with attributes of `column-number` to specify the column under discussion and `column-width` set to a value using the `proportional-column-width` function. There should be one entry per column of the table being set out, prior to the `fo:table-header` entry. This isn't a percentage, but, to quote the specification, "The column widths are first determined ignoring the proportional measures. The difference between the `table-width` and the sum of the column widths is the available proportional width. One unit of proportional measure is the available proportional width divided by the sum of the proportional factors." For example:

```
<fo:table width="3in">
<fo:table-column
column-number="1"
column-width="proportional-column-width(50)"/>
<fo:table-column
column-number="2"
column-width="proportional-column-width(25)"/>
<fo:table-column column-number="3"
column-width="proportional-column-width(25)"/>
<fo:table-body>
```

This is often a good choice because it doesn't have to add up to 100% and it is easier to use where fixed-width columns and proportional-width columns are mixed.

Proportional-width table columns may be specified using a `column-width` value of proportional-column-width, as in Example 5-25.

Example 5-25. Proportional-width columns

```
<table-column column-width="proportional-column-width(1)"/>
  <table-column column-width="proportional-column-width(3)"/>
  <table-column column-width="proportional-column-width(1)"/>
```

This will make the middle column three times the width of each other column.

Fixed columns

An alternative approach to table layout is to specify the required width of a table column. The `table-column` element is a first child of `table` and has attribute values that apply to the named column and spans. Example 5-26 shows a simple extract, using the `column-width` attribute values set to percentages. The values may take percentages or widths, although percentages are generally easier to handle. A table column is specified by number, starting at one, with each column width specified using the `column-width` attribute. Note that this property is ignored if the `number-columns-spanned` is greater than one.

Example 5-26. Fixed columns, variable width

```
<fo:table>
        <fo:table-column column-number="1" column-width="20%"/>
        <fo:table-column column-number="2" column-width="60%"/>
        <fo:table-column column-number="3" column-width="20%"/>
        ... Remainder of table specification.
```

An alternative use of this element is to ensure that table columns are of equal width. This may be specified using the `number-columns-repeated` attribute of `table-column`. This is simply a shorthand to save rewriting the `table-columns` for all succeeding columns. The effect is to take this `table-column` specification and repeat it, with the column-number increasing by increments of one. So for this three-column table, a simple specification requiring one third for each column is shown in Example 5-27.

Example 5-27. Fixed columns, constant width

```
<fo:table>
        <fo:table-column
          column-number="1"
          column-width="33%"
          number-columns-repeated="3"/>

        ... Remainder of table specification.
```

Spanning Columns and Rows

Two attributes are used for spanning. To span columns, use the `number-columns-spanned` property on either `table-column` or `table-cell` elements to specify the number of columns required to be spanned. The default value is 1. This provides a flexible way to mix single and multiple spans. Similarly for rows, use the `number-rows-spanned` property of `table-cell` to span rows.

As an example, consider a 5 by 5 table, R1C1 to R5C5, where the requirement is to span R2C1 and R2C2 (column span) and to span R4C1 and R5C1 (row span). So, the `table-cell` that specifies R2C1 will have the property `number-columns-spanned` set to 2, with R2C2 omitted (its area now covered by R2C1). The `table-cell` that specifies R4C1 will have the property `number-rows-spanned` set to 2, with cell R5C1 omitted.

Hence, the relevant stylesheet parts will be as shown in Example 5-28.

Example 5-28. Row and column spanning

```
<fo:table-row>
    <fo:table-cell border="solid black 1px"
                   border-collapse="collapse"
                   number-columns-spanned="2">
     <fo:block>R2C1</fo:block>
    </fo:table-cell>
 <!-- R2C2 omitted-->

.... and for row 4,

<fo:table-row>
    <fo:table-cell
                   border="solid black 1px"
                   border-collapse="collapse"
                   number-rows-spanned="2">
     <fo:block>R4C1</fo:block>
    </fo:table-cell>
... and for row 5
<fo:table-row>
 <!-- R5C1 omitted  -->
```

This produces the table shown in Figure 5-15.

R1C1	R1C2	R1C3	R1C4	R1C5
R2C1, with column span of 2		R2C3	R2C4	R2C5
R3C1	R3C2	R3C3	R3C4	R3C5
R4C1, with rowspan 2	R4C2	R4C3	R4C4	R4C5
	R5C2	R5C3	R5C4	R5C5

Figure 5-15. Row and column spanning in a table

Note that the borders on each of the relevant table cells are realigned as needed to provide for the spanning.

Empty Cells in Tables

Two options are offered for empty cells. The empty-cells property may be set to either show or hide. This will affect borders that are either hidden or shown for each empty cell.

Cell Alignment

Within any cell, content may be aligned horizontally using the text-align property, as mentioned earlier—for example, to center the contents of a cell—with values of start, center, end, or justify.

Vertical alignment within a cell is achieved using the display-align property, with a value of before, center, or after. Figure 5-16 repeats the previous example, with R5C3 having the two attributes set as in Example 5-29.

Example 5-29. Cell alignment

```
<fo:table-cell border="solid black 1px"
               display-align="center"
               border-collapse="collapse"
               text-align="center">
    <fo:block font-weight="bold">XXX</fo:block>
    </fo:table-cell>
```

Other Table Issues

Other properties needed to address table layout problems include keeps and breaks, which keep content together over page breaks or ensure a break after or before a specific row, respectively.

R1C1	R1C2	R1C3	R1C4	R1C5
R2C1, with column span of 2		R2C3	R2C4	R2C5
R3C1	R3C2	R3C3	R3C4	R3C5
R4C1, with rowspan 2	R4C2	R4C3	R4C4	R4C5
	R5C2, set long to wrap text	**XXX**	R5C4	R5C5

Figure 5-16. Cell alignment

Within any table cell, the blocks that contain the content may use any of the available properties to lay out the cell content.

Additional Material

While the descriptions above work well in most situations, there are a few more details about blocks that are worth explaining.

A Minor Aside on Lengths

One of the ways to specify lots of things in XSL-FO is via the length specification.

The spec says:

> <length> A signed length value where a 'length' is a real number plus a unit qualification. A property may define additional constraints on the value.

Got that? No? One approach is just to see what your formatter makes of your attempts and adjust as necessary. Remember that fonts, for example, are not infinitely flexible, so a request for 11.6 point text is highly likely to result in 12 point text. Section 5.9.13 of the Recommendation lists the permitted units of measurement, providing centimeters (cm), millimeters (mm), inches (in), points (pt), picas (pc), pixels (px), and em (em). A pixel is taken as 0.28mm; a point, as 1/72 of an inch; and a pica is a printer's unit of type size, equal to 12 points or about 1/6 of an inch.

Short forms

Throughout the specification, you can read the dotted notation used for properties, for example, space-before.optimum. Generally, the first term may be used alone to set the value. The fuller, dotted form is used when tight requirements on formatting are needed, and it is required that some value lie between the X.minimum and X.maximum values.

A short form provides a value for all the length specifications and the initial value to all the non-length specifications.

Section 5.11 of the Recommendation details the various datatypes, should you need them. The shortform of each length is quite acceptable in most cases, for example, space-before="4pt". This is shown fully expanded in Example 5-30.

Example 5-30. Full form

```
space-before.minimum="4.0pt"
space-before.optimum="4.0pt"
space-before.maximum="4.0pt"
space-before.precedence="0"
space-before.conditionality="discard"
```

The optimum, minimum, and maximum values together comprise a length-range that provides the formatter with limits which should meet your needs.

Inline Elements

In this chapter, we will cover what is perhaps the simplest area of XSL-FO: styling the inline content. This is analogous to the word processor's application of bold or italics to particular words.

Inline content can be defined as content that, *when formatted*, does not extend beyond the formatted line extent, i.e., it does not wrap into a new line. Typical source content that may need marking for fo:inline might include content that needs to be emphasized for a specific purpose, such as emphasis, computer commands, instructions, and cross-references. The formatted output might be italicized, underlined, boldface, or hyperlinked. Other visual forms of emphasis include font changes and nontext output, such as inline graphics, horizontal lines, or dot leaders. These are all possible within fo:inline. It's sometimes difficult to decide between using fo:block and fo:inline. In such cases, if the content in question falls into a typeset line of content, use the fo:inline tag, otherwise, use fo:block.

A simpler view of an inline element is as a wrapper to apply style to phrases or individual words. A word of advice: if you use a style change, make a note of it and stick to it. If one specific font is used to represent a certain type of content, stick to it. Try the options out on sample input and find a scheme that is identifiable by the schema in use, and produces output that looks cohesive. A good example of this is provided in Donald E. Knuth's *The TEXbook* (Addison Wesley). Throughout the book, two symbols are used. The first symbol is similar to a bend roadsign; the other has two such symbols, referring to a dangerous bend! This simple scheme is used regularly and produces a nice visual reminder.

Content

The content model for fo:inline is rather loose, permitting both other inline elements and block elements. It makes sense to restrict content to #PCDATA plus other inlines elements, in most cases. I'll leave it to you to experiment. If you start out with this principle, you will break it, though usually for good reason, and emerge with greater understanding. I only ask that you consider why you are breaking it.

Inline Styling

Starting with the familiar, the stylesheet snippet of bullet 2 in Examples 6-1 and 6-2 demonstrates basic fo:inline usage.

Example 6-1. Inline example, XML source

```
<para>Some base content, containing an inline warning,
  <emphasis role="warning">Do not touch blue paper</emphasis>,
  a fairly straightforward piece requiring emphasis
  <emphasis>TEXT</emphasis>, and some instructions which
  require presenting in a different way, such as
  <instruction>Now light the blue paper</instruction>.
</para>
```

Example 6-2. Inline example, stylesheet snippet

```
      <xsl:template match="para">
❶      <fo:block>
           <xsl:apply-templates/>
          </fo:block>
        </xsl:template>

        <xsl:template match="emphasis[@role='warning']">
❷      <fo:inline background-color="red">Warning:</fo:inline>
              <xsl:apply-templates/>
          </xsl:template>

        <xsl:template match="emphasis[not(@role) or @role='']">
❸      <fo:inline font-weight="bold">
              <xsl:apply-templates/></fo:inline>
          </xsl:template>


        <xsl:template match="instruction">
❹      <fo:inline font-style="italic">
              <xsl:apply-templates/>
           </fo:inline>
          </xsl:template>
```

❶ This is the containing block.

❷ The warning generates literal content using an inline.

❸ The simple emphasis tag generates bold content.

❹ The instruction tag generates italics.

This provides simple inline usage, probably the most common requirement, with the output as shown in Figure 6-1.

> Some base content, containing an inline warning, **Warning:** Do not touch blue paper, a fairly straightforward piece requiring emphasis **TEXT**, and some instructions which require presenting in a different way, such as *Now light the blue paper*.

Figure 6-1. Inline output example

Other straightforward styles that may be applied in this manner are the `font-style` attributes of `normal`, `italic`, `oblique`, and `backslant`; the `font-weight` attributes, which split into relative values, are `normal`, `bold`, `bolder`, `lighter`, as well as the absolute values of 100, 200, 300, 400, 500, 600, 700, 800, and 900. Decoration is applied in the same way, using the `text-decoration` attribute of the `fo:inline` element.

The values for `text-decoration` are `underline`, `overline`, and `line-through`, which are the affirmative requests to the formatter, requesting a line under, above, or through the marked content, respectively. Each is effectively removed by the use of the `no-` prefix, so that an inline with mixed underline can be produced, as in Example 6-3. This nests inline content to (potentially) reduce the level of markup needed. Figure 6-2 shows the text decoration being switched on and off.

Example 6-3. Text decoration

```
<fo:block text-decoration="underline">Underline on for all
    but one <fo:inline text-decoration="no-underline">word</fo:inline>
    of the sentence.
</fo:block>
```

> <u>Underline on for all but one word of the sentence.</u>

Figure 6-2. Text decoration being switched on and off

In Figure 6-2, the containing block has the `underline` property set; the contained inline turns it off for the single word.

The ability to select either the affirmative requirement (`underline`) or its inverse (`no-underline`) is more readily appreciated when transforming from XML. The utility of the specification becomes apparent only when you need it.

Other values for `text-decoration` are `overline` and `line-through`. This is very useful when marking up content for insertion and deletion in a manuscript. New content could be shown with either the background or the content colored and with content set for deletion shown as strike-through.

When decorating content, each case should be judged on its merits and future use. If you're designing stylesheets for a general purpose schema, it might be wise to allow for both cases, such that either may be applied. Which one you choose should be determined more by the case than by any rules. This is where your understanding of blocks and line layout will be tested.

`text-shadow` is available as an extended compliance option for text decoration; it is applicable to all elements, though it's most appropriate on inline content. It takes two length specifications and a color attribute. It is not widely implemented. The two lengths specify the horizontal and vertical offset, and the color specifies the color to be used for the shadow, as in Example 6-4. The first length is the horizontal offset from the text, the second, the vertical. Negative values indicate an offset left and up, positive values, down and right

Example 6-4. Text shadow effect

```
<fo:block>
        <fo:inline
          text-shadow="red 1mm 1mm">
        Text with a red shadow down and to the right by 1mm
        .</fo:inline>
</fo:block>
```

Inapplicable Properties

Certain properties appear (to me) to be largely inapplicable to inlines. I hate to make general rules, because it's all too likely that they will be broken, but it is a reasonable starting point. Borders are of less use inline than they are in blocks. Padding provides rather ugly whitespace around an inline and is best suited to blocks. Equally, breaks are best left to the blocks. This is not the way to terminate a page or column. Finally, whitespace preservation properties do not apply to inlines.

Inline Containers

`fo:inline-container` is available as an inline wrapper for content with a different writing mode to that of the bulk of the content. This matches the provision of a block with a change in writing mode, this time for inline content. A simple example is shown in Example 6-5. Note that the content of this element is a block.

Example 6-5. The use of fo:inline-container

```
<fo:block>
  <fo:inline-container writing-mode="rl-tb">
    <fo:block>
      Some text with writing mode st to rl-tb.</fo:block>
  </fo:inline-container>

</fo:block>
```

Inline Graphics

Sometimes the formatter may not provide what you want. A classic response to this has been the use of graphics as a replacement. For example, it has been common practice to insert mathematical expressions into HTML as graphics. Another formatter might not have a glyph in the font you wish to use. XSL-FO provides a means of including external graphics with fo:external-graphic, within the fo:inline element. This can be used to provide graphic content that has the appearance of normal inline content. A classic aspect of PDF that produces inaccessible content is the use of graphics to replace the first letter of a word. When exported to provide plain text, of course, the first letter is are omitted. Example 6-6 shows how you would obtain the graphic.

Example 6-6. An inline graphic

```
<fo:inline id="ls1">The main
    <fo:external-graphic src="url(images/image.png)"/> is ....
</fo:inline>
```

This form needs due care and attention because various facets tend to conspire against it. First, the resolution of the surrounding content is likely to be higher than that of the graphic. The graphic itself will need scaling and cropping to match the surrounding text. XSL-FO has a property that aids with this aspect, permitting use of two properties that size the graphic with respect to the font in use, using something such as Example 6-7.

Example 6-7. Scaled graphic

```
<fo:external graphic
content-height="1em"
content-width="1em"
src="url(images/image.png)"
/>
```

Other uses of graphics are discussed further in Chapter 7.

The fo:instream-foreign-object has developed quite well to permit the use of vector graphics, due to the efforts and needs of the FOP group, who embedded Scalable Vector Graphics (SVG) as a namespace-identified inclusion. This permits high-quality graphics, particularly line graphics, to be included as an integral element of a high-quality print document. You can read more about SVG on the W3C site or in *SVG Essentials* by David Eisenberg (O'Reilly).

Word and Letter Spacing

Both word and letter spacing are tasks for the formatter. XSL-FO provides both. The letter-spacing property specifies spacing behavior between text characters. When a length is specified, the value indicates inter-character space, in addition to the default space between characters. Similarly, the word-spacing property indicates inter-word space, in addition to the default space between words. See Example 6-8.

Example 6-8. Letter spacing

```
<fo:inline
 letter-spacing="2mm">This is text with 2mm letter-spacing,</fo:inline>
<fo:inline word-spacing="1cm">  this has 1cm word spacing.</fo:inline>
```

Figure 6-3 is the result.

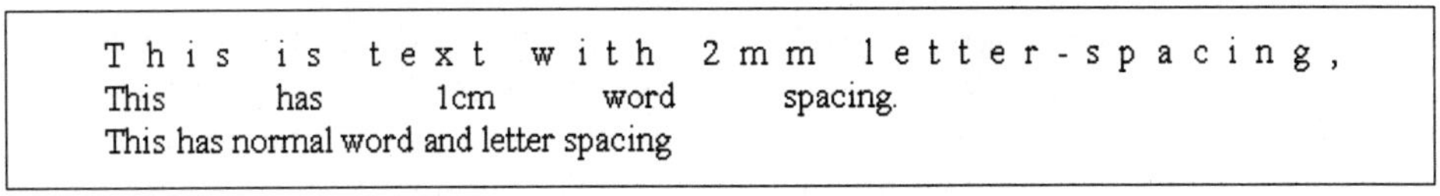

T h i s   i s   t e x t   w i t h   2 m m   l e t t e r - s p a c i n g ,
This   has   1cm   word   spacing.
This has normal word and letter spacing

Figure 6-3. Character spacing

Other Styling Properties

The line-height property can emphasize certain content within a large surrounding block of text, without other styling. This use of whitespace clearly outlines the content without otherwise distinguishing it. Note that if it is used within a block of content, the entire line will be laid out with the additional spacing. This is useful for content that does not stretch over a line boundary, after which point it simply looks strange. I find the percentage value most useful in this application, because it will adjust to any changes in surrounding font size, being a percentage of the font size itself.

The Horizontal Rule and Its Variants

The way a line is drawn in HTML is commonly known as the horizontal rule. XSL-FO provides a more subtle way of producing the same effect. The uses of the fo:leader element are generally decorative and might include breaks between sections of a book, signature lines, dot leaders in a table of contents, or text spacing. fo:leader is not allowed as a top-level element; it must be used within a block.

The basic, full-length line is shown in Example 6-9.

Example 6-9. Leaders for lines

```
     <fo:block>
❶    <fo:leader
❷      leader-length="100%"
❸      leader-pattern="rule"
❹      rule-style="solid"
❺      rule-thickness="0.1mm"  color="black"/>
     </fo:block>
```

❶ Wrapper element

❷ Length of the leader

❸ Its pattern

❹ Its style

❺ How thick and what color the result should be

The length of the resulting line is a standard length specification. I've chosen percentage here. Any form of length range can be used.

The pattern is specified using the leader-pattern attribute, which accepts the following options: space, rule, dots, use-content, and inherit. The pattern used in the example is the rule option. The style of the rule (rule-style) can be one of the following: none, dotted, solid, double, groove, ridge, or inherit. Each provides a variant decoration.

The thickness of the leader is specified using a length specification on the rule-thickness attribute. The example uses millimeters.

Note that the default for leader-length is 100% when a situation occurs where the width of the content area is determined by something other than the content itself. For example, when text-align-last is justify, the default rule-style is solid. In these circumstances, use the following to get a full-width rule:

```
<fo:block text-align-last="justify">
  <fo:leader leader-pattern="rule"/>
</fo:block>
```

A variation on this is to use two leader lines with a decorative character or graphic centered within the line. Figure 6-4 shows such an example, using a character from the Zapf family and two leader lines on either side, each half slightly less than 50% wide.

Figure 6-4. Decorative rule

The various options for decorative characters are nearly self-explantory. The pattern to be used is one from the selection space, rule, dots, or use-content. space uses the space character; rule uses a plain line; dots produces the dot leaders often used in lists; use-content produces a series of characters that are specified as actual content of the fo:leader element. Example 6-10 shows an example of this, using the character o.

Example 6-10. Leader pattern example

```
<fo:leader  leader-pattern="use-content" leader-length="60%">o</fo:leader>
```

The style of the rule is one from a selection list: none, dotted, solid, double, dashed, groove, or ridge. Each selects a particular style of line. Figure 6-5 shows a variety of these.

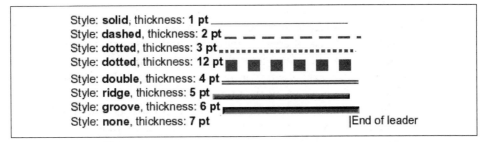

Figure 6-5. Line styles

The final use is the table of contents example shown in Example 6-11 and Figure 6-6.

Example 6-11. Table of contents usage

```
<fo:block
  text-align-last="justify">Chapter 10
    <fo:leader leader-pattern="dots" />Page 25</fo:block>
```

Chapter 10 ....Page 25

Figure 6-6. Table of contents usage

This demonstrates that inline styling may also be applied to blocks. This styling appears as a line of content, which is why it's in this chapter. Note the use of the text-align-last property, which ensures that the content is expanded to fill the available block width.

Another use of fo:leader is to produce a blank space on a form for someone to fill in. This makes use of the leader-pattern="space" and style="none" attribute settings, with an appropriate length specification, and produces a blank space in which the respondent can write. Note that if the font size is small, the line-height should be adjusted to ensure sufficient space is left to hand-write a response. Another option might be to use leader-pattern="dots" to provide a line on which to write, if the line is surrounded by whitespace.

Line Layout

Within any individual line, there may be layout issues requiring resolution. Some of these relate to block layout, such as those specific to first and last line layout; while others are specific to inline content. Other issues may be a case of appropriate selection. Typical of this last group are cross-references, footnotes and their references, and keeps and breaks.

Although covered in Chapter 9, I'll mention briefly the use of page numbers as typical inline content. The two aspects of this element, fo:page-number and fo:page-number-citation, are not obvious. fo:page-number-citation creates a page number reference. So when you want to talk about some material on another page, it becomes a case of referencing the remote content and/or the page number on which that content appears. The task of creating the page number is part of the formatting stage; the task of creating the reference to the section is part of the transformation stage. As in other such contexts, the use of ID values is a great help here. If you wish to reference Chapter 6 on page 34, or the title of that chapter, then if its ID value is known, it can be done easily in XSLT, using XSLT constructs and the fo:page-number-citation element from the XSL-FO syntax. The XSLT function id(string) takes a string value as a parameter, which is the ID needed, and returns the node-set that contains that ID value. This can then be used to obtain, for example, the title of the chapter using an XPath expression. The notable difference about fo:page-number-citation is that the ID value is not an ID value in the source document, but one in the intermediate document made up from the transform, such that the for-matter has this information to determinine the page number on which this particular content is laid out. The implications of this are that for any content having an ID value in the source file, it is worthwhile generating an ID value on the derived block or inline. This is done easily with a simple, named template that adds the ID value to the block or inline only if the context node actually has an ID value. Such a tem-plate, and its call, are shown in Example 6-12.

Example 6-12. ID generation

```
<xsl:template match="p">
    <fo:block>
      <xsl:call-template name="gen-id">
        <xsl:with-param name="id-val" select="@id"/>
      </xsl:call-template>
      <xsl:apply-templates/>
    </fo:block>
  </xsl:template>

 <xsl:template name="gen-id">
    <xsl:param name="id-val" select="@id"/>
    <xsl:if test="$id-val">
      <xsl:attribute name="id"><xsl:value-of
          select="$id-val"/></xsl:attribute>
    </xsl:if>
  </xsl:template>
```

As an example of ID generation, consider the snippet of XML in Example 6-13.

Example 6-13. Cross-reference generation

```
<section id="sect1">
   <head>Introduction</head>
   <p>A plain paragraph</p>

   <p id="referenced-para">A paragraph which is referenced,
   hence has the id value.</p>
```

The section element is identifiable, and a particular paragraph is identified. Later on in the document, we may see something similar to Example 6-14.

Example 6-14. Source XML example

```
<p>See  <link target="sect1"/>
on page <pgref target="referenced-para"/>.</p>
```

Although single media, this shows the principles in use. The transformation requirement is to generate the head element contents in place of the link element and to replace the pgref element with the page number on which that particular paragraph is placed. The transform to execute this is shown in Example 6-15.

Example 6-15. Link usage

```
<xsl:template match='section'>
<fo:block id='{@id}'>
  <xsl:apply-templates/>
</fo:block>
</xsl:template>

<xsl:template match='para'>
  <fo:block id='{generate-id( )}'>
   <xsl:apply-templates/>
  </fo:block>
</xsl:template>

 <xsl:template match="link">
    <xsl:value-of select="id(@target)/head"/>
 </xsl:template>

 <xsl:template match="pgref">
   <fo:page-number-citation ref-id="{@target}"/>
 </xsl:template>
```

Note that because the ID value is copied across from the source XML document to the transformed document, we can use it as the target of page-number-citation.

Keeping Line Content Together

Some applications require you to keep a block of content within one line. The line wrapping options in XSL-FO will let you know about this, but it's up to the stylesheet author to manage it. The keep property keep-together.within-line attribute can be set to always to control wrapping. Note that if content cannot be fitted to the line, the overflow property can be used. If it is set to error-if-overflow, the formatter will report the error.

Other Uses

Some uses of inlines may not be obvious. For example, lists may be built using leaders with a fixed length to provide the spacing between the list marker and the list item content. Example 6-16 shows an example of this. There may be occasions when you simply need the line format that a list provides, but you don't want the block layout of a list.

Example 6-16. Leaders for lists

```
<fo:inline>
  <fo:character
  character="&#x2022;" font-family="ZapfDingbats"/> <fo:leader
      leader-pattern="space"
      leader-length="1.5cm"/> The list item contents</fo:inline>
```

Here, I have used the bullet character, U+2022, a fixed-length leader, and then the element content. Note that this is viable only for lists with short content because wrapping will not occur as in a proper list.

Page Headers

One of the requirements of a page header is often to contain two or three items. These might be the page number, the running header, and perhaps the book title. A number of options are available to do this, although the specification does not address this need directly. Unfortunately, one of these options involves implementation dependency. The end result of this is a loss of portability. The layout you test with one implementation may not work in another.

Use the `text-align-last` property of a block to stretch the block over the full line. The specification does not say where this stretching should take place (assuming you have content that can be stretched). To quote the recommendation, "The algorithm for resolving the adjusted values between word-spacing and letter-spacing is User Agent dependent." Thus, one implementation may stretch the space between words, and another may stretch the character spacing. Additionally, this is fraught with danger if the actual content is unknown and results in unequal content. Given these caveats, I have provided examples that can provide this layout. In Example 6-17, I have used leaders to provide the stretchable spaces. Try them out with your formatter, and be careful.

Example 6-17. Stretchable spaces for three area headers

```
<fo:block text-align-last="justify">
    <fo:inline> start1 </fo:inline>
    <fo:inline> center </fo:inline>
    <fo:inline> end </fo:inline>
</fo:block>
```

Example 6-17. Stretchable spaces for three area headers (continued)

```
<fo:block text-align-last="justify">
    <fo:inline letter-spacing="0pt" word-spacing="0pt"> start2 </fo:inline>
    <fo:inline letter-spacing="0pt" word-spacing="0pt"> center </fo:inline>
    <fo:inline letter-spacing="0pt" word-spacing="0pt"> end </fo:inline>
</fo:block>

<fo:block text-align-last="justify">
    <fo:inline> start3 </fo:inline>
    <fo:leader />
    <fo:inline> center </fo:inline>
    <fo:leader />
    <fo:inline> end </fo:inline>
</fo:block>

<fo:block text-align-last="justify">
    <fo:inline> start4 longer </fo:inline>
    <fo:leader />
    <fo:inline> center </fo:inline>
    <fo:leader />
    <fo:inline> end </fo:inline>
</fo:block>


<fo:list-block>
  <fo:list-item>
    <fo:list-item-label>
      <fo:block id="A" text-align="left">start5</fo:block>
    </fo:list-item-label>
    <fo:list-item-body>
      <fo:list-block>
        <fo:list-item>
          <fo:list-item-label>
            <fo:block id="B" text-align="center">Center</fo:block>
          </fo:list-item-label>
          <fo:list-item-body>
            <fo:block id="C" text-align="right">Right</fo:block>
          </fo:list-item-body>
        </fo:list-item>
      </fo:list-block>
    </fo:list-item-body>
  </fo:list-item>
</fo:list-block>
```

The first part of the example uses whitespace as the stretchable item; the second part uses word spacing—this guarantees that only spaces between inlines are expanded (inlines with explicitly specified letter-spacing and word-spacing are not subject to justification). The third part of the example uses a leader; the fourth part abuses the list structure. Note the impact of the longer start direction in the third part of the example on the centered area.

Stretching the block can also be achieved within an inline using two properties of inlines and leaders. First, the balanced spacing is achieved using a leader with its pattern set to space, and the inline element uses the text-align-last attribute set to justify. This spreads the three elements out over the inline giving the desired effect. Using fo:block to replace the fo:inline will provide the full page width, as might be used for a header or footer with content at the left, right, and center of the header. Example 6-18 shows how this spreading is accomplished.

Example 6-18. Header justification

```
<fo:inline text-align-last="justify">
    Left-hand text
    <fo:leader leader-pattern="space" />
    Centre Text using inlines
    <fo:leader leader-pattern="space" />
    Right-hand text
  </fo:inline>
```

This produces output shown in Figure 6-7. The width depends on the content.

Left-hand text	Centre Text using inlines	Right-hand text

Figure 6-7. Header justification

An alternative, when the content of each header area is unequal, is to misuse the list. Misuse is probably too strong a term. One XSL Working Group member suggested a better title might be side-by-side formatting objects and provided Example 6-19, which shows a static-content example that enables unbalanced content to be nicely formatted in three areas, with all three correctly placed. This is written to be used as a callable template, with a parameter (listed here as a variable $header-width) for the actual header width.

Example 6-19. Lists in headers

```
<xsl:template name='head1'>
<xsl:param name='header-width'>

<fo:static-content flow-name="xsl-region-before">
    <!-- header-width is the width of the full header in picas -->
    <xsl:variable name="header-width" select="36"/>
    <xsl:variable name="header-field-width">
    <xsl:value-of select="$header-width * 0.3333"/><xsl:text>pc</xsl:text>
    </xsl:variable>
    <fo:list-block font-size="8pt" provisional-label-separation="0pt">
        <xsl:attribute name="provisional-distance-between-starts">
            <xsl:value-of select="$header-field-width"/>
        </xsl:attribute>
```

Example 6-19. Lists in headers (continued)

```
        <fo:list-item>
            <fo:list-item-label end-indent="label-end( )">
                <fo:block text-align="left">
                    <xsl:text>The left header field which is long </xsl:text>
                </fo:block>
            </fo:list-item-label>
            <fo:list-item-body start-indent="body-start( )">
                <fo:list-block provisional-label-separation="0pt">
                    <xsl:attribute name="provisional-distance-between-starts">
                        <xsl:value-of select="$header-field-width"/>
                    </xsl:attribute>
                    <fo:list-item>
                        <fo:list-item-label end-indent="label-end( )">
                            <fo:block text-align="center">
                                Page - <fo:page-number/>
                            </fo:block>
                        </fo:list-item-label>
                        <fo:list-item-body start-indent="body-start( )">
                            <fo:block text-align="right">
                                <xsl:text>short right</xsl:text>
                            </fo:block>
                        </fo:list-item-body>
                    </fo:list-item>
                </fo:list-block>
            </fo:list-item-body>
        </fo:list-item>
    </fo:list-block>
</fo:static-content>
</xsl:template>
```

This produces the output shown in Figure 6-8, illustrating the balancing effect.

Figure 6-8. Header justification 2

Inlines are only presented here in terms of what is practical and what is likely to be needed. Many more properties are covered elsewhere in this book that can be used with inlines.

As stated earlier, the overlap between inlines and blocks is significant. Most of the properties available with inlines are also available with blocks, so use them as you need them.

CHAPTER 7

Graphics and Color

Graphics are mentioned briefly in Chapter 3 and Chapter 6 in the discussions of blocks and inlines. You will need to consult your formatter's documentation to determine what graphics formats are viable. All the formatters I've used are happy with JPEG.

Color is one of the most generally applicable properties in the specification, which makes it somewhat harder to describe concisely. If you have a CSS background, you might already be familiar with its use on web pages. The coverage is just as broad as in CSS, and indeed many of the properties carry over directly from CSS. The specification of color is quite similar to that in CSS; colors can be specified by name or as Red-Green-Blue (RGB) color value numbers. However, XSL-FO includes additional, more sophisticated ways to specify colors.

While color can add value to presentation, it can also spoil it. It should support your message, not overwhelm it. Use it carefully and it will work well.

Graphics

The fo:external-graphic formatting object is always inline. If you want it to act like a block, you have to wrap it in a block.

The fo:instream-foreign-object is often used to include Scalable Vector Graphics (SVG) directly in the file, and it has all the same properties as an external-graphic.

fo:external-graphic provides the wrapper for graphics. Why external? Because the actual graphic's file is external to the XML source document. If wrapped in a block or inline, the graphic is appropriately laid out by the formatter, as shown in Example 7-1 and illustrated in Figure 7-1. The size is determined naturally by the actual graphic size; text-align and display-align are used to align the graphic with respect to its area. You can use the content-height and content-width properties to resize a graphic.

Example 7-1. Graphics example

```
<fo:block>
 <fo:block >Title for the figure</fo:block>
   <fo:external-graphic
     src="url(images/pig.jpg)"
        content-height="300%"
     scaling="uniform"/>
 </fo:block>

     <fo:block>fo:external-graphic wrapped in a block, and</fo:block>
     <fo:block>a block containing the graphic wrapped in
              an inline container,
        <fo:inline>
           <fo:external-graphic  src="url(images\1.png)"/>
        </fo:inline>
              with content both before and after the graphic.
     </fo:block>
```

❶ Applies the scaling

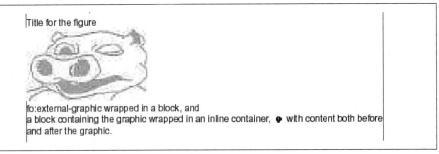

Figure 7-1. A block with fully specified borders

The external graphic formatting object acts like a big character, meaning it generates an area with a certain size. The actual size may be defined in a number of ways, which may seem confusing at first. There are, in fact, two pairs of properties that affect the size of the generated area and how the image is displayed in that area. To understand how that works, you need to understand one of the basic concepts underlying the XSL formatting model: the concept of a viewport area/reference area pair. This pair acts like a scrollable window, and the content (in this case, your graphic) is viewed in that window. The viewport area defines the size of the window area, and the reference area defines the size of the graphic area. The viewport area is used when positioning the graphic with respect to other elements in the same line.

The height and width properties of fo:external-graphic (or the writing-mode neutral equivalents, block-progression-dimension and inline-progression-dimension) define the dimensions of the viewport area. The content-height and content-width properties define the dimensions of the reference (graphic) area. Both sets of properties can be specified as fixed-length values or as the special value auto. If the viewport size properties are set to auto, the content size of the graphic determines both the reference area and the viewport area dimensions. If both the content-height and content-width properties are set to auto, the intrinsic size of the graphic, as modified by the value of the property scaling, determines the size.

 Some graphic formats don't have any information about the intrinsic size and some tools don't include it. In those cases, it's up to the formatter to make a judgement call.

If one of the content-height or content-width properties is not auto (the default), the formatter should calculate a scale factor and apply it to both dimensions. If both are specified, the behavior depends on whether the property scaling is set to uniform (the default value) or non-uniform. uniform implies that the aspect ratio should be maintained.

If you know how much space you want your graphic to occupy, set the dimensions using width and height, and set the values of content-width and content-height to scale-to-fit. This will make the reference area the same size as the viewport area by scaling the graphic appropriately.

If you have set a specific value for the viewport dimensions and left the content dimensions set to auto, or set them to a different specific value, the reference area is aligned with respect to the viewport area using the text-align and display-align traits. If it is too large for the viewport-area, the graphic is aligned as if it would fit and the overflow trait controls the clipping. If the graphic is smaller than the viewport area, the space around it will be filled according to the background-color or background property.

You might be wondering how the processor knows what to do with the graphic. The content-type property may be used to specify the format explicitly. It may be either a mime-type, specified as content-type='content-type:binary/jpeg', or a namespace prefix. If no content-type attribute is specified, the processor will use an implementation-dependent way of recognizing the graphic format.

What formats does your XSL-FO processor support? If you are lucky, the documentation will tell you. It might also say which compression options are supported for formats both on input and output. When creating PDF files, for example, some graphic formats can be compressed quite effectively (for example, JPEG, bilevel TIFF with the CCITT compression). Try out the combinations until you reach what is probably a compromise: the output satisfies your needs and the processor supports that format, combined with the bandwidth impact on your delivery methods. The higher the quality resolution of the graphic, the greater the space needed for that graphic. (All the examples in this book were created in PNG format, simply because I know the processor I'm using supports it.)

Basic Color Usage

XSL-FO has several properties where color values can be specified. The most common is `background-color`, which can be specified on most formatting objects. The `color` property describes the foreground color of text and text decorations, such as under- or over-scoring. It can be specified on `fo:block` or `fo:character` (see Chapter 8) and a number of inline formatting objects (see the section "Applicability" later in this chapter). In addition to these, color may be specified in the various `border` properties and in the `text-shadow` property.

Of the various color-related properties, only the `color` property itself is automatically inherited. That means that if you specify `color='red'` on an `fo:block`, all text in that block and any of its descendants will be red, except where a different color value is specified for a nested flow object. Although the `background-color` property isn't inherited, you may be fooled into thinking that it is, because the default value for this property is `transparent`. So if you have specified `background-color='red'` on an `fo:block`, its background will be red. Any nested objects for which you don't specify `background-color` will thus let the underlying color show through.

Which object's `background-color` is visible depends on the layering of the areas that are generated by formatting objects. This is fairly intuitive, but it can become complicated when using absolutely positioned objects (as with `block-container`) and in tables where there are several levels. Tables, rows, and columns can each have a `background-color`. This can mean that different parts of a spanning cell could have different background colors!

Following are a few basic examples to show color use in its more common application. An initial warning: if you are not used to using color in document delivery, please don't get carried away with it. XSL-FO can apply color nearly anywhere and everywhere. Use it carefully and it will enhance you document; abuse it and it will spoil your document. Example 7-2 shows the use of background and border colors, and Figure 7-2 shows the results.

Example 7-2. Background and border colors

```
<fo:block background-color="aqua"
          border-after-color="red"
          border-after-width="1.2em"

          border-before-color="blue"
          border-before-width="1em"

          border-end-color="silver"
          border-end-width="1em"

          border-start-color="green"
          border-start-width="1em"

          border-style="solid"
          padding="6pt"
```

Example 7-2. Background and border colors (continued)

```
                start-indent="1in"
                end-indent="2in"

>

     A paragraph with a completely specified border.
     Style is not specified.
     color varies on each edge</fo:block>
```

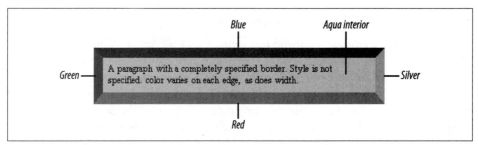

Figure 7-2. A block with fully specified borders

Example 7-3 shows the use of background-color and color when flow objects are nested. Figure 7-3 shows the result.

Example 7-3. Color and nesting

```
<fo:block
     background-color="yellow" color="blue">
     A paragraph with blue text on a yellow border.
     Nested in the text are two inline objects, one of which
     specifies a different 'color' and
     one which specifies a different 'background-color' value.
     Here is the
     <fo:inline color='green'>green inline</fo:inline>.
        And here is the
        <fo:inline background-color='white'>white background inline
     </fo:inline>. More text in the block after the inlines.</fo:block>
```

Figure 7-3. Color in nested FOs

Color Specification

The XSL-FO specification uses the keyword color to designate the value type for color-related properties. There are several ways of specifying the actual color value.

As in CSS, a predefined color keyword may be used. The list of keyword color names is as follows: aqua, black, blue, fuchsia, gray, green, lime, maroon, navy, olive, purple, red, silver, teal, white, and yellow. These 16 colors are defined in HTML.

When this range of base colors fails to meet your needs, you may specify the color more exactly using a hexidecimal RGB form such as #FFCCAA. Note that it is not case-sensitive. The format of an RGB value in hexadecimal notation is a # immediately followed by either three or six hexadecimal characters. The three-digit RGB notation (#rgb) is converted into six-digit form (#rrggbb) by replicating digits, not by adding zeros. For example, #fb0 expands to #ffbb00. This ensures that white (#ffffff) can be specified with the short notation (#fff) and removes any dependencies on the color depth of the display.

The specification also defines three built-in functions that may be used to specify a color value. These are:

- rgb(*numeric, numeric, numeric*)
- rgb-icc(*numeric, numeric, numeric*, NCName, *numeric, numeric, ...*)
- system-color(*NCName*)

The rgb function gives the same result as the hexidecimal form of the specification. In other words, color="#FFCCAA" has the same effect as color="rgb(255, 204, 176)".

The rgb-icc function returns a color from an International Color Consortium (ICC) color profile. The profile to use is defined by the NCName parameter, which is the fourth argument to the function. This must match the name declared in the fo:color-profile element, which is part of the declarations section described in the section "Color Profiles." The first three arguments designate a fallback RGB value, and the fifth and following arguments designate a color in the ICC profile. The number and value of the arguments depend on the specific profile being used. This function is intended for more sophisticated color specifications, such as CMYK, often used in printing.

The system-color function, as the name indicates, provides a way to obtain a system-dependent color value. For example, in an X Window environment this might be one of the colors defined in the X Color database. Or a specific formatter might provide a list of extra named colors accessible in this way.

Color Profiles

The fo:color-profile formatting object appears in the fo:declarations formatting object (which appears after the fo:layout-master-set). An XSL-FO stylesheet may contain several color-profile declarations. Each defines a profile named using the color-profile-name attribute. The actual profile definition is designated with the src attribute, which is a URI value. The URI may be a conventional value that is interpreted by the processor or may name an actual external resource containing the ICC profile description. Example 7-4 shows a color profile in use.

Example 7-4. Color profile example

```
<fo:declarations>
<fo:color-profile src="url('./myprofile.icc')" color-profile-name="cp1"/>
</fo:declarations>
 <-- Intervening stuff -->
    <fo:block color='icc-color(200, 200, 50, cp1, 1.45, 2.22)'>
   A block whose text color is defined using the profile named cp1
    </fo:block>
```

The color-profile declaration can also bear a rendering-intent attribute. The specification says in Section 7.17.3:

> rendering-intent permits the specification of a color-profile rendering-intent other than the default. rendering-intent is applicable primarily to color-profiles corresponding to CMYK color spaces. The different options cause different methods to be used for translating colors to the color gamut of the target rendering device.

Applicability

This section outlines the applicability of color to the various formatting objects available in XSL-FO and provides a few examples.

The various color properties may be applied to the formatting objects listed in Table 7-1.

Table 7-1. Color properties and the formatting objects to which they may be applied

Color property	Formatting objects
background-color	All page-region objects, block, block-container, all table objects, list-block, list-item, inline, inline-container, external-graphic, foreign-instream-object, character, leader, initial-property-set, bidi-override, page-number, page-number-citation
border-{side}-color	Same formatting objects as background-color, except for page-region objects and some special cases in tables
color	block, character, inline, leader, initial-property-set, bidi-override
text-shadow (colors the shadow)	character, leader, page-number, page-number-citation, initial-property-set

Summary

The application of color to your document content is a personal thing. It's highly likely that whatever you do with color, some of your readers will object. The only advice is to avoid overdoing it. Color adds visual presentation value, up to a point. Use it sparingly and wisely to enhance your documents.

Styling at the Character Level

XSL-FO provides a number of features aimed at formatting text and dealing with characters, which provide fine-grained control over presentation. You can manage content on a character-by-character basis, or you can apply properties to larger chunks of text.

In this chapter, I discuss the options available for formatting at the character level and when you should use this level of formatting. I also introduce font usage.

 Be aware that, as formatters are introduced, the available fonts are not likely to match those available for desktop publishing packages or word processors. Most packages allow you to add fonts, either purchased or downloaded. See the vendor literature for instructions on adding new fonts and for the list of included fonts.

General Character Properties

In many cases, what can be done at the character level could also be done at the inline level. This gives the stylesheet designer the choice of using either one. In some cases, the choice will be very clear. If you need to style only a single character, it makes sense to use the `fo:character` element. If it's necessary to style a block of text that is all inline, use the `fo:inline` element. Many of the characteristics available at the inline level are equally applicable at the character level, so the number of them to remember doesn't increase dramatically! The only properties unique to `fo:character` are `treat-as-word-space`, `character`, `glyph-orientation-horizontal`, `glyph-orientation-vertical`, and `suppress-at-line-break`. I'll describe each of these in this chapter.

The `fo:character` element is always empty. The character to be formatted is specified as an attribute of the element. While it is possible to specify more than one character, using the `character="ABC"` form, the working draft does say that this attribute specifies the Unicode *character* to be presented! This implies a single character but does not require it.

The fo:character element is the fundamental unit of formatting for the formatting engine, creating an area on the page whose size is determined by the font metrics for the glyph representing the Unicode code point specified. Presently, the Antenna House implementation permits this to be seen by indicating the borders around each character-level element when specified as a unit. This indicates, to some extent, the work being done by the formatter when laying out page after page!

Usage

The need to format a specific character in some special way is a rare occurrence, though it is handy to have that capability. When a single character has to stand out in some way, marked off from other inline text, it first needs to be identified in the source XML document, then provided with sufficient characteristics to provide the stylesheet writer with the information necessary to enable the appropriate formatting. This might be, for instance, a single character in another language or an example character that, though inline, is required to be shown in some detail. For example, you might specify that this character outlined in a large font, perhaps with a different background color. This can be done with the properties discussed in Chapter 7, using border or background-color and color attributes. Example 8-1 shows a single character in 20-point text, a pale blue background, and the character in red:

Example 8-1. A color-contrasted character

```
<fo:character
    character="&x067;"
    font-size="20pt"
    background-color="skyblue"
    color="red"/>
```

This creates output as shown in Figure 8-1.

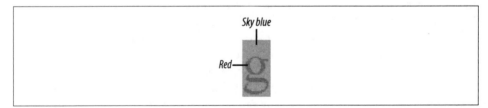

Figure 8-1. A color-contrasted character

Now, let's move on to those characteristics specific to fo:character. The basic form of fo:character is shown Example 8-2.

Example 8-2. fo:character example

```
    <fo:character
❶       character="&#x0067;" />
```

❶ Shows the primary, required attribute: the actual character to be displayed. This may be entered as either an actual character or, as shown, in its Unicode entity format. The x indicates that it is a hexadecimal number. If the special character is to be referred to, you might want to add an `id` attribute to identify it.

When discussing a single character, it may be required to present it in a way other than the normal inline-progression-direction. For a single character, this is specified using the `glyph-orientation-horizontal` attribute.

A more unusual property, `treat-as-word-space`, has the specific function of using characters, not whitespace, to separate words. Unicode has a group of code points, U+2000 to U+200A, which may be used as word seperators in certain circumstances. These are known, respectively, as:

- U+2000, EN QUAD
- U+2001, EM QUAD
- U+2002, EN SPACE
- U+2003, EM SPACE
- U+2004, THREE-PER-EM SPACE (a.k.a. thick space)
- U+2005, FOUR-PER-EM SPACE (a.k.a. mid space)
- U+2006, SIX-PER-EM SPACE (sometimes known as thin space)
- U+2007, FIGURE SPACE (equivalent to the digit width of a font)
- U+2008, PUNCTUATION SPACE (equivalent to the narrow punctuation of a font)
- U+2009, THIN SPACE (one fifth of an em)
- U+200A, HAIR SPACE (often the thinest space available)

So, why are we interested in them? The information is provided to tell the formatter that these are not printable characters that provide glyphs, but that they are used to separate two words. This is done using the `treat-as-word-space` attribute on `fo: character`, as shown in Example 8-3. A colleague informs me that in Thai texts, the interword gaps are not always whitespace; perhaps this is a case where `treat-as-word-space` is needed.

Example 8-3. treat-as-word-space example

```
<fo:inline>Words with<fo:character
    character="&#x2001;"
    treat-as-word-space="true"
    />spaces.
</fo:inline>
```

(Note that I'm cheating here! The specification says that this group of characters is treated as if true has been specified anyway.) This gives the output shown in Figure 8-2.

```
┌─────────────────────────────────────────────────────────┐
│                                                           │
│              Words with□spaces.                           │
│                                                           │
└─────────────────────────────────────────────────────────┘
```

Figure 8-2. treat-as-word-space example

The `suppress-at-line-break` attribute takes one value from a fixed number of values. This property determines what happens to this character when it is the last character on either end of a line. The character may be retained or suppressed depending on the setting of the attribute value. The values are:

`auto`
> Action is dependent on the character.

`suppress`
> The character is suppressed.

`retain`
> The character is retained.

When the action is character dependent, the value of the character is inspected to determine whether it is a normal space character, U+0020, in which case the character is suppressed. `suppress` implies that if it is at either end of a line, the glyph is not presented. `retain` implies that the character will always be retained and presented.

Writing Mode

If you write from the top left to the bottom right as in English, writing mode is not an issue. Writing mode is only necessary when you need to specify writing direction to a formatter. The W3C is serious about internationalization, so this has been accounted for in XSL-FO. The terminology is explained in Chapter 3, but I want to bring this down to its impact on character orientation. Remember that when we are dealing with characters, some properties are already available. Starting at the top of the hierarchy, we have the block-progression-direction. At right angles to this is the inline-progression-direction. These are both set by the `writing-mode` attribute. If we take the Latin example of left to right, top to bottom, then when we come down to the character level, we finish with a default glyph orientation. This has the top of the glyph oriented towards the top of the page.

Writing modes specify the manner in which text flows down the page. Unicode includes the default writing mode for each character. Thus, Arabic is automatically presented right to left. If you want it presented left to right, you need to use the `bidi-override` attribute of `fo:inline`. This also allows you to embed left-to-right text into right-to-left data (e.g., English words embedded in an Arabic stream).

`glyph-orientation` (horizontal or vertical) sets the orientation of a glyph with respect to this default glyph orientation. The variance is that vertical, as used here, relates to vertical and horizontal writing modes. Latin scripts where the glyphs are laid out on the page from top to bottom, left to right use a horizontal writing mode.

For vertical writing mode, where text is laid out top to bottom, use the glyph-orientation-vertical attribute. The rotation obtained should be one from the following list: 0, 90, 180, or –90. The formatter is supposed to round to the nearest one of these values. Used for single characters, the result is that the character is rotated relative to the zero at the top of the page. Using the clock face analogy, 90 degrees has the top of the glyph oriented to 3 on the clock face. From that, it's easy to work out that the top of the glyph is at 6 on the clock face for 180 degrees and at 9 on the clock face for –90 (or +270) degrees. Figure 8-3 should explain it clearly.

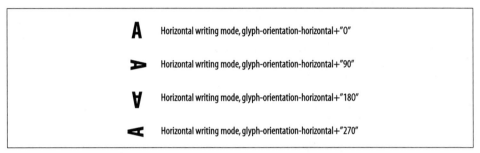

Figure 8-3. Writing mode

Note that this applies to horizontal writing mode. Although the vertical writing mode is similar at the character level, the effect is different when applied at block or inline level using the closely related properties set by the writing-mode property. For fo:character level operation, it is fairly straightforward.

When vertical writing mode is used, the actual rotations are identical for single characters to that shown in Figure 8-3. Character sequencing and layout are modified due to common layout properties, as specified in the font tables.

Superscript and Subscript

Although not specific to fo:character, the ability to use superscript and subscript is handy at the character level. Typical uses might include references to footnotes, glossary items, or where a single character reference is needed. This is achieved readily, as shown in Example 8-4. Because the size of the superscripted character is often set smaller than the main content, the font-size property would normally be applied here, too.

Example 8-4. Superscript

```
<fo:character
    character="1"
    baseline-shift="super"
    font-size="8pt"
    font-family="'MS Serif'"/>
```

The value 1 specifies that the `baseline-shift` attribute be set to the value super. This provides the shift upwards relative to the reference baseline suitable for a superscript. Example 8-5 combines this with an inline.

Example 8-5. Character-level superscript

```
<fo:inline>See note
 <fo:character
     character="1"
     baseline-shift="super"
     font-family="'MS Serif'"/>
</fo:inline>
```

This provides the output shown in Figure 8-4.

See note ¹

Figure 8-4. Character-level superscript

Subscript is similar but has the alternate attribute value `baseline-shift="sub"`. If the extent of the shift is not right for you, the alternative is to specify the amount by which the character is required to be shifted, using the `baseline-shift="120%"` form. The specification also permits an absolute value stated as a length, but I don't recommend it unless the document is fixed in terms of font size, etc. The percentage solution works relative to the size of the font and, hence, would scale if the font were changed. Note that a negative value, such as `baseline-shift="-120%"`, provides the subscript version.

Fonts

Font selection considerations are primarily dependent on the formatter used. Each formatter may have certain built-in fonts readily available to the stylesheet writer, other fonts may be added either by the user or by the provider. Fonts may be found on the Web, purchased from font foundries, or developed specifically for a task. The two prerequisites for use within a stylesheet are that the font metrics are available to the formatter in the style selected and that the font chosen is identified correctly by the stylesheet.

While discussion of the general characteristics of fonts is beyond the scope of this book, a good reference is the approach used by LaTeX. One I found particularly useful is Chapter 7 of *The Latex Companion* by Goosens, Mittelback, and Samarin (Addison Wesley).

Some of the preparatory tasks when writing the stylesheet for a document are to determine if the source file contains characters not likely to be found in the primary font chosen for the document, find a font that contains an entry for that character, and ensure that all characters can be mapped to a presentation form. The result of not doing these tasks is likely to be a missing character glyph, often difficult to spot in anything other than a small document. It's often easier to search the source XML document for entities than to peruse the formatted document for the missing character glyph.

The reference section of XSL refers to a font model called OpenType, developed by Microsoft and Adobe. The reference is to the OpenType specification v1.2 (see *http://www.microsoft.com/truetype/tt/tt.htm*). This technology model has been adopted by XSL-FO.

Some of the terminology takes getting used to. As in all XML, the starting point is a given Unicode code point, such as U+0041, its name, LATIN CAPITAL LETTER A, the actual glyph representing that code point, and the font chosen to represent it, Arial Black, for instance. The XSL document defines a glyph as "…a recognizable abstract graphic symbol which is independent of any specific design." Therefore, we can tell that a particular symbol represents the letter A, even when it's in a strange font that we may have never seen before. The recognition is critical. A font is simply a collection of glyphs. The font designer determines which set of glyphs to include in his font.

The font tables for any particular font include the information necessary to map characters to glyphs, to determine the size of glyph areas, and to position the glyph area precisely on the page to align with its neighbors. Alignment of an individual character with its neighbors uses reference points, called *alignment points*, such that any two glyphs that are direct neighbors appear correct when viewed together. Vertical alignment information is also provided. For instance, Western glyphs are aligned on the bottoms of the capital letters while other scripts have differing alignment points. The table also holds information about the writing modes supported by the font. If you intend to present a vertically oriented piece of text, ensure that this writing mode is available.

Each font table consists of the font characteristics, such as the `font-weight` and `font-style`. The formatter uses this information to place the individual glyph precisely on the page, aligned both to the sides of its neighbors and to any lines of text above or below it.

The space a character takes up is defined as the design space. It is the box within which the character fits, and within which given reference points are measured in the design space coordinate system. Each line and curve of the glyph is drawn within this box. This allows a single 20-point character in a line of 12-point characters while maintaining legible presentation.

In XSL-FO, font selection is based on the font properties: `font-family`, `font-style`, `font-variant`, `font-weight`, `font-stretch`, and `font-size`. The `font-family` specifies a font set from which the stylesheet designer wishes to select characters. This addresses the issue of font coverage. A font set is a list of fonts that will be tried, in turn, to find a glyph for the particular character. The first available font that contains the character is used. The fonts listed should be the same style and size. The two types of values for this attribute are a specific family name, such as Baskerville, and a generic family, either serif, sans-serif, cursive, fantasy, or monospace. When specifying one of these generic families, do not use quotes. These act as a fallback mechanism, coming into action when none of the font families contain the character you are seeking.

The Serif family are typically proportionately spaced and have finishing strokes. Examples include Times New Roman, Bodoni, Garamond from the Latin family, and Bitstream Cyberbit from the Hebrew and Arabic families.

Sans Serif fonts have stroke endings that are plain. Examples include MS Verdana, Univers, and Futura from the Latin families, and Helvetica Cyrillic, ER Univers, and Lucida Sans Unicode from the Cyrillic fonts.

The font-family attribute is specified by a list as in Example 8-6.

Example 8-6. Font example

```
    <fo:inline
❶          font-family="Arial, Garamond, serif"/>
    </fo:inline>
```

❶ Shows the font-family selection in use.

This selects the Arial font as first choice, Garamond as second choice, and the fallback of using any available Serif fonts. Where the font family name contains spaces, enclose in the alternate quote marks, for example, 'Times Extravaganza Fabuleux'.

font-style selects one style from a small number of variants. These are normal, the upright form of the character; italic, often used for emphasis; oblique, slightly different visually from italic and sometimes known as slanted; and backslant, the inverse of oblique.

Use is shown in Example 8-7 in a simple inline.

Example 8-7. Font style

```
<fo:inline
     font-style="normal">This is normal.</fo:inline>
<fo:inline
     font-style="italic">Italic.</fo:inline>
<fo:inline
     font-style="oblique">Oblique.</fo:inline>
<fo:inline
     font-style="backslant">Backslant.</fo:inline>
```

The font-variant attribute selects the small capital variant of the font, which could be generated by the formatter or provided by the font. Example 8-8 shows its use.

Example 8-8. Font variant

```
<fo:inline
     font-variant="small-caps">A small-caps example</fo:inline>
```

Although content is mixed case, the formatter converts these to small capitals as shown in Figure 8-5.

A SMALL-CAPS EXAMPLE

Figure 8-5. Small capitals

The `font-weight` attribute follows this pattern, the options being one from a reasonably complete list, including: `normal`, `bold`, `bolder`, and `lighter`, coupled with a numeric alternative, ranging from 100 to 900, in steps of 100. `bolder` and `lighter` provide the option of making relative changes. These are all relative to the inherited `font-weight`, which is useful in a text that may be modified. Each change increases or decreases the weight by 100 on this 100 to 900 scale, until either limit is reached. The equivalents provided set `font-weight="normal"` at either 400 or 500, with `font-weight="bold"` at 700. Trying these will often not produce a noticable difference between two adjacent values. Some fonts may only have the two basic types, `normal` and `bold`. So be aware of this when designing a stylesheet.

The `font-stretch` attribute expands characters horizontally. Currently, this is not well supported in implementations. Its utility is viable, because it is one aspect of layout that enables content to precisely fill a line. Its use is identical to the previous attributes, setting `font-stretch` to a range from `ultra-condensed` to `ultra-expanded`, again providing the relative options of wider and narrower, when compared to the inherited property. The ranged list is: `normal`, `wider`, and `narrow`. These provide the relative aspects and the initial value or default. The specified stretch range includes: `ultra-condensed`, `extra-condensed`, `condensed`, `semi-condensed`, `normal` (the mid-range default), `semi-expanded`, `expanded`, `extra-expanded`, and `ultra-expanded`. These should satisfy most requirements.

The `font-size` utility attribute provides basic sizing, selecting the potentially complex mix of availability and other modifications. Watch out for formatter font size availability and the parent element's font value inherited by the element under scrutiny.

As with the previous related attributes, this one can be provided in a number of ways, each having its uses. The full list of options include `absolute-size`, `relative-size`, a length specification, and a percentage. The meaning of these relates back to the CSS origins and may not be immediately obvious.

Let's start with a simple length specification, shown in Example 8-9.

Example 8-9. Simple font size example

```
<fo:inline
      font-size="12pt">Length specification.</fo:inline>
```

I've chosen the point length specification here. Other absolute length alternatives are the pixel (`px`), the pica (`pc`, 1 pica is equal to 12 points), inches (`in`), centimeters (`cm`), millimeters (`mm`). These forms of specification enable content to be presented to the user with an absolute size. When using XSL-FO in combination with XSLT to style an XML document, there are potential problems when using this form as anything other than an initial value to specify basic body text sizes. These relate to nested structures within the source document, where the visual aspects of the presented text size are important. Using the analogy of XHTML, headings will probably want to scale down from the largest (XHTML has its H1 element) through to any minor headings (XHTML has its H6 element). If absolute lengths are specified directly for any given level of nesting or class of text content, a number of factors come into play. If the content is modified to introduce, say, another level of usage, it is often easier to specify the font size relative to its direct neighbors. So, use absolute values (length specifications) with caution.

The length specification of a `font-size` shouldn't be confused with absolute-size, which includes the options: `xx-small`, `x-small`, `small`, `medium`, `large`, `x-large`, and `xx-large`.

These are not relative. Because they are computed values, they are specific, and the specification states that each relates to the other, with a scaling factor of 1.2 between each one and may, in fact, vary from font to font. These options are known as absolute while the 12-point specification is known as a length. So, we might see `<fo:inline font-size="xx-small">Pretty small text</fo:inline>`.

The relative alternative is shown in Example 8-10.

Example 8-10. Relative font changes

```
<fo:inline
      font-size="smaller">Relative Specification of font size.</fo:inline>
```

This form uses the previous range of values, `xx-small` to `xx-large`, such that each increment causes a change of value in one of the two directions, obviously limited to either end. This is useful when styling one piece of content with respect to its parent. Experience has proven the ratio to be successful.

The use of relative specification of size is a looser version of the larger or smaller specification in that it can range over a larger change in value. You might use this to specify the font sizes in a document as part of a range of variables that are then used throughout the document as needed. This permits a single change to alter the whole document.

The basis for this is shown in Example 8-11.

Example 8-11. Attribute sets for font variants

```
<xsl:variable name="base-font">12</xsl:variable>

<xsl:attribute-set name="head1">
  <xsl:attribute name="font-size"><xsl:value-of
    select="concat(round($base-font *1.2),'pt')"/></xsl:attribute>
```

Example 8-11. Attribute sets for font variants (continued)

```
<xsl:attribute name="font-weight">bold</xsl:attribute>
<xsl:attribute name="font-family">Helvetica</xsl:attribute>
....
<!-- other attributes as required. -->
</xsl:attribute-set>
```

With various attribute sets named like this, a clear specification is set up that may then be used throughout the document quickly and easily, as shown in Example 8-12.

Example 8-12. Attribute set usage

```
<fo:block
    xsl:use-attribute-sets="head1"
    keep-with-next.within-page="always">
    <xsl:apply-templates/>
</fo:block>
```

This makes use of the attribute set, adding, as needed, any other properties, without explicitly stating the font within the body of the stylesheet. This provides the global version equivalent to using the percentage option locally, setting any block or inline to a fixed percentage of its parent element's font size.

The specification gives the formatter the right to determine the tolerance when trying to determine what 13.56894-point text should look like. Be aware of this and don't expect too much, even for scalable fonts.

The font-size-adjust property, which is used to tweak the aspect ratio of a character, is not used often. This is defined in the specification as the ratio of the font size to its x height. The x height is the height of a letter x within a font. By adjusting this ratio, fonts can appear clearer. The calculations are provided in the specification, and the CSS specification provides clear indications of usage, enabling you to substitute fonts that have differing aspect values. The specification refers to the examples in the CSS2 specification:

> For example, if 14px Verdana (with an aspect value of 0.58) was unavailable and an available font had an aspect value of 0.46, the font-size of the substitute would be 14 * (0.58/0.46) = 17.65px.

If this level of adjustment is necessary on any scale, it may be worthwhile to purchase the required font in the needed sizes.

The decoration (as it's called in the specification) of text provides for a more readily usable set of modifications to the presented content. This uses the text-decoration property, where the list of options includes: none, underline, no-underline, overline, no-overline, line-through, no-line-through, blink, and no-blink.

You may wonder about the last two options. These can be directly attributed to CSS2 and are of little use in paper-based output, as they're targeted for screen use. A quick word on the negations in this list of properties: when a sequence of content is presented to a user, you may need to use an on/off sequence. For instance, when identifying content for deletion, you could mark the first four words with line-through, remove the strike through with the no-line-through property, then reapply it to words 7 through 10. The negation options provide for this. Example 8-13 illustrates nested inlines using this feature.

Example 8-13. Negating decorations

```
<fo:inline
   text-decoration="line-through">Continuing,
         <fo:inline
            text-decoration="no-line-through">with
         </fo:inline> font-weight bold
</fo:inline>
```

The nested inlines use the no-line-through property to turn off the strike-through for the word with. The other properties work the same way, decorating the content as described. The output is shown in Figure 8-6.

~~Continuing,~~ with ~~font weight bold~~

Figure 8-6. Negating decorations

The text-shadow property provides the type of shadow often seen on containing boxes or window buttons on a graphical user interface. It is specified by an optional color and three length values, which specify the horizontal and vertical offsets from the character (to the right and down being positive) and an implementation-dependent blur radius. The syntax might be as shown in Example 8-14.

Example 8-14. Text shadow

```
<fo:inline
   text-shadow="red 0.3px -0.3px 5px">Eclipse
</fo:inline>
```

This provides a red shadow 0.3px to the right, 0.3px up, and a blur radius of 5px.

The final property associated with characters, though also applicable to other elements, is text-transform. This enables the capitalization and case of selected content to be modified. Capitalization changes case on the first letter of bicameral fonts. The Latin alphabet is an example of a bicameral font; it has an uppercase and lowercase. Unicameral alphabets (such as Arabic and Hebrew) have only one case. The uppercase and lowercase values ensure content is fixed to that particular case. As usual, the transformation may be turned off with the none value, if this is required.

Shorthand Attribute Specification

The font attribute is a slightly lazy way of specifying a nearly complete set of font-related traits. The properties that can be set are: font-family, font-size, font-weight, font-style, font-variant, line-height, font-size-adjust, and font-stretch.

Use of the font attribute is demonstrated in Example 8-15.

Example 8-15. Font short form usage

```
font="italic 11pt/1.5 Times"
```

The syntax of this attribute is a space-separated list of values in the following order, extracting the relevent part of the specification:

```
[ <font-style> || <font-variant> || <font-weight> ]?
    <font-size> [ / <line-height>]? <font-family> ]
```

The || indicates that you can have any of the options in any order, so you don't necessarily need the font-style before the font-weight, although these do have to occur before the font-size. Note the sequencing and the exception, shown in Example 8-15, of the inclusion of the line-height value. This has the forward slash predecessor and must follow the font-size. line-height is a multiplier and may be an explicit length. Be aware that the shorthand sets all these values to their default values prior to applying those specified. So, if you don't set a value, it has a default applied. If you want to maintain a value (perhaps set by a parent element), ensure that it is included. Be careful: silently overriding line-height or font-size-adjust by this property can easily give rise to confusion. The side effect here is that two other properties are reset to default values. These are font-stretch and font-size-adjust.

CHAPTER 9

Cross-Document Links

To quote from the specification:

> Because XML, unlike HTML, has no built-in semantics, there is no built-in notion of a
> hypertext link.

So why does XSL-FO address links? Certainly for a paper-based output, an active
hyperlink isn't much use, though for a screen-based presentation using PDF, it might
be. While XSL-FO is used primarily for paper-based output today, it would be a mistake to think this is XSL-FO's only purpose. XSL-FO is designed to present XML
across several media, including interactive media; to do that, it needs to support
hyperlinking. In its simplest form, the link is useful to cross-reference to content,
locations within the document, and specific structural elements. For web-based
delivery, it is handy to have an active link, and for print output, the actual content of
the active element needs to be meaningful. This facility is offered in the first version
of the specification.

XSL-FO has a formatting object named fo:basic-link, which provides the basic linking capability. Example 9-1 and Figure 9-1 show this in use.

Example 9-1. A basic link

xml source

```
<para>...see the figure on page <link idref="fig53"/>
</para>
```

and the stylesheet

```
<xsl:template match="link">
<fo:basic-link background-color="lightblue"
    internal-destination="{@idref}">Page
    <fo:page-number-citation ref-id="intro"/>
  </fo:basic-link>

</xsl:template>
```

> Some base content linking out to another block on a different page, hot-linked to
> Page 3, which is on another page.

Figure 9-1. A basic link

Here, the link is shown inline and shaded, referencing a page number. The formatter replaces the `page-number-citation` with the page number on which the link target is present while laying out the document. Some formatters will create a clickable link, others will not. Be warned: there is no requirement to do so! Note the use of the attribute value template in this example to insert the `id` value of the link target, using the `idref` attribute value on this element.

Now, let's have a look at the various uses for links.

Cross-Document Links

The simplest syntax for this use is the `id`/`idref` pair. This is for a case in which the document being transformed contains both the source and target of the link. This way, the XSLT engine can resolve the link target using the `id( )` function.

> Note that for `id`/`idref` to work properly, the `id` attribute must be declared by the DTD as being of type ID. A common error (and one that I frequently make) is to style a part of a document and forget the DTD inclusion.

When the link is between documents that are only styled to form a single document for paper, other cross-document linking forms should be used. If the source documents are parsed as a single entity, this presents no problem. If they are to be used in other ways, to avoid unresolved cross-references the source of the link needs to use something other than the `IDREF` attribute.

The contents of the `basic-link` element could be literal content or content retrieved from the target, such as the title of a chapter, a page, or a section number, using the functionality of XSLT. Examples 9-2 and 9-3 show such an example, with the generated `fo` shown in Example 9-4.

> The cross-references are actually within the `fo` file. If you receive warnings about unresolved `page-number-citations` or reference id values, it's possible that you have forgotten to add the `id` values to the targets.

Example 9-2. Cross-references using target content, XML source

```
<chapter>
<para>A link to <xref idref="ch2" />.
    </para></chapter>
```

Example 9-2. Cross-references using target content, XML source (continued)

```
<chapter id="ch2">
  <title>Second chapter</title>
</chapter>
```

Example 9-3. Cross-references using target content, XSLT stylesheet

```
      <xsl:template match="chapter">
❶            <fo:block id="{@id}">
          <xsl:apply-templates/></fo:block>
      </xsl:template>


      <xsl:template match="xref">
       <fo:inline ><fo:basic-link
❷            internal-destination="{@idref}">
       Chapter
❸            <xsl:for-each select="id(@idref)">
          <xsl:number level="multiple" count="chapter" format="1 "/>
       </xsl:for-each>,
       <xsl:value-of select="id(@idref)/title"/>
       on Page
      <fo:page-number-citation ref-id="{@idref}"/>,
       </fo:basic-link>
      </fo:inline>
      </xsl:template>
```

❶ The example shows the chapter being wrapped in a block. An alternative is to use an empty block with the id value set.

❷ The xref template creates the source link, with content obtained from the target (Chapter 2 title); its number is calculated from its position within the document, and the page number is added.

❸ Note the need to change context, using xsl:for-each, to obtain the right context.

Example 9-4. Cross-references using target content, resulting FO

```
<fo:block font-family="Times"
   font-size="12pt" space-before="12pt" space-after="12pt"
❹      text-align="justify">A link to <fo:inline>
      <fo:basic-link
      internal-destination="ch2">Chapter 2, Second chapter on Page
      <fo:page-number-citation ref-id="ch2"/>, </fo:basic-link>
            </fo:inline>.
      </fo:block>
          </fo:block>
```

❹ The resulting output in the fo namespace indicates the processing that the formatter has to do, replacing the page-number-citation while generating the link.

Note that the whitespace in this example is there for readability.

Page Numbering

Page numbering can sometimes cause problems. As mentioned earlier in the book, page-number restarts are possible for any layout. Another thing to consider is the actual appearance of page numbers. Front matter and main matter may require different formats, for example; Roman for the front matter and Arabic for the main matter. This is not defined in XSL-FO, but rather in XSLT, which provides that facility and is referenced from the XSLT-FO Recommendation. `xsl:number` has an attribute named `format`, which takes an option of 1, a, A, i, or I, and applies formatting to the string to return Arabic numerals, lowercase letters, uppercase letters, lowercase Roman numerals, and uppercase numerals, respectively. This attribute is available on the `fo:page-sequence` element, with a default beginning value of 1. Select one of the other options to format the page number in Roman or other formats. For example, to have a page-sequence numbered using Roman uppercase, you might specify `<fo:page-sequence master-reference="only" format="I"> <fo:flow flow-name="xsl-region-body">` ....

Next, let's put the basic link to use.

Indexing and Tables of Contents

The most common use of links, index, and table of contents generation, share two characteristics. First, they answer the old problem of changing content. If the table of contents or index is generated automatically, there is no frantic rush near publishing time to get all the page numbering correct. Second, the actual page numbers (or section or chapter numbers) don't need to be hardcoded into the document. This way, content reorganization is not a problem. Take a book with chapters and sections within chapters: if all cross-references are to chapter id values, then no matter how much reorganization is done, the cross-references will remain valid, the table of contents will be accurate, and the indexing is done as part of the transformation.

Let's take the previous example further, by producing a table of contents showing the title and page number. We need to do that for chapters and the contained sections. Dot leaders are needed for each entry, which are second-level entries indented by four character widths with respect to the parent. The source might look like Example 9-5.

Example 9-5. Source XML requiring a table of contents

```
<chapter><title>one </title>
 <section><title>one one </title></section>
 <section><title>one two </title></section>
 <section><title>one three </title></section>
</chapter>

<chapter><title>two </title>
 <section><title>two one</title></section>
<section><title>two two</title></section>
<section><title>two three, with a long title to show
```

Example 9-5. Source XML requiring a table of contents (continued)

```
  the effect of wrapping on long lines in this mode.
    Normal layout provides a reasonable solution</title></section>
<section><title>two four</title></section>
<section><title>two five</title></section>
<section><title>two six</title></section>
```

The stylesheet section to generate the table of contents needs to be called at the appropriate time in the output generation and might look like Example 9-6. The example uses templates with a mode attribute set to the value toc, to enable out-of-line processing. An appropriate header must be included.

Example 9-6. Table of contents stylesheet extract

```
<xsl:template match="chapter" mode="toc">
  <fo:block text-align-last="justify">
    <fo:inline><xsl:value-of select="title"/>
    <fo:leader        leader-pattern="dots"/>
    <fo:page-number-citation ref-id="{@id}"/>
  </fo:inline>
 </fo:block>
<xsl:apply-templates select="section" mode="toc"/>
</xsl:template>

<xsl:template match="section" mode="toc">
  <fo:block text-align-last="justify"
        text-indent="-1em" start-indent="1em">
    <fo:inline padding-start="1em"><xsl:value-of select="title"/>
    <fo:leader        leader-pattern="dots" />
    <fo:page-number-citation ref-id="{@id}"/>
  </fo:inline>
 </fo:block>
</xsl:template>
```

Leaders are used to separate the title contents from the page number. The only other difference is the use of the text-align-last attribute. This expands content across the page to give the presentation shown in Figure 9-2.

Table of Contents

Figure 9-2. A table of contents example

Figure 9-2 shows how to control the wrapping of long lines by using the text-indent and start-indent combination. The first line is outdented, with the whole block indented by the same amount.

Indexing is managed in a similar manner. Each term is identified, perhaps with a specific attribute or even using an id attribute. The index is then generated automatically, using the id/idref pair again. More complex indexing would require both primary and secondary (or even tertiary) annotations to indicate the level of indexing for that usage. This is simply a case of using indentation to layout the index, perhaps using bold to indicate the primary entries and normal weight for other levels. Example 9-7 shows a simple text example illustrating the source XML.

Example 9-7. Source XML

```
<para>This is a page layout using the
    <term id="front-page">page </term> format....
....
    <idx>
      <item idref="front-page">Background Image</item>
      <item idref="b">Bold</item>
      <item idref="cen">Centered text</item>
      <item idref="sect4">Columns</item>
    </idx>
```

The indexed term is identified and referenced by page number. At the end of the document, the term is identified and the index text is inserted, which in this case expands on the content for clarity. The XSLT stylesheet to produce the overall index is shown in Example 9-8.

Example 9-8. Stylesheet for the index

```
<xsl:template match="idx">
<fo:block
  start-indent="0.5in"
  end-indent="0.5in"
  font-size="{$base-font-spec}"
  text-align-last="justify">
  <fo:inline font-weight="bold">Item</fo:inline>
    <fo:leader leader-pattern="dots"/>
  <fo:inline font-weight="bold">Page</fo:inline>
</fo:block>
  <xsl:apply-templates/>
</xsl:template>

<xsl:template match="idx/item">
<fo:block
  start-indent="0.5in"
  end-indent="0.5in"
  font-size="{$base-font-spec}"
  text-align-last="justify">
  <xsl:apply-templates/>
<fo:leader leader-pattern="dots"/><fo:basic-link
```

Example 9-8. Stylesheet for the index (continued)

```
internal-destination="{@idref}">
   <fo:page-number-citation
   color="blue" ref-id="{@idref}"/></fo:basic-link>
</fo:block>
 </xsl:template>
```

The example provides the header for the index, the column headings, the term, and page number. Note that I have used a variable to specify `font-size` to permit varying the whole document font size for different readers. The content of the `item` element is left-justified with an indent, followed by the `leader` with a pattern set to `dots` to provide the dot leaders out to the right margin, where the page number is included using the `page-number-citation` property. This produces the actual page number. The result is shown in Figure 9-3.

Item	Page
Background Image	1
Bold	7
Centred text	4
Columns	13

Figure 9-3. Resultanting index output

If secondary terms are required, the method shown for the table of contents example could be used (see Example 9-6, earlier).

Running Headers

Because the method used to produce running headers is effectively a link, it is included here with other cross-referencing techniques. For those not familiar with the term, running headers are the lines of text that run across the tops of book pages, sometimes including chapter titles.

XSL-FO uses a scheme that I don't find particularly clear. As explained earlier in this book, headers are seen as static content related to page layout, rather than to flowed content. This is reasonable for the majority of cases. I find it counter-intuitive for running headers. As of Release 1 of the Recommendation, little has been provided that is dependent on the page position. The XSL Working Group has openly stated that there are clear requirements for this that will be addressed, but have yet to address them.

A key point here is that static content is defined in the page layout specification and remains *static* until a new page layout is used. This means items such as page numbers and running headers that are required to change over a single layout must be treated specially. The running header issue is resolved in XSL-FO by means of two formatting objects, `marker` and `retrieve-marker`.

Let's first identify the content for the running header (or footer—the same principles apply). Assuming that a chapter title is required for the running header, we may have something like Example 9-9 as the XML source file.

Example 9-9. XML source for a running header

```
<chapter><title>Introducing markers</title>
  ....
```

The stylesheet for this "Introducing markers" header is as shown in Example 9-10.

Example 9-10. Marker usage

```
<xsl:template match="chapter/title">
  <fo:block xsl:use-attribute-sets="head1"
   break-before="page">
    <fo:marker marker-class-name="sect-head" >
      <fo:block><xsl:value-of select="."/>
        </fo:block>
    </fo:marker>
    <xsl:apply-templates/>
  </fo:block>
</xsl:template>
```

Within the `title` block, a marker is specified, given a class name of `sect-head` and its contents are enclosed in a block (which is not strictly necessary). The `marker-class-name` must be unique within the layout area. Note that this will not produce output prior to the contents of the title in the formatted output. It simply says, "Use this content when you want the contents of the marker named `sect-head`." This identifies the content, so now we need to use it.

As part of the page layout, the header is specified as `static-content`. Assuming a justified layout of title contents, we can use `text-align-last` for this justification, with each element as a child of the block with that property set to `justify`. The header stylesheet might look like Example 9-11.

Example 9-11. Retrieve marker usage in a header

```
<fo:static-content
    flow-name="xsl-region-head">
      <fo:block>
        <fo:retrieve-marker
           retrieve-class-name="sect-head"/>
      </fo:block>
</fo:static-content>
```

The static content for the header is specified to contain the contents of the marker named `sect-head`, contained within a block. This produces a header that changes within the same page-sequence to reflect the changing contents of the chapter title. I'll leave it up to you to format the other typical contents of a header.

Footnotes

Though footnotes are not links, it seems appropriate to discuss them here. The element (in the fo namespace) to use is fo:footnote. The two first children of this element are the inline for the footnote reference and the footnote-body for the actual content of the footnote. In Example 9-13, I've used a decorative horizontal rule to separate the footnotes from the page text and created a list to lay out the footnote content. I'll leave the addition of superscripting to you.

Both the reference and the content of the footnote is included at the same place, with the formatter doing the hard work of laying it out on the same page. Examples 9-12 through 9-14 show the XML source, the transformation, and the resulting FO.

Example 9-12. Footnote example, source XML

```
<para> the bicameral<footnote>The Latin
  alphabet, which you are reading, is an example of a
  bicameral font; it has an uppercase and
  lowercase. Unicameral alphabets (the Arabic and Hebrew
  alphabets) only have one case.</footnote> font presents us with two forms of
  presentation..</para>
```

Example 9-13. Footnote example, the transformation

```
      <xsl:template match='para'>
      <fo:block><xsl:apply-templates/></fo:block>
      </xsl:template>


      <xsl:template match='footnote'>
        <fo:footnote>
❶           <fo:inline>1</fo:inline>
        <fo:footnote-body>
❷           <fo:block text-align-last="justify">
              <fo:leader leader-pattern="rule"/>
            </fo:block>

            <fo:list-block>
              <fo:list-item>
                <fo:list-item-label end-indent="label-end( )">
❸           <fo:block>1</fo:block>
                </fo:list-item-label>
                <fo:list-item-body start-indent="body-start( )">
❹           <fo:block><xsl:apply-templates/></fo:block>
                </fo:list-item-body>
              </fo:list-item>
            </fo:list-block>

          </fo:footnote-body>
        </fo:footnote>

      </xsl:template>
```

❶ The marker, which is an inline.

❷ A leader separates footnotes.

❸ A list presents footnote.

❹ The actual footnote content.

Example 9-14. Footnote example, the resulting FO

```
<fo:block>the bicameral font presents us with two forms of presentation
        <fo:footnote>
        <fo:inline>1</fo:inline>

        <fo:footnote-body>
          <fo:block text-align-last="justify">
            <fo:leader leader-pattern="rule"/>
          </fo:block>

          <fo:list-block>
            <fo:list-item>
              <fo:list-item-label end-indent="label-end( )">
                <fo:block>1</fo:block>
              </fo:list-item-label>
              <fo:list-item-body start-indent="body-start( )">
                <fo:block>The Latin
                    alphabet, which you are reading, is an example of a
                    bicameral font; it has an uppercase and
                    lowercase. Unicameral alphabets (the Arabic and Hebrew
                    alphabets) only have one case.</fo:block>
              </fo:list-item-body>
            </fo:list-item>
          </fo:list-block>

        </fo:footnote-body>
        </fo:footnote>
font presents us with two forms of presentation..
</fo:block>
```

The output is shown in Figure 9-4. The body content is simply the inline number one, to which a prefix could be added during the transformation stage.

---

1   The Latin alphabet, which you are reading, is an example of a bicameral font; it has an uppercase and lowercase
      Unicameral alphabets (the Arabic and Hebrew alphabets) only have one case.

Figure 9-4. Resultant footnote presentation

CHAPTER 10
Putting It All Together

A small, complete document uses much of the previously described functionality and illustrates the power of XSL-FO.

Outline

As source content, I'm going to use an imaginary book outline. In terms of layout, the major elements are the front matter, which requires attention and is a one-off; the main chapters, which share layout but have one or two special treatment areas; and the rear matter, for which separate treatment is needed for an index.

The pagination needed is shown in Figures 10-1 and 10-2.

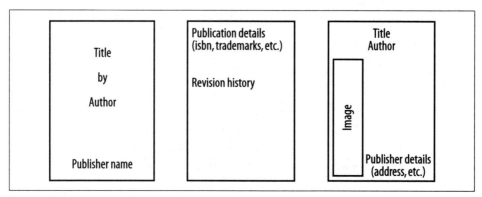

Figure 10-1. Frontmatter layout

No page headers are needed for the first three pages, page numbers are needed only for the preface and table of contents, then we use a header (no footer), as shown, for the remainder of the chapters. Now we can specify these and define some of the attribute sets that will be used throughout.

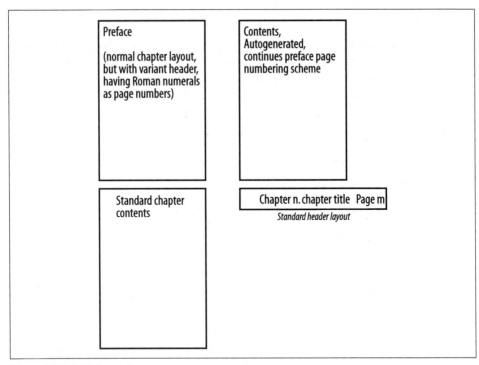

Figure 10-2. Initial page layout

So let's put an outline together. I'm presuming a fairly complex stylesheet, so I'll partition it early. The main stylesheet will hold only the content templates and will import separate stylesheets for the page layout (layout master set), the primary element templates. I'll start with a trial for the layout master set.

First, separate `simple-page-masters` will be needed for the first three pages that share a common layout. Others will be needed for the preface and contents pages and another for the bulk body content. I'll prepare those first and try them out.

Rather than include the first layout inline, it is a separate page with comments. Now we can convert it to something that is usable with content. Let's have a quick look at the format I'm using for the book itself. This is shown in outline in Appendix F. The next task is to convert the outline into a stylesheet that matches this schema. First, the root template is placed around what was an XML document in the `fo` namespace, then templates are applied, or called, to replace the dummy content.

So far, there are three files. The page layout stylesheet is derived directly from the test layout, *pl.xsl* (page layout). Another stylesheet is created with the majority of the templates, *main.xsl*. A third is created to hold all the standard property sets to be used, *ps.xsl* (property sets). The main stylesheet is the second of these; the other two are imported from that.

Page Layout

The page layout stylesheet is the key to the whole layout process, and it is important to see how the application of templates relates to this file. The primary flows are in the title page, the front matter for the preface, table of contents, and finally, the body matter, which picks up both chapter content and rear matter. Within each page-sequence, the right apply-templates statements are needed.

For the page-sequence named first3, the flow content is as shown in Example 10-1.

Example 10-1. Flow contents for the first three pages

```
<fo:page-sequence master-reference="first3">
  <fo:flow flow-name="xsl-region-body">
    <xsl:apply-templates select="/book/frontmatter/title"/>
    <xsl:apply-templates select="/book/frontmatter/dedication"/>
    <xsl:call-template name="tPage"/>
  </fo:flow>
</fo:page-sequence>
```

Remember that, prior to this point in the stylesheet, all content is a literal result element. All you need is to apply selected templates for the needed content and to ensure that other templates don't duplicate the content elsewhere. Hence the use of the select attribute on apply-templates. This takes care of the first three pages, or it will when templates are provided to match this content.

The next flow area includes the preface and table of contents. This is shown in Example 10-2.

Example 10-2. Preface and table of contents flow

```
    <fo:page-sequence
       master-reference="prefAndToc"
❶     initial-page-number="1"
❷     format="I">


❸            <fo:static-content
                     flow-name="xsl-region-after">
         <fo:block text-align="outer"><fo:page-number/></fo:block>
       </fo:static-content>

       <fo:flow flow-name="xsl-region-body">
       <xsl:apply-templates select="/book/frontmatter/preface"/>
       <xsl:apply-templates select="/" mode="toc"/>
       </fo:flow>
    </fo:page-sequence>
```

❶ The page numbering is reset to 1.

❷ The format is specified as Roman uppercase.

❸ The region-after contains the page number only.

The only content needed here is the preface and table of contents. Again, a full path to each is provided. The toc needs the full document to access each section, but is moded to ensure proper processing. Only the footer is used here; there is no header. The page number is reset to 1, and its format is set to Roman numbering.

Finally, the main body content is applied to the remaining page-sequence, as shown in Example 10-3.

Example 10-3. Chapter page-sequence

```
        <fo:page-sequence
            master-reference="chaps"
              initial-page-number="1"
❶             format="1">

        <fo:static-content
          flow-name="xsl-region-before">
❷        <fo:block text-align="outside">
         Chapter      <fo:retrieve-marker
❸            retrieve-class-name="chapNum"/>
        <fo:leader leader-pattern="space" />
          <fo:retrieve-marker
❹            retrieve-class-name="chap"/>
        <fo:leader leader-pattern="space" />
❺        Page <fo:page-number font-style="normal" />
❻        of <fo:page-number-citation ref-id='end'/>
       </fo:block>
        </fo:static-content>

        <fo:flow flow-name="xsl-region-body">
        <fo:block  xsl:use-attribute-sets='font'>
        <xsl:apply-templates select="/book/bodymatter"/>
        <xsl:apply-templates select="/book/rearmatter"/>
       </fo:flow>
      </fo:page-sequence>
```

❶ The page number is formatted in Roman.

❷ This block forms the header on these pages.

❸ The chapter number is retrieved as a marker.

❹ The chapter title is retrieved as a marker.

❺ The page number is added.

❻ Last page number of document.

Markers are used for the static content in the header, both for the chapter title and the chapter number. The last page is identified by a block with an id value of end, whose page number is retrieved here.

The Template File

The template file is where the stylesheet author will spend most of his or her time. I like to keep mine as uncluttered as possible. I've laid it out almost in document order, so that if I'm looking for a template that matches front matter, I'll expect it near the top of the file. I keep all general templates near the end of the file, finishing up with the default template. This is what works for me.

I almost always write a default template first, which helps to identify missing templates. It reads as in Example 10-4.

Example 10-4. The default template

```
   <xsl:template match="*">
❶     <fo:block color="red">
      Element <xsl:value-of
             select="name(..)"/>/ <xsl:value-of
             select="name( )"/> found, with no template.
      </fo:block>
   </xsl:template>
```

❶ A block with red content.

All this tells me is the parent and element in question by pointing them out in red. Note that there is no child processing, hence, it catches the parent prior to a child. This way, I know I need to keep writing templates until I have no more red text displayed.

Within this file, I want to keep separate the actual style (appearance) of the various blocks and inlines. I separate these out, for the most part, by means of attribute sets, in the *ps.xsl* file (I will define page breaks within this file). One approach is to start at the front and, for each element of the source document, work through until the formatting has been achieved. Prior to this, I want to set up some property sets for the major items, such that they are available for use when this file is worked on. This prevents a random approach, which results in styles being spread all over the file. As I consider each separate style, I want to review it as a candidate for either using an existing style or for forming the basis for another style.

Let's start with the title page. This needs to be on a separate page with sufficient spacing. The content is obtained from the source content by using the pull method. Because it's a one-off, all styling will be applied directly within the template. This requires something such as what's shown in Example 10-5.

Example 10-5. Template for the front page

```
<xsl:template name="tPage">
<fo:block  xsl:use-attribute-sets='font'>
  <fo:block
    font-size='36pt'
    space-before = '50mm'
```

Example 10-5. Template for the front page (continued)

```
    space-after =  '25mm'
    ><xsl:value-of select='/book/title'/>
 </fo:block>
 <fo:block
   font-size='18pt'
   space-before = '25mm'
   space-after =  '12mm'
>by </fo:block>
 <fo:block
   font-size='18pt'
   space-before = '25mm'
   space-after =  '12mm'>
   <xsl:value-of select='/book/frontmatter/author'/>
 </fo:block>
    </fo:block>
    <fo:block text-align='end'
      font-size='10pt'
      space-before = '50mm'>
    &#x00A9; <xsl:value-of
        select="/book/frontmatter/pubdetails/pubname"/>
    </fo:block>
      <fo:block text-align='end'
        font-size='10pt'>
  <xsl:value-of
        select="/book/frontmatter/pubdetails/pubads"/>
      </fo:block>

 </xsl:template>
```

Next, for the dedication page. Literal text is needed here for a title, but otherwise, this is a simple, separate page, styled in the same manner as the title page. The contents of the dedication can be handled by the standard paragraph template.

Next comes the fancy title page. This sits between the dedication and the preface, hence, it needs to be inserted manually, again using the pull technique. A template using XSLT modes inserts the content at the right time in the output. I have to force the styling to obtain the side-by-side appearance of the image and the publisher data because I don't have the appropriate float properties available in my formatter. I'm going to use a table containing the image and the text, as shown in Example 10-6.

Example 10-6. Fancy title page template

```
    <xsl:template match='/' mode='ffp'>
      <fo:block break-before="odd-page" >
        <fo:block
          xsl:use-attribute-sets="title font"
          space-after="20mm">
❶         <xsl:value-of select='/book/title'/>
        </fo:block>
        <fo:table width='130mm'>
          <fo:table-body>
```

Example 10-6. Fancy title page template (continued)

```
                <fo:table-row>
                  <fo:table-cell>
                    <fo:block>
                    <fo:external-graphic
                          src="images\ttlpg.jpg"
❷                         content-height="100%"
                          scaling="uniform"/>
                    </fo:block>
                  </fo:table-cell>
                  <fo:table-cell display-align='bottom'>
                    <fo:block/>
                    <fo:block space-before='90mm'>
❸                      &#x00A9; <xsl:value-of
                      select='/book/frontmatter/pubdetails/pubname'/>
                    </fo:block>
                    <fo:block>
                        <xsl:value-of
                          select='/book/frontmatter/pubdetails/pubads'/>
                    </fo:block>
                  </fo:table-cell>
                </fo:table-row>
              </fo:table-body>
          </fo:table>
          <fo:block
      font-size='{$small-sz}'>Image courtesy of Aries Cheung, Toronto
      </fo:block>
       </fo:block>

      </xsl:template>
```

❶ Title

❷ Image

❸ Text content

With the new page layout for the preface and contents, the styling for these pages can be applied. The preface is styled the same as the body of the book, so standard templates can be used. The table of contents requires the moded template.

Because we don't have ID values in each chapter, appendix, etc., we need to generate them to obtain the page number. This means that for the preface, each chapter, and each appendix, the template must generate the id value. Within the table of contents, it is necessary to change context to generate an id value. The template for the table of contents is shown in Example 10-7.

Example 10-7. Table of contents template

```
      <xsl:template match="/" mode="toc">
       <fo:block break-before="odd-page" >
        <fo:block xsl:use-attribute-sets="title font">
❶          Table of Contents
```

Example 10-7. Table of contents template (continued)

```
      </fo:block>

      <xsl:for-each select='book/frontmatter/preface'>
       <fo:block text-align-last="justify">
        <fo:inline><xsl:value-of select="title"/>
         <fo:leader          leader-pattern="dots"/>
❷        <fo:page-number-citation ref-id="{generate-id
        </fo:inline>
       </fo:block>
      </xsl:for-each>


❸     <xsl:for-each select='book/bodymatter/chapter'>
       <fo:block text-align-last="justify">
        <fo:inline><xsl:value-of select="title"/>
         <fo:leader          leader-pattern="dots"/>
         <fo:page-number-citation ref-id="{generate-id( )}"/>
        </fo:inline>
       </fo:block>
      </xsl:for-each>

❹     <xsl:for-each select='book/rearmatter/appendix'>
       <fo:block text-align-last="justify">
        <fo:inline><xsl:value-of select="title"/>
         <fo:leader          leader-pattern="dots"/>
         <fo:page-number-citation ref-id="{generate-id( )}"/>
        </fo:inline>
       </fo:block>
      </xsl:for-each>
     </fo:block>
    </xsl:template>
```

❶ Table of contents title

❷ Preface

❸ Chapters

❹ Appendixes

This uses the standard table of contents methods discussed earlier in the book.

The remainder of the book's formatting is fairly straightforward, using already defined property sets. If the early definitions are right, there needs to be less special formatting as the stylesheet grows. Chapters repeat the preface format, and most of the basic formatting is now available.

Property Sets

This file holds base variables, attribute sets, and little else. It is included by the *main.xsl* file. The *ps.xsl* file is shown in Appendix F.

A quick glance at the source documents indicates some ready candidates for repeated styling:

- Chapter titles
- The basic paragraph element

Let's start with the basics for these. First, begin with the font and some base sizes that I can add to as needed. The intent is never to specify an absolute size in the *main.xsl* file.

The first four variables set out a base size and three variants on that size, each a multiple of the base font. To call these sizes up, next come strings used as the attribute value font-size. The font attribute set, which comes next, defines the base font for the whole document. This is called up frequently throughout the document. A lengthy attribute-set follows for the title formatting. This, in turn, uses previously defined variables. I've specified a padding attribute set, though it hasn't been used so far. The same goes for the border attribute set. Finally, the paragraph attribute set is specified. This file can be expanded to contain all the actual styling details, which are then called up from the main stylesheet.

This chapter has shown a general approach that may be used to create a complete stylesheet. For reference, all the files are included in Appendix F: the outline source document is in Example F-2, the main stylesheet is in Example F-3, the property sets file is in Example F-4, and the page layout file is in Example F-5.

Stylesheet Organization

Now that you have all the parts needed to create XSL stylesheets, you need to think about how best to assemble them. XSLT provides very few constraints on how to structure stylesheets, but building stylesheets that can be reused and maintained requires some extra consideration and discipline.

Classes of Stylesheets

Generally, stylesheets tend to be either specialized or broad-based general purpose. The implications of this should be considered early. Examples of the first category are the one-off stylesheets created for a specific task, possibly used only for a single class of document. These will be tailored to the needs of the DTD in question and contain only as much flexibility as the DTD enables. The second category could include a base stylesheet and specialization layers to provide for specialist adaptations or a base stylesheet that can quickly be adapted to a whole range of document classes with minimal effort. These two forms require different approaches.

Specialized Stylesheets

If you are styling a single DTD or schema for print output, some finer considerations come into play. If you have a firm requirement that is well thought-out and likely to be stable once designed, you've just hit stylesheet heaven. It's far more likely that you will design the stylesheet, it will be in use for a few iterations, then the end users of the output or the information providers will decide they want to *tweak* this bit, subdivide that part, or adapt the schema. If your stylesheet is well thought-out, it may take the strain of such modifications. If it's monolithic and undocumented, you may find the effort needed to update it is almost as great as the effort that was needed to create it.

A second consideration is the environment in which the stylesheet will be used. Stylesheets that are created and used by the same person can often get away with less formal structures and documentation than stylesheets meant for use in a production environment, where the creators of the stylesheets may be unavailable. Similarly, stylesheets that are written with the expectation that their parts may be reused or changed on a regular basis may need more attention to structural detail than stylesheets meant to be written once and never modified or reused.

General-Purpose Stylesheet

If the stylesheet is to live for some time, it should be documented, using either XML comments or namespaced inline documentation. An example of this latter style of documentation may be found in the DocBook Stylesheets now hosted on SourceForge at *http://docbook.sourceforge.net*. When a particular facet of a stylesheet is designed, the ideas in the designer's mind may be very clear but that clarity is unlikely to remain over time. Make it easier for yourself and others by documenting and updating as you work.

Partitioning is the key to designing a successful, reusable stylesheet that can be quickly adapted. If you can swap modules in and out of your stylesheet quickly and easily, your previous work can be reused. If it's also well documented, you will be able to use that stylesheet extract efficiently. The design requirements of XSLT and XPath support this reuse by being side-effect–free languages. It is still possible to write bad stylesheets that are unlikely to be reusable, but some of the nastier aspects of procedural languages won't get in the way. If small, clean, closely related templates are grouped into a single file, the chances of them being reused increases. How you group them is up to you, whether it's by DTD relationships or some other association will depend on circumstance. Moded templates come into their own when prior selection determines the formatting needed, and the moded templates are then called with clear, well-known formatting requirements.

Local Modifications

If you are providing a stylesheet for others to extend or modify, certain considerations must be applied.

The stylesheet must be well documented if you want to avoid frequent requests for support. If possible modifications could change the operation of the stylesheet, let users know of the risks they are taking.

Templates that are not meant to be modified must be identified as such, preferably with a clearly understandable rationale for that identification. Try to control stylesheet operation by using parametric variables. This keeps the stylesheet users away from prime code while satisfying their need to be able to customize stylesheet operation. Note the interaction between parameters. A good example is the use of DocBook table of contents (toc) related parameters. A single parameter is set to enable or disable toc generation. Once you've enabled toc generation, individual parameters are used to switch toc generation on or off within the various major container level divisions such as parts, chapters, and appendixes.

If your files are imported into the modifiers stylesheets, the importing stylesheet will take precedence. If an element is found for which you haven't provided a template, let the user know that it's not being formatted. Example 11-1 shows such a template.

Example 11-1. Unexpected element processing

```
<xsl:template match="*">
  <xsl:message>
    <xsl:value-of select="name(.)"/>
    <xsl:text> with no styling.</xsl:text>
  </xsl:message>
  <fo:block color="red" >
    <xsl:text>
      <xsl:value-of select="name(..)"/>/<xsl:value-of select="name(.)"/>
    </xsl:text>
  </fo:block>
</xsl:template>
```

This produces a block of red text (via the message) that lets the output reader and whomever is processing the stylesheet know that this element has not been processed. The red text helps the message to stand out.

Overall Stylesheet Organization

Stylesheets may be crudely divided into two major parts: the part of the stylesheet that specifies the page layout and the part that specifies the content styling. Of course, these two are fairly intimately related, but it is possible to isolate them for design and update purposes. The other advantage of this separation is the refresh rate. Relatively, the second block of templates is most likely to require modification. With this in mind, when starting from a blank page, one early decision should be how many files you will create. Factors influencing this will be the size of the Schema or DTD, context sensitivity (if similar elements will be processed differently in different contexts), stylesheet life, and likely development period. Each of these impacts the file count. If you are used to dealing with large chunks of code, it will be easier. If you are fairly new to stylesheets, it may be easier to develop incrementally, adding more templates slowly, in smaller files, keeping your work focused on small sections of the Schema at any one time, and relying on default handler templates for the elements you haven't processed yet.

A suggested starting point, given just *too* many options, might be to encapsulate all paging templates in one file, then to look at either one or more files to hold all other templates below the root of the document instance. This provides a basis on which to build. As the stylesheet grows, it may then be split out further, grouping templates either by similar layout style or by some schema-related division. Further considerations, depending on the circumstances for isolation and inclusion might be:

- Font properties, using attribute-set elements
- Parameter values, which control stylesheet operation

- Locale-specific processing
- Literals, if internationalization is an issue
- Special page-level processing, for instance, front matter, back matter, or any major branches of the Schema that require special handling
- Elements from the Schema that are likely to require similar processing (these could be similar block-related formats, inlines, or elements with special whitespace requirements)

If elements are to be formatted differently within each of the contexts within which they occur, as opposed to being formatted identically in any context, groupings of templates will occur naturally by context. This often happens with Schema that make high levels of reuse of lower-level structures (sometimes inappropriately). An example of this might be a block-level element that is formatted as a float, in one context and an inline block in another.

Page Layout

One way to gain a view of a stylesheet's structure is to use the collapsable tree view provided by Internet Explorer from Microsoft. If you think of your page definitions in this way, the candidates for modularization can be seen. Figure 11-1 shows the overall structure.

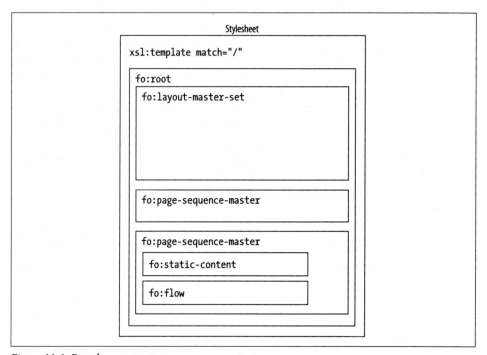

Figure 11-1. Page layout structure

Standard XML inclusion methods may be used to keep each file a managable size using entities for any of these sections. An example of such usage is shown in Example 11-2.

Example 11-2. Use of entities in a stylesheet

```
<?xml version="1.0" ?>
<!DOCTYPE xsl:stylesheet [
  <!ENTITY  lms SYSTEM "lms.xml">
]>
<xsl:stylesheet
  xmlns:xsl="http://www.w3.org/1999/XSL/Transform"
  xmlns:fo="http://www.w3.org/1999/XSL/Format"
version="1.0">

<fo:root>
<-- Include the layout-master-set -->
&lms;
......
```

The entity `lms` contains the `layout-master-set` for the stylesheet. The remainder of the stylesheet is not shown. The included entity is a well-formed XML file containing the `layout-master-set` itself.

This technique reduces the clutter in the main stylesheet (or one of its inclusions) and enables the author to focus on the task at hand. Don't overdo it or you will find yourself constantly opening other files just to see what is included! This can be done incrementally, developing a major section of the stylesheet, then, once it's finalized, separating that section into an included entity.

This is perhaps most useful for the larger sections of the page layout information, which, once working, tend not to be disturbed.

Main Flows

Selecting the flow into which a particular content is included is perhaps one of the most critical aspects of stylesheet design. If you are applying single-document–specific templates within a particular flow, to ensure that the specific content is formatted within a specific page-sequence, don't select it by its current position within the document; instead, use an `id` value assigned to that element. This allows other siblings to be inserted or reorganized without changing the stylesheet.

How content is selected for flows can be varied. An example is shown in Example 11-3.

Example 11-3. Selecting content for flows

```
<fo:page-sequence
    master-name="rest">
        <xsl:call-template name="page-sequence">
        <xsl:with-param
```

Example 11-3. Selecting content for flows (continued)

```
            name="head-R">Page <fo:page-number/> </xsl:with-param>
            <xsl:with-param name="foot-L">Chapter title</xsl:with-param>
            </xsl:call-template>
        <fo:flow flow-name="xsl-region-body">
            <xsl:comment>2D</xsl:comment>
                <!-- Process section contents -->
            <xsl:apply-templates select="simpdoca/section[@id='chap03']" />
        </fo:flow>
</fo:page-sequence>
```

Example 11-3 uses a named template, page-sequence, to specify the header and footer, uses the xsl-region-body flow specify the page layout, and then applies the selected templates that process the section with an id value of chap03.

Inclusion and Importing

For a definitive rationale on whether to select including or importing, read Michael Kay's book, *XSLT Programmers' Reference* (Wrox Press). Take particular note of the relative precedence. When importing, the importing stylesheet takes precedence. This is extremely useful for overrides. Tailoring a stylesheet for a particular case is possible using the import statement. The base stylesheet (which is imported) provides standard processing, the importing stylesheet then tailors that standard processing by only specifying templates that require non-standard formatting.

How Do I Do That?

This appendix covers some of the common questions that are asked about XSL-FO, but are not answered by the Recommendation. Usually someone has thought about it and found an answer by using (or misusing, depending on your point of view) one aspect or another of the Recommendation.

I'm used to using <xsl:preserve-space> to keep my whitespace in XSLT. Why doesn't it work in XSL-FO?

This is a case of working in the right domain. The `xsl:*` elements control spaces in the resulting XSL-FO file only; these hints don't even arrive at the formatter.

Whitespace handling in XSL-FO is controlled by a substantial set of specialized properties: `space-treatment`, `linefeed-treatment`, `white-space-collapse`, `wrap-option`, and `white-space` (a CSS2-compatibility shorthand).

I can't find a particular property on a particular element.

Note that not all properties are listed for all elements. Often the Recommendation will list them by some form of abstraction, such as *border properties*. This means that it's necessary to go hunting to find out if the property is available. Often, it is quicker to try it and see if it is supported by your formatter. Another option is to use the DTD provided by RenderX, and see if the `fo` file will validate to it. This is not guaranteed to work, but is very helpful. It does mean working in the `fo` namespace, but that often provides the answer that you can take back to the XSLT domain.

Can I create a newspaper-style layout: part of the page with one column, the rest with multiple columns?

Simply put, no. The present Recommendation focuses on content-driven layout, not layout-driven formatting. The former simply pours the content into predefined areas, the latter dictates where the content should go. It is a known issue that I hope will be addressed in the next version of the Recommendation.

Presently, you can fix this by using tables for layout, as in HTML, but don't expect content to wrap from one fake column to another.

How do I fix the position of some content?

Document appearance may change because of varying content. If you need to fix the position of content (perhaps the signature line on a letter at the bottom of the page), make use of the `absolute-position` property to ensure that the content appears where you want it. Remember that absolute positions are calculated with respect to the containing block, not the page. Example A-1 gives an example of this.

Example A-1. Fixed-position blocks

```
            <fo:block-container
❶              absolute-position="fixed"
❷                   top="200mm">
        <fo:block>Yours sincerely:
          <fo:inline font-style="italic">Dave Pawson</fo:inline>
        </fo:block>
    </fo:block-container>
```

❶ The `absolute-position` property ensures that content in this block is fixed.

❷ This block is fixed 200mm from the top.

How can I center a block across the page—for instance, a table?

You can indent the table by half the width of the item, as in:

```
<fo:block width="4in" start-indent="(100% - 4in) div 2">
 <xsl:apply-content/>
 </fo:block>
```

This provides a block of 4 inches, indented by half that value. If you have a mathematical bent, please realize that the formatter can deal with `start-indent`.

How do I number my footnotes consistently and automatically?

XSLT addresses this. If you want footnotes to be numbered automatically within, say, a chapter, use the `xsl:number` attributes (`count`, `format`, and `level`) to select the numbering system. For example:

```
<xsl:number count="footnote" from="chapter" format="i"/>
```

This will count all footnotes within a chapter, numbering them with lowercase Roman numerals.

How do I get text to spread out over the line, creating the appearance of left- and right-justified text?

You can achieve this by using a `leader-pattern` of space, as in the following example. The lefthand text is separated from the righthand text by means of the leader, which being formed of whitespace, does not show.

```
<fo:block text-align-last="justify">
  Left-hand text
  <fo:leader leader-pattern="space" />
  Right-hand text
</fo:block>
```

How do I start page numbering at something other than 1?

You can specify the number at which page numbering begins with:

```
<fo:page-sequence initial-page-number="42">
```

This specifies that all the pages in this sequence should be numbered starting at 42. Specify this in the page layout and specification section of the stylesheet. This can also be used to reset the page number to one, where it would normally (by default) continue numbering from the previous page sequence, simply by specifying the initial-page-number as 1.

What happens if I want to say page 42 of 120, where I don't know the last page number of the document?

In this case, you need to have a marker of some description at the *end* of the document. This is done by putting an empty block as the last item of content right at the end of the document and providing an id attribute on that block. Then you can use:

```
<fo:page-number-citation ref-id="theEnd"/>
...
<fo block id="theEnd"></fo:block>
```

which the formatter then replaces with the page number of the very last page.

How do I number my front matter pages using Roman numerals?

For the page master in question, use the format attribute to specify that Roman numerals are wanted:

```
<fo:page-sequence master-name="frontmatter" format="i">
```

How do I use a prefix for page numbering?

The prefix is a literal string, so add it as you would any other literal, for example, in Appendix C, to have the page numbers use the C prefix, try

```
<fo:static-content
 flow-name="xsl-region-after">
 <fo:block text-align="outside">C<fo:page-number/></fo:block>
 </fo:static-content>
```

If you need the prefix calculated automatically, use the XSLT functions for numbering, with Arabic format, i.e. count the number of appendixes and format the number using the format attribute.

How do I get running headers where the chapter title is placed in the header?

Use the marker element, as in:

```
<fo:marker marker-class-name="rh"><xsl:value-of select="title"/> </fo:marker>
```

This must be in the block containing the chapter, normally a wrapper for the whole chapter. This is within the template for chapter. Then, in the static content for the header, use the marker, like so:

```
<fo:static-content flow-name="xsl-region-before">
 <fo:block font=" 10pt Helvetica">
 <fo:retrieve-marker retrieve-marker-name="rh"
```

```
        retrieve-boundary="page"
        retrieve-position="first-starting-within-page"/>
    </fo:block>
    </fo:static-content>
```

This puts the chapter title on each page, and it changes as new chapters are formatted.

How do I create superscript and subscript?

The Recommendation specifically provides for this, either at the character level using:

```
<fo:character
 character="1"
 baseline-shift="super"
 font-family="'MS Serif'"/>
```

which provides the number 1 in superscript (subscript is similar), or, as a standard inline, using:

```
<fo:inline
 vertical-align="sub"
 font-size="8pt"> <xsl:apply-templates/> </fo:inline>
```

which takes any content within the inline and formats it as subscript.

How do I keep two pieces of content together (on the same page, column, etc.)?

There is a property that may be applied very broadly that ties content (in terms of blocks, lists, tables, inlines, etc.) together. It's named keep-with-*, where * can be previous or next. This uses the dot notation to provide a family of properties, such as keep-with-next.within-page and keep-with-previous.within-line. This set of properties are known as the keep properties. So, to keep a heading on the same page as the first paragraph, when styling the heading, try:

```
<fo:block
 ... other properties
 keep-with-next.within-page='5'>
<xsl:apply-contents/>
</fo:block>
```

This tells the formatter that this and the following block should be kept together. The default value for this property is always. It can be set to either a number or always. The always value is the strongest way of expressing your need to keep these items together, even if it means starting a new page, for instance.

Finding Your Way Around the Specification

This description applies to the W3C Recommendation of October 15, 2001, found at *http://www.w3.org/TR/xsl/*.

At this URL, you will find various formats of the document. Unless you are lucky enough to be permanently connected, it's probably wise to have a copy on your desktop. For that purpose, the specification is provided in alternate formats, specifically, a single large file, a zip file, which splits up the HTML into a number of smaller files, and a PDF version, should you be brave enough to print it out, kindly provided by RenderX.

Within the main specification, you will find frequent (annoyingly so, in my opinion) references to *http://www.w3.org/TR/1998/REC-CSS2-19980512/*, the CSS2 specification. You should download that too. Each time you come across such a reference, if you are using a local copy on your PC, the link in the HTML will be to a web document. I resolved this by using a command line editor to change all the strings *http://www.w3.org/TR/REC-CSS2/* to read *../CSS2*. In other words, I made them local references. Do this for all *.html* files in the directory in which you have stored the XSL specification. In a similar manner, I have stored the CSS specification in the same root directory, hence, the *../CSS2*.

Personally, I found it worthwhile to have a paper copy. I also had access to a double sided printer and binding facilities, which helped. You decide. The PDF produced by the RenderX stylesheets is good. All cross-references are to page numbers and section numbers, so it really is a joy to use, and sometimes the screen is just not enough, until we all have Annotea in place! Otherwise, the notes on the paper copy provides as good a place as any to keep your jottings.

Overview

First, the downside! This document is not meant for end users of XSL-FO. Its target audience is an implementor. For that reason, it is written in a style that is meant to be accurate, precise, and clear (to an implementor), rather than explanatory. Keep that in mind when you read it and you'll appreciate why its phrasing is so concise.

To quote the specification, "This document is intended for implementors of such XSL processors. Although it can be used as a reference manual for writers of XSL style sheets, it is not tutorial in nature."

index.html

The *index.html* file is most useful for its table of contents and is hyperlinked to each of even the most minor sections. It is wonderfully complete, a real gem. My thanks to the XSL Working Group for this. Use it to find almost any aspect of the specification.

Section 1

Section 1 of the specification outlines what happens with the conversion process, XML through to print (and screen-based media). If you want the whole thing in perspective, this is the only chapter that deals at that level. It dives straight into the jargon of formatting objects, so don't expect an easy ride.

Section 2

This section appears as a waste of space, referring out to XSLT and also formally defining the fo namespace.

Section 3

This section introduces the process of formatting. Some terminology is introduced, areas are discussed, and then it moves on to a *conceptual* model of what happens. The XSL Working Group says what might happen, but carefully avoids telling an implementor just what to do. This avoids implementation conflicts. The specification is supposed to say what happens, not how to do it.

The rider here is that there are implementor interpretation conflicts; that is, the recommendation has been interpreted differently by different implementations. It will take some time (and probably a revision of the recommendation) to resolve this.

The formatting process is explained, in very broad terms, which is more than likely of little interest to the end user! Look to Section 4 for a pictorial model of the area tree introduced here.

Section 4

Section 4 begins to put some meat on the bones. Further terminology is introduced, and there is more on areas, with the introduction of block and inline areas block-progression-dimension and inline-progression-dimension. The majority of this section relates to the management of areas, specifying how any adjacent areas should resolve traits to produce the final output. The concept of conditionality (include or forget) is introduced, spaces are defined and resolved, and the layout of blocks and inlines are expressed in terms of their relationships to one another. Keeps and breaks (when to keep two areas together and when to break them) are defined and the final stages, converting to the final presented output, are discussed. Borders and padding are brought into the layout equation, explaining how they are added to content to offset one piece of content from another. This section provides clear definitions of the terms that may be creating problems for you.

Section 5

This section is one I rarely visit. Come here when you need to care about inheritance! The shorthand of XSL-FO is introduced (though not explained fully), and the section explains how actual final values of, for instance, indents and widths are calculated.

This section, for some reason I can't figure, explains units you'll come across. If you want to know how to specify a length, this is the section to which you should refer. The few XSL-FO functions are covered here as well, including the color functions. Compound data types, specified with a minimum, maximum, and optimum set of values are explained, including resolution.

Section 6

Section 6 starts with interesting material for the end user. Here, you will find the basic formatting objects defined in reasonably plain English, both with the detailed content you will use most and with the page level objects. The diagram in this section explains how to specify your pages in document tree form. I guess it was from this section that RenderX derived their document type definition that I find so useful.

This section is worth browsing to absorb the details of page layout, which are diagrammed and explained. Also included are the first examples in the specification. The common uses entries for each of the formatting objects are particularly useful. It won't tell you of the devious ways you can use some of them, but states their most common application.

This should be your starting point when you are trying to determine whether or not you can use a particular property. Look up the particular formatting object of concern and you'll find a full list of applicable properties. This is of particular application in the usage of tables and lists, which are not the most intuitive of structures.

This section is possibly the second most used section for the stylesheet author.

Section 7

Compared to the others, this section is home. When you want to find out about a particular property, you can either look it up in the table of contents and go directly to it, or use the table of contents at the front of the document.

My personal usage of this section is actually centered on the table of contents. I have highlighted the ones I repeatedly go back to because, due to its density of information, it can take a while to trawl through the list to find the one I want.

Section 8

This section provides the source of the compliance tables available for most of the processors. This section defines the three levels of conformance by which most of the implementations define their compliance.

Appendix A

This appendix addresses internationalization. It's worth a quick skim to find out the pains to which the XSL Working Group went to address an international audience.

Appendix B

This appendix is the *other half* of Section 8. It assigns each of the formatting objects to one of the three levels of compliance.

Appendix C

This appendix lists all the properties and candidate values. It's useful as a summary, and is fully linked to the section in which properties and candidate values are fully specified.

Appendix D

This appendix lists references made from within the specification. They are mostly hyperlinked to the web address where they can be found.

Appendix E

This appendix has a list of hyperlinks or page references to each of the properties.

Appendix F

This appendix lists the most recent set of changes.

Appendix G

This appendix lists the acknowledgments from the XSL Working Group.

Today's Tools

This appendix covers the tools that are currently available. I've placed this in an appendix simply because I didn't want the book to appear dated within months of it being on the shelves. Please keep in mind the general comments I made about tools in Chapter 2 when reading this.

RenderX XEP Formatter

XEP is an engine that converts XSL-FO documents to a printable form (PDF or Post-Script). An evaluation package with limited functionality is freely available. It aligns with the November 2001 Recommendation. Extensions are included and partial SVG support is now available.

I think XEP is the most established product; it was certainly the first one I came across. Developed by a small and dedicated team, it's a commercial product, with an evaluation version available for download. The evaluation version is restricted in the number of pages it will output. It produces PDF and PostScript output. Its command-line interface is convenient, and it has good error reporting. It's developers, who are contributors on the XSL-FO related lists, are very helpful. Inputting of an XML file in the fo namespace, will deliver PDF in the evaluation version. An implementation features list is available on their web site, *http://www.renderx.com*. XEP is written in Java and runs on any system that supports Java 2 (JDK/JRE 1.1.8) and above. Their web site hosts many demonstration files, and they have provided the W3C with a PDF version of the Recommendation ready for printing.

Antenna House Formatter

Nearly a year old, the Antenna House Formatter is a fast implementation with a GUI. Ideal for testing, it's probably the fastest processor today. It's developers respond well to feedback. It is available as an evaluation download and as a commercial product. It provides the two-step process of conversion, direct from XML through the visual presentation, and it makes use of the Microsoft parser to transform to the fo namespace, which restricts its use to Windows. It provides a stylesheet to convert XHTML into the fo vocabulary. I like it as a product and find it very convenient. It is probably a prime choice for finding out all about XSL-FO. Its implementation feature list is available from their web site, *http://www.antennahouse.com/*.

FOP Formatter

This is an open source project. IT was originally based around James Tauber's early work, but was reorganized and taken well beyond the original. FOP is part of Apache's XML project. The goals of the Apache XML FOP Project are to deliver an XSL-FO to PDF formatter that is compliant to at least the basic conformance level described in the W3C Candidate Recommendation November 21, 2000, and that complies with the March 11, 1999, Portable Document Format Specification (Version 1.3) from Adobe Systems. An implementation features list is available on the web site, although, because it moves so fast, users do have problems determining if their problems are their interpretation of the specification, or if they are trying to use a feature not implemented in FOP. I guess this is an issue with most implementations, until specification interpretation becomes settled. It has the additional feature of supporting embedded SVG, but FOP is now subcontracting that work to the Batik project instead of handling it directly. It can be run from the command line or called via a Java interface. The home page of FOP is *http://xml.apache.org/fop*.

PassiveTEX Formatter

PassiveTEX is a partial implementation of the November 2001 XSL-FO Recommendation, using TEX. It is not complete or conformant but implements things from all three levels of conformance. I am not sure whether it has a long-term future, but for now, you can rely on it to do anything from straightforward pages to TEX's normal high standards of, for example, hyphenation and justification. It understands a subset of MathML. PassiveTEX relies on David Carlisle's xmltex XML processor written in TEX.

As its author, Sebastian Rahtz says, "If you have never installed TEX before, expect to have to do some work!" If you do have a decent TEX setup (and you understand it), it should be easy. Because Sebastian Rahtz and David Carlisle are very familiar with TEX, it makes full use of the strength of TEX. MathML is also processed, though not completely.

At the home page, *http://users.ox.ac.uk/~rahtz/passivetex/*, there are stylesheets for the Text Encoding Initiative, along with examples. A conformance matrix is also provided.

Unicorn Formatting Objects Formatter

Unicorn Formatting Objects (UFO) implements a substantial subset of the Extensible Stylesheet Language (XSL) Version 1.0 specification (W3C Working Draft (March 27, 2000).

The UFO formatter is optimized for composition of business-style documents (e.g., catalogs, orders, invoices, banking statements, etc.). Extensive support is provided for various features (for instance, collapsing border model in tables), which are not yet supported by many existing XSL implementations.

The XSL-FO backend, written in TEX macro language, implements XSL-FO transformation algorithms. The interface between the C++ frontend and TEX backend is well documented. Alternative backend implementations may be created by independent developers. The generation of TEX code from an arbitrary source XML document can be done in one pass, without creating intermediate files.

The software is free (see the license included in the distribution) and can be obtained at the Unicorn web site, *http://www.unicorn-enterprises.com/*. It runs on Windows NT 4.0 and Windows 95.

Formatting Objects Authoring Tool

Formatting Objects Authoring (FOA) is a graphical XSL-FO authoring tool. It is a Java application that gives users a graphical interface to author XSL-FO stylesheets. With FOA, you can generate pages and page sequences and fill them with content provided into one or more XML files. FOA will generate the XSLT stylesheet that transforms the XML content into an XSL-FO document.

This product approaches stylesheet design from quite a different angle. Using a Java GUI, a fill-in-the-gaps approach takes you through form filling to define page layouts and styles (attribute sets), then you can apply those styles to a selected document structure. If you come to XSL-FO from editing XML in the fo namespace, it takes some getting used to. It introduces the idea of *bricks*, which might be described as the building blocks of XSL-FO (i.e., blocks, images, inlines, etc.), which are then used to style the source document. The authors describe these as *translation elements*. I'm not sure whether this would appear natural if you came to XSL-FO with no manual stylesheet generation experience, though I guess, once familiar with the principles, it is a sound approach. A tutorial is provided, though no compliance matrix is available. The current FOA version does not support tables and tables of content, which some may find a shortcoming. The documentation is still being developed along with the product.

In use, the multiple open windows provide a complex interface, with a need to switch between windows frequently. Again, familiarity with the interface will make this easier. The intuitive XSL-FO approach, taking a part of the source XML structure and painting it with a particular style is the goal of this project (as I see it), and the product makes a very solid start in this direction.

The home page is at *http://www-uk.hpl.hp.com/people/fabgia/foa/foa.html*, and it includes the tutorial, which is worth watching for a novel approach to stylesheet generation.

As of February 2001, the project has become open source and moved to Sourceforge.

Render Engine from XML/XSL to PDF

Render Engine from XML/XSL to PDF (REXP) provides the functionality to render complex documents with good quality.

The development started from an early implementation of FOP (Version 0.9.2) but has made several architectural modifications. The product addresses the processing of complicated documents, such as commercial letters, and focuses on adding support for page breaking, keeps, absolute positioning, and images (block level and inline level). Properties, such as `keep-with-next`, `keep-with-previous`, and `page-break-inside="avoid"`, allow an efficient control on the document flow to designers. Special attention has been made around the line-rendering algorithm, to readjust the line height and baseline accurately, especially with inline images. REXP includes good document flow control (pagination rules and keeping support), absolute and relative positioning, inline and block level images (precise line-height and baseline calculation), but is compliant only with the April 1999 Working Draft Specification and lacks table and link support. The web site lists implemented properties, although not in the compliance format of the specification.

It is completely written in Java and is, therefore, portable across operating systems; its output is PDF and it is open source. Again, SVG is partially supported for vector graphics. REXP is engineered to be flexible and to support the expansion to other output formats such as PostScript and other Page Description Language (PDL) languages.

The home page for REXP is *http://www.esng.dibe.unige.it/REXP/*.

jfor, Java XSL-FO to RTF converter

jfor is licensed under the Mozilla Public License V1.1., is written in Java, and produces Microsoft Word 97 RTF output documents. It's a SourceForge project, still at an early version, so it has limited support of FO blocks, inline elements, lists, tables, and images. Personally, I'm quite pleased to see a Microsoft-compatible output. Because this project is just starting, there is very little to report.

The home page is *http://www.jfor.org/*, which is worth watching if you or your customers are confirmed Office users.

XMLmind FO Converter

The XMLmind FO Converter (XFC) is an XSL-FO to RTF converter. It takes an XSL-FO source file as input and converts it to RTF. XFC is a pure Java application/library.

Both personal and professional editions are offered. The first release is aimed at getting some feedback from the XSL-FO community. Though XFC is deemed usable in its current state, there's still much to be done, in my opinion. If everything goes right, expect a release of the commercial product in 2002. This version should add support of headers and footers as far as allowed by RTF, and should provide better support of tables. Note that RTF has less capability than XSL-FO, so remember that it must operate within those bounds.

For more information and to download the personal edition, please see the XFC home page at, *http://www.xmlmind.com*.

XSLfast

Based at *http://www.xslfast.com*, this product is based on FOP and written in Java. Described as a design and authoring tool for XSL-FO, this is another graphics-based application based around the FOP formatter. This product is very new, so I don't know it at all well. It was announced just before this book went to print. I like the idea of visual layout and see this as another step towards hiding the FO processing behind a visual layer. Good luck to the team developing it.

XSLfast is an editor for creating XSL-FO stylesheets visually. It allows you to place elements such as text, images, and tables on the page and edit properties such as font-family, font-style, and table-cell. These elements can be positioned absolutely or relatively.

XSLfast gives you the option to enter XSL-Code within the layout areas defined on a layout. You can add external template collections that produce partial or full FOs. For instance, a template for creating auto-layout tables with variable column sizes depending on the input data. You then use xsl:call-template to create these tables.

Another important feature is the Multi Layout Manager, which allows you to combine several layouts into one, driving the creation of FOs on a certain selection by expressions (Boolean XPath expressions). For instance, you create a front page, one or more content layouts, and a table of contents layout, then combine all these into one bigger layout with the Multi Layout Manager to get one PDF.

These layouts then produce the XSL-FO stylesheet, which then produces the FO file, which is then rendered to PDF.

Epic Editor V4.2

Epic is well known as the Rolls Royce of XML (and SGML) editors. The latest release (Version 4.2) is designed for creating XML and SGML content. The challenge of showing something other than a tags-based user view meant that Arbortext provided a styled view of content. In addition to an older standard called FOSI, Arbortext now provides XSL-FO capability, using what they call the Turbo Styler feature. The editor is just one piece of a full publishing system, detailed on the Arbortext web site, *http://www.arbortext.com/html/products.html*. Windows NT 4.0, 95, 98, 2000, and Sun Solaris 7 and 8 are supported. The editor continuously applies a stylesheet that gives the content a print or web appearance. Arbortext has been in the SGML and XML business for 12 years and has staff on the XSL Working Group of the W3C, which provides something of an inside track that strengthens its position. The XSL-FO offering is new, and with Arbortext's background and experience, I had expected something quite special and was not disappointed.

The stylesheet aspects of this product are similar to using a word processor. Each element of the source schema is presented in a list, where you are offered base options of block or inline styling. Block type elements are further sub-divided into categories, such as divisions, lists, basic blocks, etc. As one of these is selected, the associated styling options are modified live, presenting appropriate refinement options. For example, divisions can be numbered, start a new page, be indented, or have preceding literal content. This is about as familiar as it gets when trying to make the association between this form of styling and XSL-FO. For the technical author, this interface may well be ideal. Base categories are presented as block, graphic, table, inline, link, or even hidden (for items such as revision histories that should not be presented to the user). Block categories are basic, document, division, title, paragraph, list, list item, table of contents, or preformatted. To further guide the user, inappropriate options are grayed out when inappropriate. Unstyled elements are marked as such (which saves having that default template and going through the loop time after time!) to inform the stylesheet writer.

The integration with the editor is what makes this product different. For an organization that requires cooperative team authoring with high-quality print output, this product could provide the solution. Equally, for a user unused to the programmatic interface of XSLT and XSL-FO, this tool provides an interface that, although complex, is competent and comprehensive. Be aware of what you are buying though. You get the basics and extras don't come cheap. Check out the options list before committing.

IBM XSL Formatting Objects Composer (XFC)

This is a processor that does the same job as other formatters, plus a little more. The user can choose whether to create a PDF file or a Java2D output for online viewing in a Java environment. The PDF output is business as usual, but the Java2D is added-value for those working (and at home) in a Java environment.

XSL Formatting Objects Composer (XFC) is a typesetting and display engine that implements a substantial portion of XSL-FO. A compliance table is available and can be found at the IBM web site, *http://www.alphaworks.ibm.com/tech/xfc*.

Summary

Now that the specification has become a W3C Recommendation, the tool developers should have the confidence to carry on at less risk, which may provide incentive for others to follow. If you are curious and want to have a look at XSL-FO, the tools are available in the public domain at zero cost. If you are convinced and prepared to invest as an organization, commercial tools are available with support. Whether you pick up a text editor to write on your own or invest in a site license for the Arbortext product, there are many options available.

My personal choice, today, would extend from the open source PassiveTEX, through the commercial RenderX or Antenna House products for the programmers, to the Epic Editor suite (when I have a need for a standards-based integrated environment). Each has a place; no single implementation will be suitable for all users.

Because this information will date rather quickly, please keep an eye on the web page for this book, the author's web site, at *http://www.dpawson.co.uk*.

Objects, Properties, and Compliance Levels

Basic, Extended or Complete?

The following tables list formatting objects and properties, along with whether the XSL Recommendation considers them necessary for basic, extended, or complete compliance.

Table D-1. Layout formatting objects

fo:root	basic
fo:page-sequence	basic
fo:page-sequence-master	basic
fo:single-page-master-reference	basic
fo:repeatable-page-master-reference	basic
fo:repeatable-page-master-alternatives	extended
fo:conditional-page-master-reference	extended
fo:layout-master-set	basic
fo:simple-page-master	basic
fo:region-body	basic
fo:region-before	extended
fo:region-after	extended
fo:region-start	extended
fo:region-end	extended
fo:declarations	basic
fo:color-profile	extended
fo:flow	basic
fo:static-content	extended
fo:title	extended

Table D-2. Block formatting object compliance

fo:block	basic
fo:block-container	extended

Table D-3. Inline formatting objects

fo:bidi-override	extended
fo:character	basic
fo:initial-property-set	extended
fo:external-graphic	basic
fo:instream-foreign-object	extended
fo:inline	basic
fo:inline-container	extended
fo:leader	basic
fo:page-number	basic
fo:page-number-citation	extended

Table D-4. Table formatting objects

fo:table-and-caption	basic
fo:table	basic
fo:table-column	basic
fo:table-caption	extended
	caption-side="start" becomes caption-side="before"
	caption-side="end" becomes caption-side="after"
	caption-side="left" becomes caption-side="before"
	caption-side="right" becomes caption-side="after"
fo:table-header	basic
fo:table-footer	extended
fo:table-body	basic
fo:table-row	basic
fo:table-cell	basic

Table D-5. List formatting objects

fo:list-block	basic
fo:list-item	basic
fo:list-item-body	basic
fo:list-item-label	extended

Table D-6. Link and multi formatting objects

fo:basic-link	extended
fo:multi-switch	extended, need not be implemented for extended conformance for non-interactive media
fo:multi-case	basic: needed as wrapper for fallback for multi-switch
fo:multi-toggle	extended, need not be implemented for extended conformance for non-interactive media
fo:multi-properties	extended, need not be implemented for extended conformance for non-interactive media
fo:multi-property-set	extended, need not be implemented for extended conformance for non-interactive media

Table D-7. Out-of-line formatting objects

fo:float	extended
fo:footnote	extended
fo:footnote-body	extended

Table D-8. Other formatting objects

fo:wrapper	basic
fo:marker	extended
fo:retrieve-marker	extended

Property Summary

Table D-9. Property table

Name	Values	Core
absolute-position	auto | absolute | fixed | inherit	Complete
active-state	link | visited | active | hover | focus	Extended
alignment-adjust	auto | baseline | before-edge | text-before-edge | middle | central | after-edge | text-after-edge | ideographic | alphabetic | hanging | mathematical | <percentage> | <length> | inherit	Basic
alignment-baseline	auto | baseline | before-edge | text-before-edge | middle | central | after-edge | text-after-edge | ideographic | alphabetic | hanging | mathematical | inherit	Basic
auto-restore	true | false	Extended
azimuth	<angle> | [[left-side | far-left | left | center-left | center | center-right | right | far-right | right-side] | behind] | leftwards | rightwards | inherit	Basic
background	[<background-color> | <background-image> | <background-repeat> | <background-attachment> | <background-position>]] | inherit	Complete
background-attachment	scroll | fixed | inherit	Extended
background-color	<color> | transparent | inherit	Basic
background-image	<uri-specification> | none | inherit	Extended

Table D-9. Property table (continued)

Name	Values	Core
background-position	[[[<percentage> | <length>]{1,2} | [[top | center | bottom] | [left | center | right]]] | inherit	Complete
background-position-horizontal	<percentage> | <length> | left | center | right | inherit	Extended
background-position-vertical	<percentage> | <length> | top | center | bottom | inherit	Extended
background-repeat	repeat | repeat-x | repeat-y | no-repeat | inherit	Extended
baseline-shift	baseline | sub | super | <percentage> | <length> | inherit	Basic
blank-or-not-blank	blank | not-blank | any | inherit	Extended
block-progression-dimension	auto | <length> | <percentage> | <length-range> | inherit	Basic
border	[<border-width> | <border-style> | <color>] | inherit	Complete
border-after-color	<color> | inherit	Basic
border-after-precedence	force | <integer> | inherit	Basic
border-after-style	<border-style> | inherit	Basic
border-after-width	<border-width> | <length-conditional> | inherit	Basic
border-before-color	<color> | inherit	Basic
border-before-precedence	force | <integer> | inherit	Basic
border-before-style	<border-style> | inherit	Basic
border-before-width	<border-width> | <length-conditional> | inherit	Basic
border-bottom	[<border-width> | <border-style> | <color>] | inherit	Complete
border-bottom-color	<color> | inherit	Basic
border-bottom-style	<border-style> | inherit	Basic
border-bottom-width	<border-width> | inherit	Basic
border-collapse	collapse | collapse-with-precedence | separate | inherit	Extended
border-color	[<color> | transparent]{1,4} | inherit	Complete
border-end-color	<color> | inherit	Basic
border-end-precedence	force | <integer> | inherit	Basic
border-end-style	<border-style> | inherit	Basic
border-end-width	<border-width> | <length-conditional> | inherit	Basic
border-left	[<border-width> | <border-style> | <color>] | inherit	Complete
border-left-color	<color> | inherit	Basic
border-left-style	<border-style> | inherit	Basic
border-left-width	<border-width> | inherit	Basic
border-right	[<border-width> | <border-style> | <color>] | inherit	Complete
border-right-color	<color> | inherit	Basic

Name	Values	Core
border-right-style	<border-style> | inherit	Basic
border-right-width	<border-width> | inherit	Basic
border-separation	<length-bp-ip-direction> | inherit	Extended
border-spacing	<length> <length>? | inherit	Complete
border-start-color	<color> | inherit	Basic
border-start-precedence	force | <integer> | inherit	Basic
border-start-style	<border-style> | inherit	Basic
border-start-width	<border-width> | <length-conditional> | inherit	Basic
border-style	<border-style>{1,4} | inherit	Complete
border-top	[<border-width> | <border-style> | <color>] | inherit	Complete
border-top-color	<color> | inherit	Basic
border-top-style	<border-style> | inherit	Basic
border-top-width	<border-width> | inherit	Basic
border-width	<border-width>{1,4} | inherit	Complete
bottom	<length> | <percentage> | auto | inherit	Extended
break-after	auto | column | page | even-page | odd-page | inherit	Basic
break-before	auto | column | page | even-page | odd-page | inherit	Basic
caption-side	before | after | start | end | top | bottom | left | right | inherit	Complete
case-name	<name>	Extended
case-title	<string>	Extended
character	<character>	Basic
clear	start | end | left | right | both | none | inherit	Extended
clip	<shape> | auto | inherit	Extended
color	<color> | inherit	Basic
color-profile-name	<name> | inherit	Extended
column-count	<number> | inherit	Extended
column-gap	<length> | <percentage> | inherit	Extended
column-number	<number>	Basic
column-width	<length> | <percentage>	Basic
content-height	auto | scale-to-fit | <length> | <percentage> | inherit	Extended
content-type	<string> | auto	Extended
content-width	auto | scale-to-fit | <length> | <percentage> | inherit	Extended
country	none | <country> | inherit	Extended
cue	<cue-before> | <cue-after> | inherit	Complete
cue-after	<uri-specification> | none | inherit	Basic
cue-before	<uri-specification> | none | inherit	Basic

Table D-9. *Property table (continued)*

Name	Values	Core
destination-placement-offset	<length>	Extended
direction	ltr | rtl | inherit	Basic
display-align	auto | before | center | after | inherit	Extended
dominant-baseline	auto | use-script | no-change | reset-size | ideographic | alphabetic | hanging | mathematical | central | middle | text-after-edge | text-before-edge | inherit	Basic
elevation	<angle> | below | level | above | higher | lower | inherit	Basic
empty-cells	show | hide | inherit	Extended
end-indent	<length> | <percentage> | inherit	Basic
ends-row	true | false	Extended
extent	<length> | <percentage> | inherit	Extended
external-destination	<uri-specification>	Extended
float	before | start | end | left | right | none | inherit	Extended
flow-name	<name>	Basic
font	[[<font-style> | <font-variant> | <font-weight>]? <font-size> [/ <line-height>]? <font-family>] | caption | icon | menu | message-box | small-caption | status-bar | inherit	Complete
font-family	[[<family-name> | <generic-family>],]* [<family-name> | <generic-family>] | inherit	Basic
font-selection-strategy	auto | character-by-character | inherit	Complete
font-size	<absolute-size> | <relative-size> | <length> | <percentage> | inherit	Basic
font-size-adjust	<number> | none | inherit	Extended
font-stretch	normal | wider | narrower | ultra-condensed | extra-condensed | condensed | semi-condensed | semi-expanded | expanded | extra-expanded | ultra-expanded | inherit	Extended
font-style	normal | italic | oblique | backslant | inherit	Basic
font-variant	normal | small-caps | inherit	Basic
font-weight	normal | bold | bolder | lighter | 100 | 200 | 300 | 400 | 500 | 600 | 700 | 800 | 900 | inherit	Basic
force-page-count	auto | even | odd | end-on-even | end-on-odd | no-force | inherit	Extended
format	<string>	Basic
glyph-orientation-horizontal	<angle> | inherit	Extended
glyph-orientation-vertical	auto | <angle> | inherit	Extended
grouping-separator	<character>	Extended
grouping-size	<number>	Extended
height	<length> | <percentage> | auto | inherit	Basic
hyphenate	false | true | inherit	Extended

Table D-9. Property table (continued)

Name	Values	Core
hyphenation-character	<character>	inherit	Extended
hyphenation-keep	auto	column	page	inherit	Extended
hyphenation-ladder-count	no-limit	<number>	inherit	Extended
hyphenation-push-character-count	<number>	inherit	Extended
hyphenation-remain-character-count	<number>	inherit	Extended
id	<id>	Basic
indicate-destination	true	false	Extended
initial-page-number	auto	auto-odd	auto-even	<number>	inherit	Basic
inline-progression-dimension	auto	<length>	<percentage>	<length-range>	inherit	Basic
internal-destination	empty string	<idref>	Extended
intrusion-displace	auto	none	line	indent	block	inherit	Extended
keep-together	<keep>	inherit	Extended
keep-with-next	<keep>	inherit	Basic
keep-with-previous	<keep>	inherit	Basic
language	none	<language>	inherit	Extended
last-line-end-indent	<length>	<percentage>	inherit	Extended
leader-alignment	none	reference-area	page	inherit	Extended
leader-length	<length-range>	<percentage>	inherit	Basic
leader-pattern	space	rule	dots	use-content	inherit	Basic
leader-pattern-width	use-font-metrics	<length>	<percentage>	inherit	Extended
left	<length>	<percentage>	auto	inherit	Extended
letter-spacing	normal	<length>	<space>	inherit	Extended
letter-value	auto	alphabetic	traditional	Basic
linefeed-treatment	ignore	preserve	treat-as-space	treat-as-zero-width-space	inherit	Extended
line-height	normal	<length>	<number>	<percentage>	<space>	inherit	Basic
line-height-shift-adjustment	consider-shifts	disregard-shifts	inherit	Extended
line-stacking-strategy	line-height	font-height	max-height	inherit	Basic
margin	<margin-width>{1,4}	inherit	Complete
margin-bottom	<margin-width>	inherit	Basic
margin-left	<margin-width>	inherit	Basic
margin-right	<margin-width>	inherit	Basic
margin-top	<margin-width>	inherit	Basic

Name	Values	Core
marker-class-name	<name>	Extended
master-name	<name>	Basic
master-reference	<name>	Basic
max-height	<length> | <percentage> | none | inherit	Complete
maximum-repeats	<number> | no-limit | inherit	Extended
max-width	<length> | <percentage> | none | inherit	Complete
media-usage	auto | paginate | bounded-in-one-dimension | unbounded	Extended
min-height	<length> | <percentage> | inherit	Complete
min-width	<length> | <percentage> | inherit	Complete
number-columns-repeated	<number>	Basic
number-columns-spanned	<number>	Basic
number-rows-spanned	<number>	Basic
odd-or-even	odd | even | any | inherit	Extended
orphans	<integer> | inherit	Basic
overflow	visible | hidden | scroll | error-if-overflow | auto | inherit	Basic
padding	<padding-width>{1,4} | inherit	Complete
padding-after	<padding-width> | <length-conditional> | inherit	Basic
padding-before	<padding-width> | <length-conditional> | inherit	Basic
padding-bottom	<padding-width> | inherit	Basic
padding-end	<padding-width> | <length-conditional> | inherit	Basic
padding-left	<padding-width> | inherit	Basic
padding-right	<padding-width> | inherit	Basic
padding-start	<padding-width> | <length-conditional> | inherit	Basic
padding-top	<padding-width> | inherit	Basic
page-break-after	auto | always | avoid | left | right | inherit	Complete
page-break-before	auto | always | avoid | left | right | inherit	Complete
page-break-inside	avoid | auto | inherit	Complete
page-height	auto | indefinite | <length> | inherit	Basic
page-position	first | last | rest | any | inherit	Extended
page-width	auto | indefinite | <length> | inherit	Basic
pause	[<time> | <percentage>]{1,2} | inherit	Complete
pause-after	<time> | <percentage> | inherit	Basic
pause-before	<time> | <percentage> | inherit	Basic
pitch	<frequency> | x-low | low | medium | high | x-high | inherit	Basic
pitch-range	<number> | inherit	Basic

Table D-9. Property table (continued)

Name	Values	Core
play-during	<uri-specification> mix? repeat? | auto | none | inherit	Basic
position	static | relative | absolute | fixed | inherit	Complete
precedence	true | false | inherit	Extended
provisional-distance-between-starts	<length> | <percentage> | inherit	Basic
provisional-label-separation	<length> | <percentage> | inherit	Basic
reference-orientation	0 | 90 | 180 | 270 | -90 | -180 | -270 | inherit	Extended
ref-id	<idref> | inherit	Extended
region-name	xsl-region-body | xsl-region-start | xsl-region-end | xsl-region-before | xsl-region-after | xsl-before-float-separator | xsl-footnote-separator | <name>	Basic
relative-align	before | baseline | inherit	Extended
relative-position	static | relative | inherit	Extended
rendering-intent	auto | perceptual | relative-colorimetric | saturation | absolute-colorimetric | inherit	Extended
retrieve-boundary	page | page-sequence | document	Extended
retrieve-class-name	<name>	Extended
retrieve-position	first-starting-within-page | first-including-carryover | last-starting-within-page | last-ending-within-page	Extended
richness	<number> | inherit	Basic
right	<length> | <percentage> | auto | inherit	Extended
role	<string> | <uri-specification> | none | inherit	Basic
rule-style	none | dotted | dashed | solid | double | groove | ridge | inherit	Basic
rule-thickness	<length>	Basic
scaling	uniform | non-uniform | inherit	Extended
scaling-method	auto | integer-pixels | resample-any-method | inherit	Extended
score-spaces	true | false | inherit	Extended
script	none | auto | <script> | inherit	Extended
show-destination	replace | new	Extended
size	<length>{1,2} | auto | landscape | portrait | inherit	Complete
source-document	<uri-specification> [<uri-specification>]* | none | inherit	Basic
space-after	<space> | inherit	Basic
space-before	<space> | inherit	Basic
space-end	<space> | <percentage> | inherit	Basic
space-start	<space> | <percentage> | inherit	Basic
span	none | all | inherit	Extended
speak	normal | none | spell-out | inherit	Basic

Table D-9. Property table (continued)

Name	Values	Core
speak-header	once | always | inherit	Basic
speak-numeral	digits | continuous | inherit	Basic
speak-punctuation	code | none | inherit	Basic
speech-rate	<number> | x-slow | slow | medium | fast | x-fast | faster | slower | inherit	Basic
src	<uri-specification> | inherit	Basic
start-indent	<length> | <percentage> | inherit	Basic
starting-state	show | hide	Extended
starts-row	true | false	Extended
stress	<number> | inherit	Basic
suppress-at-line-break	auto | suppress | retain | inherit	Extended
switch-to	xsl-preceding | xsl-following | xsl-any | <name>[<name>]*	Extended
table-layout	auto | fixed | inherit	Extended
table-omit-footer-at-break	true | false	Extended
table-omit-header-at-break	true | false	Extended
target-presentation-context	use-target-processing-context | <uri-specification>	Extended
target-processing-context	document-root | <uri-specification>	Extended
target-stylesheet	use-normal-stylesheet | <uri-specification>	Extended
text-align	start | center | end | justify | inside | outside | left | right | <string> | inherit	Basic
text-align-last	relative | start | center | end | justify | inside | outside | left | right | inherit	Extended
text-altitude	use-font-metrics | <length> | <percentage> | inherit	Extended
text-decoration	none | [[underline | no-underline] | [overline | no-overline] | [line-through | no-line-through] | [blink | no-blink]] | inherit	Extended
text-depth	use-font-metrics | <length> | <percentage> | inherit	Extended
text-indent	<length> | <percentage> | inherit	Basic
text-shadow	none | [<color> | <length> <length> <length>? ,]* [<color> | <length> <length> <length>?] | inherit	Extended
text-transform	capitalize | uppercase | lowercase | none | inherit	Extended
top	<length> | <percentage> | auto | inherit	Extended
treat-as-word-space	auto | true | false | inherit	Extended
unicode-bidi	normal | embed | bidi-override | inherit	Extended
vertical-align	baseline | middle | sub | super | text-top | text-bottom | <percentage> | <length> | top | bottom | inherit	Complete
visibility	visible | hidden | collapse | inherit	Extended

Table D-9. Property table (continued)

Name	Values	Core
voice-family	[[<specific-voice> | <generic-voice>],]* [<specific-voice> | <generic-voice>] | inherit	Basic
volume	<number> | <percentage> | silent | x-soft | soft | medium | loud | x-loud | inherit	Basic
white-space	normal | pre | nowrap | inherit	Complete
white-space-collapse	false | true | inherit	Extended
white-space-treatment	ignore | preserve | ignore-if-before-linefeed | ignore-if-after-linefeed | ignore-if-surrounding-linefeed | inherit	Extended
widows	<integer> | inherit	Basic
width	<length> | <percentage> | auto | inherit	Basic
word-spacing	normal | <length> | <space> | inherit	Extended
wrap-option	no-wrap | wrap | inherit	Basic
writing-mode	lr-tb | rl-tb | tb-rl | lr | rl | tb | inherit	Basic
xml:lang	<country-language> | inherit	Complete
z-index	auto | <integer> | inherit	Extended

Inheritance Characteristics

This appendix simply lists those formatting objects that exhibit inheritance, based on Appendix C.2 of the specification.

Why is it worth including? To quote from the specification:

> During refinement the set of properties that apply to a formatting object is transformed into a set of traits that define constraints on the result of formatting. For many traits there is a one-to-one correspondence with a property; for other traits the transformation is more complex.

And:

> The first step in refinement of a particular formatting object is to obtain the effective value of each property that applies to the object. Any shorthand property specified on the formatting object is expanded into the individual properties. ... For any property that has not been specified on the object the inherited or initial value, as applicable, is used as the effective value.

This means some properties on an area that you specify are derived from the ancestors of the current node being formatted. The inheritable properties are propagated down the formatting object tree from a parent to each child. (These properties are given their initial value at the root of the result tree even if you don't specify them.) For a given inheritable property, if that property is present on a child, that value of the property is used for that child (and its descendants until explicitly reset in a lower descendant).

The following lists show the inherited properties for the visual formatting objects. Those not listed are not inherited. They are grouped according to usage.

Font-, Character-, and Spacing-Related Properties

- font
- font-family
- font-selection-strategy

- font-size
- font-size-adjust
- font-stretch
- font-style
- font-variant
- font-weight
- glyph-orientation-horizontal
- glyph-orientation-vertical
- letter-spacing
- line-height
- line-height-shift-adjustment
- line-stacking-strategy
- word-spacing

Visibility-Related Properties

- visibility

Writing Mode–Related Properties

- direction
- reference-orientation
- writing-mode

Border- and Text Decoration–Related Properties

- border-collapse
- border-separation
- border-spacing
- score-spaces

Whitespace- and Line Break–Related Properties

- hyphenate
- hyphenation-character
- hyphenation-keep
- hyphenation-ladder-count
- hyphenation-push-character-count

- hyphenation-remain-character-count
- linefeed-treatment
- orphans
- white-space
- white-space-collapse
- white-space-treatment
- widows
- wrap-option

Leader- and Rule-Related Properties

- leader-alignment
- leader-length
- leader-pattern
- leader-pattern-width
- rule-style
- rule-thickness

Indent-Related Properties

- end-indent
- last-line-end-indent
- start-indent
- text-indent

Border-Related Properties

- border-collapse
- border-separation
- border-spacing

Caption-Related Properties

- caption-side

Color-Related Properties

- color

Alignment-Related Properties

- `display-align`
- `relative-align`
- `text-align`
- `text-align-last`

Table-Related Properties

- `empty-cells`

Keeps- and Breaks-Related Properties

- `keep-together`
- `page-break-inside`

List-Related Properties

- `provisional-distance-between-starts`
- `provisional-label-separation`

Language-Related Properties

- `country`
- `language`
- `script`
- `text-transform`
- `xml:lang`

Examples for Chapter 10

Example F-1. Initial layout

```
<fo:root xmlns:fo="http://www.w3.org/1999/XSL/Format">

  <fo:layout-master-set>

  <!-- spm for first 3 pages -->
      <fo:simple-page-master master-name="first3"
                 page-height="29.7cm"
                 page-width="21cm"
                 margin-top="1in"
                 margin-bottom="2in"
                 margin-left="2.5cm"
                 margin-right="2.5cm">
        <fo:region-body
                 padding-start="1cm"
                 padding-end="1cm"
                 margin-top="0.6in"
                 margin-bottom="0.6in"
                 margin-left="0.7in"
                 margin-right="0.5in"/>
      </fo:simple-page-master>
      <!-- No headers or footers required -->

  <!-- spm for preface and toc -->
      <fo:simple-page-master master-name="prefAndToc"
                 page-height="29.7cm"
                 page-width="21cm"
                 margin-top="1in"
                 margin-bottom="1.5in"
                 margin-left="2.5cm"
                 margin-right="2.5cm">
        <fo:region-body
                 padding-start="1cm"
                 padding-end="1cm"
                 margin-top="0.6in"
                 margin-bottom="0.6in"
                 margin-left="0.7in"
```

❶ (appears beside `<fo:simple-page-master master-name="first3"`)

❷ (appears beside `<!-- No headers or footers required -->`)

```
                        margin-right="0.5in"/>
   <fo:region-before
     extent          ="0.5in"/>  <!-- Height of the region -->
❸

   <fo:region-after
     extent          ="0.5in"/>          <!-- Height of region -->


      </fo:simple-page-master>



   <!-- spm for main chapters, odd pages -->
❹     <fo:simple-page-master master-name="chapsOdd"
                   page-height="29.7cm"
                   page-width="21cm"
                   margin-top="1in"
                   margin-bottom="0.7in"
❺                  margin-left="1.5cm"
                   margin-right="2.5cm">


        <fo:region-body


❻       border-color="red"
        border-style="solid"
        border-width="1pt"



                      padding-end="3mm"
                      padding-start="1mm"
                      margin-bottom="0.5in"
                      margin-top="1in"
                      margin-left="15mm"
                      margin-right="15mm"/>
     <fo:region-before

       border-color="red"
       border-style="solid"
       border-width="1pt"

     extent          ="0.7in"/>  <!-- Height of the region -->

   <fo:region-after
       border-color="red"
       border-style="solid"
       border-width="1pt"

     extent          ="0.4in"/>          <!-- Height of region -->

      </fo:simple-page-master>

   <!-- spm for main chapters, even pages -->
```

```
❼       <fo:simple-page-master master-name="chapsEven"
                    page-height="29.7cm"
                    page-width="21cm"
                    margin-top="1in"
                    margin-bottom="0.7in"
                    margin-left="2.5cm"
                    margin-right="1.5cm">

    <fo:region-body


   border-color="red"
   border-style="solid"
   border-width="1pt"


                    padding-end="3mm"
                    padding-start="1mm"
                    margin-bottom="0.5in"
                    margin-top="1in"
                    margin-left="15mm"
                    margin-right="15mm"/>
   <fo:region-before

     border-color="red"
     border-style="solid"
     border-width="1pt"

     extent          ="0.7in"/>  <!-- Height of the region -->

   <fo:region-after
     border-color="red"
     border-style="solid"
     border-width="1pt"

     extent          ="0.4in"/>       <!-- Height of region -->

    </fo:simple-page-master>



  <!-- Control the sequencing for odd and even pages in chapters -->



❽       <fo:page-sequence-master master-name="chaps">

     <fo:repeatable-page-master-alternatives>
      <fo:conditional-page-master-reference
              master-reference="chapsOdd"
              odd-or-even="odd" />
```

Example F-1. Initial layout (continued)

```
            <fo:conditional-page-master-reference
❾                  master-reference="chapsEven"
                   odd-or-even="even" />

        </fo:repeatable-page-master-alternatives>
      </fo:page-sequence-master>
    </fo:layout-master-set>


    <!-- page-sequence for first 3 pages -->


❿    <fo:page-sequence master-reference="first3">
       <fo:flow flow-name="xsl-region-body">
         <fo:block break-after="page">Front page</fo:block>
         <fo:block break-after="page">Dedication page</fo:block>
         <fo:block break-after="page">Title  page</fo:block>
       </fo:flow>
     </fo:page-sequence>

    <!-- Page sequence for preface and toc -->
⓫    <fo:page-sequence master-reference="prefAndToc">
       <fo:static-content
                   flow-name="xsl-region-after">
           <fo:block>Preface and toc footer with roman page numbers</fo:block>
       </fo:static-content>

       <fo:flow flow-name="xsl-region-body">
         <fo:block break-after="page">Preface</fo:block>
         <fo:block break-after="page">Table of contents 1</fo:block>
        <fo:block break-after="page">Table of contents 2</fo:block>

       </fo:flow>
     </fo:page-sequence>


    <!-- Page sequence for all chapters -->
     <fo:page-sequence master-reference="chaps">
       <fo:static-content
⓬                  flow-name="xsl-region-before">
           <fo:block>Chapter header with Arabic  page numbers</fo:block>
       </fo:static-content>


       <fo:flow flow-name="xsl-region-body">
         <fo:block break-after="page">chapter odd page</fo:block>
         <fo:block break-after="page">chapter even pages</fo:block>
        <fo:block break-after="page">chapter odd pages</fo:block>

       </fo:flow>
     </fo:page-sequence>

  </fo:root>
```

❶ simple page model for first three pages. All pages follow this model.

❷ No footers or headers.

❸ Only the footer is needed, the header is included to keep the balance.

❹ Specification for odd pages.

❺ One-centimeter difference between odd and even pages, swapped for the even pages.

❻ Borders will be removed for use. Inclusion allows the three areas to be viewed without content.

❼ Main chapters, even pages specification.

❽ Need to alternatively select odd and even pages, depending on the parity of the page number.

❾ Select the even simple page model.

❿ First flow. No headers, simple text content to ensure it works as expected. This will be replaced by templates.

⓫ Same for all areas, some temporary content is included to check that the layout works.

⓬ This will be replaced by retrieve-markers and page-number elements.

Example F-2. Source document outline

```
      <book>
        <title>Book title</title>
❶     <frontmatter>
          <author>A.N. Author</author>
          <dedication>
            <para>Dedication to all the people
        who wrote this book for me.</para>
          </dedication>
          <pubdetails>
            <pubname>A Publisher</pubname>
            <pubads>London, 2001 </pubads>
          </pubdetails>

          <preface>
            <title>Preface</title>
            <para>First para of preface</para>
      <para>Second para of preface</para>
          </preface>
        </frontmatter>
❷     <bodymatter> <!-- bodymatter -->
          <chapter>
            <title>Introduction and first chapter title</title>
            <para>Content in the first chapter.
        Additional paragraphs are necessary to check for
        inter-paragraph spacing and layout. </para>
            <para>Content in the first chapter.
        Additional paragraphs are necessary to check for
```

Example F-2. Source document outline (continued)

```
        inter-paragraph spacing and layout. </para>
      </chapter>
      <chapter>
        <title>chapter 2 title</title>
        <para>Content </para>
      </chapter>
      <chapter>
        <title>Chapter 3 title</title>
        <para>Content </para>
      </chapter>
      <chapter>
        <title>Chapter n +2</title>
        <para>Content </para>
      </chapter>
      <chapter>
        <title>Chapter n +3</title>
        <para>Content </para>
      </chapter>
      <chapter>
        <title>Chapter n +4</title>
        <para>Content </para>
      </chapter>
      <chapter>
        <title>Chapter n +5</title>
        <para>Content </para>
      </chapter>
      <chapter>
        <title>Chapter n +6</title>
        <para>Content </para>
      </chapter>
      <chapter>
        <title>Chapter n +7</title>
        <para>Content </para>
      </chapter>
      <chapter>
        <title>Chapter n +8</title>
        <para>Content </para>
      </chapter>


    </bodymatter>
❸ <rearmatter>
      <appendix>
        <title>Appendix title</title>
        <para>content</para>
      </appendix>
    </rearmatter>
    </book>
```

❶ Front matter

❷ Body matter

❸ Rear matter

Example F-3. Main stylesheet

```
<?xml version="1.0" ?>
<!DOCTYPE xsl:stylesheet [
<!ENTITY  sp  "<xsl:text> </xsl:text>">
]>
<xsl:stylesheet
  xmlns:xsl="http://www.w3.org/1999/XSL/Transform"
  xmlns:fo="http://www.w3.org/1999/XSL/Format"
version="1.0">
  <xsl:import href="pl.xsl"/>
  <xsl:import href='ps.xsl'/>
 <xsl:template match="book">
      <xsl:apply-templates/>
  </xsl:template>



  <xsl:template match="frontmatter">
    <fo:block>
      <xsl:apply-templates/>
    </fo:block>
  </xsl:template>

  <xsl:template match="author">
    <fo:block>
      <xsl:apply-templates/>
    </fo:block>
  </xsl:template>

  <xsl:template match="frontmatter/title">
    <fo:block>
      <xsl:apply-templates/>
    </fo:block>
  </xsl:template>



  <xsl:template name="tPage">
 <fo:block  xsl:use-attribute-sets='font'>
   <fo:block
     font-size='36pt'
     space-before = '50mm'
     space-after =  '25mm'
     ><xsl:value-of select='/book/title'/>
 </fo:block>
 <fo:block
   font-size='18pt'
   space-before = '25mm'
   space-after =  '12mm'
>by </fo:block>
 <fo:block
   font-size='18pt'
```

Example F-3. Main stylesheet (continued)

```
   space-before = '25mm'
   space-after =  '12mm'>
   <xsl:value-of select='/book/frontmatter/author'/>
</fo:block>
   </fo:block>

   <fo:block text-align='end'
      font-size='10pt'
      space-before = '60mm'>
   &#x00A9; <xsl:value-of
            select="/book/frontmatter/pubdetails/pubname"/>
   </fo:block>
     <fo:block text-align='end'
       font-size='10pt'        >
 <xsl:value-of select="/book/frontmatter/pubdetails/pubads"/>
     </fo:block>

</xsl:template>

<xsl:template match="dedication">
   <fo:block break-before='page'>
     <fo:block xsl:use-attribute-sets="title font">
        Dedication.
     </fo:block>
   <xsl:apply-templates/>
   </fo:block>
</xsl:template>

<xsl:template match='/' mode='ffp'>
   <fo:block break-before="odd-page" >
     <fo:block xsl:use-attribute-sets="title font"
            space-after="20mm">
      <xsl:value-of select='/book/title'/>
     </fo:block>
     <fo:table width='130mm'>
       <fo:table-body>
         <fo:table-row>
           <fo:table-cell>
             <fo:block>
             <fo:external-graphic
                  src="images\ttlpg.jpg"
                  content-height="100%"
                  scaling="uniform"/>
             </fo:block>
           </fo:table-cell>
           <fo:table-cell display-align='bottom'>
             <fo:block/>
             <fo:block space-before='90mm'>
               &#x00A9; <xsl:value-of
               select='/book/frontmatter/pubdetails/pubname'/>
             </fo:block>
             <fo:block>
```

```
            <xsl:value-of
              select='/book/frontmatter/pubdetails/pubads'/>
         </fo:block>
       </fo:table-cell>
     </fo:table-row>
   </fo:table-body>
 </fo:table>
 <fo:block font-size='{$small-sz}'>Image courtesy of
         Aries Cheung, Toronto</fo:block>
</fo:block>


</xsl:template>


<xsl:template match="preface">
  <fo:block id='{generate-id( )}'>
  <xsl:apply-templates/>
  </fo:block>
</xsl:template>

<xsl:template match="preface/title">
  <fo:block xsl:use-attribute-sets="title font">
  <xsl:apply-templates/>
  </fo:block>
</xsl:template>


<xsl:template match="/" mode="toc">
   <fo:block break-before="odd-page" >
      <fo:block xsl:use-attribute-sets="title font">
         Table of Contents
      </fo:block>

      <xsl:for-each select='book/frontmatter/preface'>
      <fo:block text-align-last="justify">
        <fo:inline><xsl:value-of select="title"/>
        <fo:leader        leader-pattern="dots"/>
        <fo:page-number-citation ref-id="{generate-id( )}"/>
      </fo:inline>
    </fo:block>
  </xsl:for-each>


      <xsl:for-each select='book/bodymatter/chapter'>
        <fo:block text-align-last="justify">
          <fo:inline><xsl:value-of select="title"/>
          <fo:leader        leader-pattern="dots"/>
          <fo:page-number-citation ref-id="{generate-id( )}"/>
        </fo:inline>
      </fo:block>
      </xsl:for-each>
```

Example F-3. Main stylesheet (continued)

```
        <xsl:for-each select='book/rearmatter/appendix'>
           <fo:block text-align-last="justify">
              <fo:inline><xsl:value-of select="title"/>
              <fo:leader         leader-pattern="dots"/>
              <fo:page-number-citation ref-id="{generate-id( )}"/>
              </fo:inline>
           </fo:block>
         </xsl:for-each>
      </fo:block>
  </xsl:template>



  <xsl:template match="bodymatter|rearmatter">
    <xsl:apply-templates/>
  </xsl:template>

  <xsl:template match="chapter">
  <fo:block break-before="odd-page" id='{generate-id( )}'>
     <fo:marker marker-class-name="chap">
        <xsl:value-of select="title"/>
     </fo:marker>
  <fo:marker marker-class-name="chapNum">
     <xsl:number count="chapter" level="any" from="bodymatter"/>

     </fo:marker>
     <xsl:apply-templates/>
     </fo:block>
  </xsl:template>

  <xsl:template match="chapter/title">
     <fo:block/>
     <fo:block xsl:use-attribute-sets="title font">
        <xsl:apply-templates/>
     </fo:block>
  </xsl:template>

  <xsl:template match="appendix">
     <fo:block id='{generate-id( )}'>
     <xsl:apply-templates/>
     </fo:block>
  </xsl:template>


  <xsl:template match="appendix/title">
     <fo:block>
        <xsl:apply-templates/>
     </fo:block>
  </xsl:template>
```

Example F-3. Main stylesheet (continued)

```
<!-- minor templates -->


 <xsl:template match="para">
    <fo:block xsl:use-attribute-sets="para font">
      <xsl:apply-templates/>
    </fo:block>
  </xsl:template>



  <xsl:template match="*">
    <fo:block color="red">
***************        Element <xsl:value-of
                 select="name(..)"/>/ <xsl:value-of
                 select="name( )"/> found, with no template. ***************
    </fo:block>
  </xsl:template>




</xsl:stylesheet>
```

Example F-4. File ps.xsl, the property sets

```
<?xml version="1.0" encoding="utf-8"?>
<!DOCTYPE xsl:stylesheet [
<!ENTITY  sp  "<xsl:text> </xsl:text>">
]>
<xsl:stylesheet
  xmlns:xsl="http://www.w3.org/1999/XSL/Transform"
  xmlns:fo="http://www.w3.org/1999/XSL/Format"
version="1.0">

<xsl:variable name='base-font-size' select='12'/>
<xsl:variable name='title-font-size' select='$base-font-size * 1.5'/>
<xsl:variable name='head-font-size' select='$base-font-size * 1.2'/>
<xsl:variable name='small-font-size' select='$base-font-size div 2'/>

<xsl:variable name='base-sz' select= 'concat ($base-font-size,"pt")'/>
<xsl:variable name='title-sz' select= 'concat ($title-font-size,"pt")'/>
<xsl:variable name='head-sz' select= 'concat ($head-font-size,"pt")'/>
<xsl:variable name='small-sz' select= 'concat ($small-font-size,"pt")'/>


<xsl:attribute-set name='font'> <!-- Font family -->
  <xsl:attribute
    name='font-family'>'Arial' 'Helvetica' Serif</xsl:attribute>
</xsl:attribute-set>
```

Example F-4. File ps.xsl, the property sets (continued)

```
<xsl:attribute-set name="title"
use-attribute-sets="font ">
    <xsl:attribute name="font-size">
      <xsl:value-of select="$title-sz"/>
    </xsl:attribute>
    <xsl:attribute name="font-weight">bold</xsl:attribute>
    <xsl:attribute name="font-style">normal</xsl:attribute>
    <xsl:attribute name="space-before.optimum">
          <xsl:value-of select="$title-sz"/>
    </xsl:attribute>
    <xsl:attribute
      name="space-before.conditionality">retain</xsl:attribute>
    <xsl:attribute name="space-after.optimum">
      <xsl:value-of select="$small-sz"/>
    </xsl:attribute>
    <xsl:attribute name="keep-with-next">true</xsl:attribute>
    <xsl:attribute name="page-break-inside">avoid</xsl:attribute>
    <xsl:attribute name="text-align">center</xsl:attribute>
    <xsl:attribute name="background-color">white</xsl:attribute>
  </xsl:attribute-set>

  <xsl:attribute-set name='pad'>
    <xsl:attribute name='padding'>
        <xsl:value-of select="$small-sz"/>
    </xsl:attribute>
  </xsl:attribute-set>

  <xsl:attribute-set name="border">
<xsl:attribute-set name='border'>
<xsl:attribute name='border-before-style>solid'</xsl:attribute>
<xsl:attribute name='border-after-style>solid'</xsl:attribute>
<xsl:attribute name='border-start-style>solid'</xsl:attribute>
<xsl:attribute name='border-end-style>solid'</xsl:attribute>


<xsl:attribute name='border-before-width>.1mm"</xsl:attribute>
<xsl:attribute name='border-after-width>.1mm"</xsl:attribute>
<xsl:attribute name='border-start-width>.1mm"</xsl:attribute>
<xsl:attribute name='border-end-width>.1mm"</xsl:attribute>
  </xsl:attribute-set>


 <xsl:attribute-set name="para"
   use-attribute-sets='font '>
    <xsl:attribute name="space-before.optimum">
      <xsl:value-of select="$base-sz"/>
    </xsl:attribute>
    <xsl:attribute name="space-after.optimum">
```

Example F-4. File ps.xsl, the property sets (continued)

```
        <xsl:value-of select="$base-sz"/>
      </xsl:attribute>
    </xsl:attribute-set>

</xsl:stylesheet>
```

Example F-5. Page layout stylesheet

```
<?xml version="1.0" ?>
<!DOCTYPE xsl:stylesheet [
  <!ENTITY  lms SYSTEM "lms.xml">
]>
<xsl:stylesheet
  xmlns:xsl="http://www.w3.org/1999/XSL/Transform"
  xmlns:fo="http://www.w3.org/1999/XSL/Format"
version="1.0">
<!-- Time-stamp: "2000-12-22 11:30:45 dave"  -->

<xsl:output method="xml" indent="yes"/>

<xsl:template match="/">
<fo:root xmlns:fo="http://www.w3.org/1999/XSL/Format">
  <fo:layout-master-set>

<!-- spm for first 3 pages -->
    <fo:simple-page-master master-name="first3"
                page-height="29.7cm"
                page-width="21cm"
                margin-top="1in"
                margin-bottom="2in"
                margin-left="2.5cm"
                margin-right="2.5cm">
      <fo:region-body
                    padding-start="1cm"
                    padding-end="1cm"
                    margin-top="0.6in"
                    margin-bottom="0.6in"
                    margin-left="0.7in"
                    margin-right="0.5in"/>
    </fo:simple-page-master>
    <!-- No headers or footers required -->

<!-- spm for preface and toc -->
    <fo:simple-page-master master-name="prefAndToc"
                page-height="29.7cm"
                page-width="21cm"
                margin-top="1in"
                margin-bottom="1.5in"
                margin-left="2.5cm"
```

```
                     margin-right="2.5cm">
      <fo:region-body
                     padding-start="1cm"
                     padding-end="1cm"
                     margin-top="0.6in"
                     margin-bottom="0.6in"
                     margin-left="0.7in"
                     margin-right="0.5in"/>
 <fo:region-before
    extent          ="0.5in"/>  <!-- Height of the region -->


 <fo:region-after
    extent          ="0.5in"/>         <!-- Height of region -->

    </fo:simple-page-master>



<!-- spm for main chapters, odd pages -->
    <fo:simple-page-master master-name="chapsOdd"
                     page-height="29.7cm"
                     page-width="21cm"
                     margin-top="1in"
                     margin-bottom="0.7in"
                     margin-left="1.5cm"
                     margin-right="2.5cm">

  <!--
    border-color="red"
    border-style="solid"
    border-width="1pt"
-->
      <fo:region-body
                     padding-end="3mm"
                     padding-start="1mm"
                     margin-bottom="0.5in"
                     margin-top="1in"
                     margin-left="15mm"
                     margin-right="15mm"/>
 <fo:region-before

    extent          ="0.7in"/>  <!-- Height of the region -->
  <!--
    border-color="red"
    border-style="solid"
    border-width="1pt"
-->
```

```
<fo:region-after

   extent          ="0.4in"/>          <!-- Height of region -->
 <!--
    border-color="red"
    border-style="solid"
    border-width="1pt"
-->
    </fo:simple-page-master>

<!-- spm for main chapters, even pages -->
    <fo:simple-page-master master-name="chapsEven"
                 page-height="29.7cm"
                 page-width="21cm"
                 margin-top="1in"
                 margin-bottom="0.7in"
                 margin-left="2.5cm"
                 margin-right="1.5cm">

      <fo:region-body

                 padding-end="3mm"
                 padding-start="1mm"
                 margin-bottom="0.5in"
                 margin-top="1in"
                 margin-left="15mm"
                 margin-right="15mm"/>


      <!--     border-color="red"
    border-style="solid"
    border-width="1pt" -->


 <fo:region-before


   extent          ="0.7in"/>  <!-- Height of the region -->
<!--    border-color="red"
    border-style="solid"
    border-width="1pt"
 -->
 <fo:region-after

   extent          ="0.4in"/>          <!-- Height of region -->
<!--    border-color="red"
    border-style="solid"
    border-width="1pt"
 -->
```

Example F-5. Page layout stylesheet (continued)

```
    </fo:simple-page-master>



<!-- Control the sequencing for odd and even pages in chapters -->
    <fo:page-sequence-master master-name="chaps">
      <fo:repeatable-page-master-alternatives>
        <fo:conditional-page-master-reference
                master-reference="chapsOdd"
                odd-or-even="odd" />

        <fo:conditional-page-master-reference
                master-reference="chapsEven"
                odd-or-even="even" />
      </fo:repeatable-page-master-alternatives>
    </fo:page-sequence-master>
  </fo:layout-master-set>


<!-- page-sequence for first 3 pages -->
  <fo:page-sequence master-reference="first3">
    <fo:flow flow-name="xsl-region-body">
   <xsl:call-template name="tPage"/>
      <xsl:apply-templates select="/book/frontmatter/dedication"/>
 <xsl:apply-templates select="/" mode="ffp"/>
  </fo:flow>
</fo:page-sequence>

<!-- Page sequence for preface and toc -->
  <fo:page-sequence
        master-reference="prefAndToc"
        initial-page-number="1" format="I">
    <fo:static-content
                    flow-name="xsl-region-after">
      <fo:block text-align="outside"><fo:page-number/></fo:block>
    </fo:static-content>

    <fo:flow flow-name="xsl-region-body">
    <xsl:apply-templates select="/book/frontmatter/preface"/>
    <xsl:apply-templates select="/" mode="toc"/>

    </fo:flow>
  </fo:page-sequence>


<!-- Page sequence for all chapters -->
  <fo:page-sequence master-reference="chaps">
    <fo:static-content
      flow-name="xsl-region-before">
```

Example F-5. Page layout stylesheet (continued)

```
      <fo:block text-align="outside"
                   xsl:use-attribute-sets='para font pad'>
        Chapter     <fo:retrieve-marker retrieve-class-name="chapNum"/>
    <fo:leader leader-pattern="space" />
        <fo:retrieve-marker retrieve-class-name="chap"/>
    <fo:leader leader-pattern="space" />
      Page <fo:page-number
            font-style="normal" /> of <fo:page-number-citation
                                    ref-id='end'/>
  </fo:block>
   </fo:static-content>
   <fo:flow flow-name="xsl-region-body">
   <fo:block xsl:use-attribute-sets='font'>
   <xsl:apply-templates select="/book/bodymatter"/>
   <xsl:apply-templates select="/book/rearmatter"/>
   </fo:block>
  <fo:block id='end'/>
  </fo:flow>
</fo:page-sequence>


</fo:root>

</xsl:template>
</xsl:stylesheet>
```

APPENDIX G

Elements and Valid Properties

In accordance with the W3C copyright, please note that this content is abstracted from Extensible Stylesheet Language (XSL) Version 1.0, "Copyright 2001 World Wide Web Consortium, (Massachusetts Institute of Technology, Institut National de Recherche en Informatique et en Automatique, Keio University). All Rights Reserved. *http://www.w3.org/Consortium/Legal/*".

This document lists all the properties available for the elements in the fo namespace (with exceptions being my error). Posted to clarify.

XSL-FO Elements and Their Properties

This table lists all elements and their associated properties, derived from section 6 of the Recommendation. Table G-1 lists all elements and their properties.

The common aural properties, which are noted in this table for many elements, include azimuth, cue-after, cue-before, elevation, pause-after, pause-before, pitch, pitch-range, play-during, richness, speak, speak-header, speak-numeral, speak-punctuation, speech-rate, stress, voice-family, and volume.

Table G-1. Properties

Element	Properties	Comments
fo:root	media-usage	
fo:declarations		
fo:color-profile	src, color-profile-name, rendering-intent	
fo:page-sequence	country, format, language, letter-value, grouping-separator, grouping-size, id, initial-page-number, force-page-count, master-reference	

Element	Properties	Comments
fo:layout-master-set		
fo:page-sequence-master	master-name	
fo:single-page-master-reference	master-reference	
fo:repeatable-page-master-reference	master-reference, maximum-repeats	
fo:repeatable-page-master-alternatives	maximum-repeats	
fo:conditional-page-master-reference	master-reference, page-position, odd-or-even, blank-or-not-blank	
fo:simple-page-master	margin-top, margin-bottom, margin-left, margin-right, space-before, space-after, start-indent, end-indent, master-name, page-height, page-width, reference-orientation, writing-mode	
fo:region-body	background-attachment, background-color, background-image, background-repeat, background-position-horizontal, background-position-vertical, border-before-color, border-before-style, border-before-width, border-after-color, border-after-style, border-after-width, border-start-color, border-start-style, border-start-width, border-end-color, border-end-style, border-end-width, border-top-color, border-top-style, border-top-width, border-bottom-color, border-bottom-style, border-bottom-width, border-left-color, border-left-style, border-left-width, border-right-color, border-right-style, border-right-width, padding-before, padding-after, padding-start, padding-end, padding-top, padding-bottom, padding-left, padding-right margin-top, margin-bottom, margin-left, margin-right, space-before, space-after, start-indent, end-indent, clip, column-count, column-gap, display-align, overflow, region-name, reference-orientation, writing-mode	
fo:region-before	background-attachment, background-color, background-image, background-repeat, background-position-horizontal, background-position-vertical, border-before-color, border-before-style, border-before-width, border-after-color, border-after-style, border-after-width, border-start-color, border-start-style, border-start-width, border-end-color, border-end-style, border-end-width, border-top-color, border-top-style, border-top-width, border-bottom-color, border-bottom-style, border-bottom-width, border-left-color, border-left-style, border-left-width, border-right-color, border-right-style, border-right-width, padding-before, padding-after, padding-start, padding-end, padding-top, padding-bottom, padding-left, padding-right clip, display-align, extent, overflow, precedence, region-name, reference-orientation, writing-mode	

Element	Properties	Comments
fo:region-after	background-attachment, background-color, background-image, background-repeat, background-position-horizontal, background-position-vertical, border-before-color, border-before-style, border-before-width, border-after-color, border-after-style, border-after-width, border-start-color, border-start-style, border-start-width, border-end-color, border-end-style, border-end-width, border-top-color, border-top-style, border-top-width, border-bottom-color, border-bottom-style, border-bottom-width, border-left-color, border-left-style, border-left-width, border-right-color, border-right-style, border-right-width, padding-before, padding-after, padding-start, padding-end, padding-top, padding-bottom, padding-left, padding-right clip, display-align, extent, overflow, precedence, region-name, reference-orientation, writing-mode	
fo:region-start	background-attachment, background-color, background-image, background-repeat, background-position-horizontal, background-position-vertical, border-before-color, border-before-style, border-before-width, border-after-color, border-after-style, border-after-width, border-start-color, border-start-style, border-start-width, border-end-color, border-end-style, border-end-width, border-top-color, border-top-style, border-top-width, border-bottom-color, border-bottom-style, border-bottom-width, border-left-color, border-left-style, border-left-width, border-right-color, border-right-style, border-right-width, padding-before, padding-after, padding-start, padding-end, padding-top, padding-bottom, padding-left, padding-right clip, display-align, extent, overflow, region-name, reference-orientation, writing-mode	
fo:region-end	background-attachment, background-color, background-image, background-repeat, background-position-horizontal, background-position-vertical, border-before-color, border-before-style, border-before-width, border-after-color, border-after-style, border-after-width, border-start-color, border-start-style, border-start-width, border-end-color, border-end-style, border-end-width, border-top-color, border-top-style, border-top-width, border-bottom-color, border-bottom-style, border-bottom-width, border-left-color, border-left-style, border-left-width, border-right-color, border-right-style, border-right-width, padding-before, padding-after, padding-start, padding-end, padding-top, padding-bottom, padding-left, padding-right clip, display-align, extent, overflow, region-name, reference-orientation, writing-mode	
fo:flow	flow-name	
fo:static-content	flow-name	
fo:title	[7.6 Common Aural Properties], source-document, role, background-attachment, background-color, background-image, background-repeat, background-position-horizontal, background-position-vertical, border-before-color, border-before-style, border-before-width, border-after-color, border-after-style, border-after-width, border-start-color, border-start-style, border-start-width, border-end-color, border-end-style, border-end-width, border-top-color, border-top-style, border-top-width, border-bottom-color, border-bottom-style, border-bottom-width, border-left-color, border-left-style, border-left-width, border-right-color, border-right-style, border-right-width, padding-before, padding-after, padding-start, padding-end, padding-top, padding-bottom, padding-left, padding-right, font-family, font-selection-strategy, font-size, font-stretch, font-size-adjust, font-style, font-variant, font-weight, space-end, space-start, color, line-height, visibility	

Table G-1. Properties (continued)

Element	Properties	Comments
fo:block	[7.6 Common Aural Properties], source-document, role, background-attachment, background-color, background-image, background-repeat, background-position-horizontal, background-position-vertical, border-before-color, border-before-style, border-before-width, border-after-color, border-after-style, border-after-width, border-start-color, border-start-style, border-start-width, border-end-color, border-end-style, border-end-width, border-top-color, border-top-style, border-top-width, border-bottom-color, border-bottom-style, border-bottom-width, border-left-color, border-left-style, border-left-width, border-right-color, border-right-style, border-right-width, padding-before, padding-after, padding-start, padding-end, padding-top, padding-bottom, padding-left, padding-right, font-family, font-selection-strategy, font-size, font-stretch, font-size-adjust, font-style, font-variant, font-weight, country, language, script, hyphenate, hyphenation-character, hyphenation-push-character-count, hyphenation-remain-character-count, margin-top, margin-bottom, margin-left, margin-right, space-before, space-after, start-indent, end-indent, relative-position, break-after, break-before, color, text-depth, text-altitude, hyphenation-keep, hyphenation-ladder-count, id, intrusion-displace, keep-together, keep-with-next, keep-with-previous, last-line-end-indent, linefeed-treatment, line-height, line-height-shift-adjustment, line-stacking-strategy, orphans, white-space-treatment, span, text-align, text-align-last, text-indent, visibility, white-space-collapse, widows, wrap-option	
fo:block-container	absolute-position, top, right, bottom, left, background-attachment, background-color, background-image, background-repeat, background-position-horizontal, background-position-vertical, border-before-color, border-before-style, border-before-width, border-after-color, border-after-style, border-after-width, border-start-color, border-start-style, border-start-width, border-end-color, border-end-style, border-end-width, border-top-color, border-top-style, border-top-width, border-bottom-color, border-bottom-style, border-bottom-width, border-left-color, border-left-style, border-left-width, border-right-color, border-right-style, border-right-width, padding-before, padding-after, padding-start, padding-end, padding-top, padding-bottom, padding-left, padding-right, margin-top, margin-bottom, margin-left, margin-right, space-before, space-after, start-indent, end-indent, block-progression-dimension, break-after, break-before, clip, display-align, height, id, inline-progression-dimension, intrusion-displace, keep-together, keep-with-next, keep-with-previous, overflow, reference-orientation, span, width, writing-mode, z-index,	
fo:bidi-override	[7.6 Common Aural Properties], font-family, font-selection-strategy, font-size, font-stretch, font-size-adjust, font-style, font-variant, font-weight, relative-position, color, direction, id, letter-spacing, line-height, score-spaces, unicode-bidi, word-spacing	

Element	Properties	Comments
fo:character	[7.6 Common Aural Properties], background-attachment, background-color, background-image, background-repeat, background-position-horizontal, background-position-vertical, border-before-color, border-before-style, border-before-width, border-after-color, border-after-style, border-after-width, border-start-color, border-start-style, border-start-width, border-end-color, border-end-style, border-end-width, border-top-color, border-top-style, border-top-width, border-bottom-color, border-bottom-style, border-bottom-width, border-left-color, border-left-style, border-left-width, border-right-color, border-right-style, border-right-width, padding-before, padding-after, padding-start, padding-end, padding-top, padding-bottom, padding-left, padding-right, font-family, font-selection-strategy, font-size, font-stretch, font-size-adjust, font-style, font-variant, font-weight, country, language, script, hyphenate, hyphenation-character, hyphenation-push-character-count, hyphenation-remain-character-count, space-end, space-start, relative-position, alignment-adjust, treat-as-word-space, alignment-baseline, baseline-shift, character, color, dominant-baseline, text-depth, text-altitude, glyph-orientation-horizontal, glyph-orientation-vertical, id, keep-with-next, keep-with-previous, letter-spacing, line-height score-spaces, suppress-at-line-break, text-decoration, text-shadow, text-transform, visibility, word-spacing	
fo:initial-property-set	[7.6 Common Aural Properties], source-document, role, background-attachment, background-color, background-image, background-repeat, background-position-horizontal, background-position-vertical, border-before-color, border-before-style, border-before-width, border-after-color, border-after-style, border-after-width, border-start-color, border-start-style, border-start-width, border-end-color, border-end-style, border-end-width, border-top-color, border-top-style, border-top-width, border-bottom-color, border-bottom-style, border-bottom-width, border-left-color, border-left-style, border-left-width, border-right-color, border-right-style, border-right-width, padding-before, padding-after, padding-start, padding-end, padding-top, padding-bottom, padding-left, padding-right, font-family, font-selection-strategy, font-size, font-stretch, font-size-adjust, font-style, font-variant, font-weight, relative-position, color, id, letter-spacing, line-height, score-spaces, text-decoration, text-shadow, text-transform, word-spacing	
fo:external-graphic	[7.6 Common Aural Properties], source-document, role, background-attachment, background-color, background-image, background-repeat, background-position-horizontal, background-position-vertical, border-before-color, border-before-style, border-before-width, border-after-color, border-after-style, border-after-width, border-start-color, border-start-style, border-start-width, border-end-color, border-end-style, border-end-width, border-top-color, border-top-style, border-top-width, border-bottom-color, border-bottom-style, border-bottom-width, border-left-color, border-left-style, border-left-width, border-right-color, border-right-style, border-right-width, padding-before, padding-after, padding-start, padding-end, padding-top, padding-bottom, padding-left, padding-right, margin-top, margin-bottom, margin-left, margin-right, space-before, space-after, start-indent, end-indent, relative-position, alignment-adjust, alignment-baseline, baseline-shift, block-progression-dimension, clip, content-height, content-type, content-width, display-align, dominant-baseline, height, id, inline-progression-dimension, keep-with-next, keep-with-previous, line-height, overflow, scaling, scaling-method, src, text-align, width	

Element	Properties	Comments
fo:instream-foreign-object	[7.6 Common Aural Properties], source-document, role, background-attachment, background-color, background-image, background-repeat, background-position-horizontal, background-position-vertical, border-before-color, border-before-style, border-before-width, border-after-color, border-after-style, border-after-width, border-start-color, border-start-style, border-start-width, border-end-color, border-end-style, border-end-width, border-top-color, border-top-style, border-top-width, border-bottom-color, border-bottom-style, border-bottom-width, border-left-color, border-left-style, border-left-width, border-right-color, border-right-style, border-right-width, padding-before, padding-after, padding-start, padding-end, padding-top, padding-bottom, padding-left, padding-right, space-end, space-start, relative-position, alignment-adjust, alignment-baseline, baseline-shift, block-progression-dimension, clip, content-height, content-type, content-width, display-align, dominant-baseline, height, id, inline-progression-dimension, keep-with-next, keep-with-previous, line-height, overflow, scaling, scaling-method, text-align, width	
fo:inline	[7.6 Common Aural Properties], source-document, role, background-attachment, background-color, background-image, background-repeat, background-position-horizontal, background-position-vertical, border-before-color, border-before-style, border-before-width, border-after-color, border-after-style, border-after-width, border-start-color, border-start-style, border-start-width, border-end-color, border-end-style, border-end-width, border-top-color, border-top-style, border-top-width, border-bottom-color, border-bottom-style, border-bottom-width, border-left-color, border-left-style, border-left-width, border-right-color, border-right-style, border-right-width, padding-before, padding-after, padding-start, padding-end, padding-top, padding-bottom, padding-left, padding-right, font-family, font-selection-strategy, font-size, font-stretch, font-size-adjust, font-style, font-variant, font-weight, space-end, space-start, relative-position, alignment-adjust, alignment-baseline, baseline-shift, block-progression-dimension, color, dominant-baseline, height, id, inline-progression-dimension, keep-together, keep-with-next, keep-with-previous, line-height, text-decoration, visibility, width, wrap-option	
fo:inline-container	background-attachment, background-color, background-image, background-repeat, background-position-horizontal, background-position-vertical, border-before-color, border-before-style, border-before-width, border-after-color, border-after-style, border-after-width, border-start-color, border-start-style, border-start-width, border-end-color, border-end-style, border-end-width, border-top-color, border-top-style, border-top-width, border-bottom-color, border-bottom-style, border-bottom-width, border-left-color, border-left-style, border-left-width, border-right-color, border-right-style, border-right-width, padding-before, padding-after, padding-start, padding-end, padding-top, padding-bottom, padding-left, padding-right, space-end, space-start, relative-position, alignment-adjust, alignment-baseline, baseline-shift, block-progression-dimension, clip, display-align, dominant-baseline,xe, height, id, inline-progression-dimension, keep-together, keep-with-next, keep-with-previous, line-height, overflow, reference-orientation, width, writing-mode	

Element	Properties	Comments
fo:leader	[7.6 Common Aural Properties], source-document, role, background-attachment, background-color, background-image, background-repeat, background-position-horizontal, background-position-vertical, border-before-color, border-before-style, border-before-width, border-after-color, border-after-style, border-after-width, border-start-color, border-start-style, border-start-width, border-end-color, border-end-style, border-end-width, border-top-color, border-top-style, border-top-width, border-bottom-color, border-bottom-style, border-bottom-width, border-left-color, border-left-style, border-left-width, border-right-color, border-right-style, border-right-width, padding-before, padding-after, padding-start, padding-end, padding-top, padding-bottom, padding-left, padding-right, font-family, font-selection-strategy, font-size, font-stretch, font-size-adjust, font-style, font-variant, font-weight, space-end, space-start, relative-position, alignment-adjust, alignment-baseline, baseline-shift, color, dominant-baseline, text-depth, text-altitude, id, keep-with-next, keep-with-previous, leader-alignment, leader-length, leader-pattern, leader-pattern-width, rule-style, rule-thickness, letter-spacing, line-height, text-shadow, visibility, word-spacing	
fo:page-number	[7.6 Common Aural Properties], source-document, role, background-attachment, background-color, background-image, background-repeat, background-position-horizontal, background-position-vertical, border-before-color, border-before-style, border-before-width, border-after-color, border-after-style, border-after-width, border-start-color, border-start-style, border-start-width, border-end-color, border-end-style, border-end-width, border-top-color, border-top-style, border-top-width, border-bottom-color, border-bottom-style, border-bottom-width, border-left-color, border-left-style, border-left-width, border-right-color, border-right-style, border-right-width, padding-before, padding-after, padding-start, padding-end, padding-top, padding-bottom, padding-left, padding-right, font-family, font-selection-strategy, font-size, font-stretch, font-size-adjust, font-style, font-variant, font-weight, space-end, space-start, relative-position, alignment-adjust, alignment-baseline, baseline-shift, dominant-baseline, id, keep-with-next, keep-with-previous, letter-spacing, line-height, score-spaces, text-altitude, text-decoration, text-depth, text-shadow, text-transform, visibility, word-spacing, wrap-option	The conversion properties are: [7.24.1 "format"], [7.24.2 "grouping-separator"], [7.24.3 "grouping-size"], [7.24.4 "letter-value"], [7.9.1 "country"], and [7.9.2 "language"].
fo:page-number-citation	[7.6 Common Aural Properties], source-document, role, background-attachment, background-color, background-image, background-repeat, background-position-horizontal, background-position-vertical, border-before-color, border-before-style, border-before-width, border-after-color, border-after-style, border-after-width, border-start-color, border-start-style, border-start-width, border-end-color, border-end-style, border-end-width, border-top-color, border-top-style, border-top-width, border-bottom-color, border-bottom-style, border-bottom-width, border-left-color, border-left-style, border-left-width, border-right-color, border-right-style, border-right-width, padding-before, padding-after, padding-start, padding-end, padding-top, padding-bottom, padding-left, padding-right, font-family, font-selection-strategy, font-size, font-stretch, font-size-adjust, font-style, font-variant, font-weight, space-end, space-start, relative-position, alignment-adjust, alignment-baseline, baseline-shift, dominant-baseline, id, keep-with-next, keep-with-previous, letter-spacing, line-height, ref-id, score-spaces, text-altitude, text-decoration, text-depth, text-shadow, text-transform, visibility, word-spacing, wrap-option	

Element	Properties	Comments
fo:table-and-caption	[7.6 Common Aural Properties], source-document, role, background-attachment, background-color, background-image, background-repeat, background-position-horizontal, background-position-vertical, border-before-color, border-before-style, border-before-width, border-after-color, border-after-style, border-after-width, border-start-color, border-start-style, border-start-width, border-end-color, border-end-style, border-end-width, border-top-color, border-top-style, border-top-width, border-bottom-color, border-bottom-style, border-bottom-width, border-left-color, border-left-style, border-left-width, border-right-color, border-right-style, border-right-width, padding-before, padding-after, padding-start, padding-end, padding-top, padding-bottom, padding-left, padding-right, margin-top, margin-bottom, margin-left, margin-right, space-before, space-after, start-indent, end-indent, space-end, space-start, relative-position, break-after, break-before, caption-side, id, intrusion-displace, keep-together, keep-with-next, keep-with-previous, text-align	
fo:table	[7.6 Common Aural Properties], source-document, role, background-attachment, background-color, background-image, background-repeat, background-position-horizontal, background-position-vertical, border-before-color, border-before-style, border-before-width, border-after-color, border-after-style, border-after-width, border-start-color, border-start-style, border-start-width, border-end-color, border-end-style, border-end-width, border-top-color, border-top-style, border-top-width, border-bottom-color, border-bottom-style, border-bottom-width, border-left-color, border-left-style, border-left-width, border-right-color, border-right-style, border-right-width, padding-before, padding-after, padding-start, padding-end, padding-top, padding-bottom, padding-left, padding-right, margin-top, margin-bottom, margin-left, margin-right, space-before, space-after, start-indent, end-indent, space-end, space-start, relative-position, block-progression-dimension, border-after-precedence, border-before-precedence, border-collapse, border-end-precedence, border-separation, border-start-precedence, break-after, break-before, id, inline-progression-dimension, intrusion-displace, height, keep-together, keep-with-next, keep-with-previous, table-layout, table-omit-footer-at-break, table-omit-header-at-break, width, writing-mode	
fo:table-column	background-attachment, background-color, background-image, background-repeat, background-position-horizontal, background-position-vertical, border-after-precedence, border-before-precedence, border-end-precedence, border-start-precedence, column-number, column-width, number-columns-repeated, number-columns-spanned, visibility	If the value of border-collapse is "collapse" or "collapse-with-precedence" for the table the border properties also apply.

Element	Properties	Comments
fo:table-caption	[7.6 Common Aural Properties], source-document, role, background-attachment, background-color, background-image, background-repeat, background-position-horizontal, background-position-vertical, border-before-color, border-before-style, border-before-width, border-after-color, border-after-style, border-after-width, border-start-color, border-start-style, border-start-width, border-end-color, border-end-style, border-end-width, border-top-color, border-top-style, border-top-width, border-bottom-color, border-bottom-style, border-bottom-width, border-left-color, border-left-style, border-left-width, border-right-color, border-right-style, border-right-width, padding-before, padding-after, padding-start, padding-end, padding-top, padding-bottom, padding-left, padding-right, relative-position, block-progression-dimension, height, id, inline-progression-dimension, intrusion-displace, keep-together, width	
fo:table-header	[7.6 Common Aural Properties], source-document, role, background-attachment, background-color, background-image, background-repeat, background-position-horizontal, background-position-vertical, relative-position, border-after-precedence, border-before-precedence, border-end-precedence, border-start-precedence, id, visibility	If the value of border-collapse is "collapse" or "collapse-with-precedence" for the table the border properties also apply.
fo:table-footer	[7.6 Common Aural Properties], source-document, role, background-attachment, background-color, background-image, background-repeat, background-position-horizontal, background-position-vertical, relative-position, border-after-precedence, border-before-precedence, border-end-precedence, border-start-precedence, id, visibility	If the value of border-collapse is "collapse" or "collapse-with-precedence" for the table the border properties also apply.
fo:table-body	[7.6 Common Aural Properties], source-document, role, background-attachment, background-color, background-image, background-repeat, background-position-horizontal, background-position-vertical, border-after-precedence, border-before-precedence, border-end-precedence, border-start-precedence, id, visibility	If the value of border-collapse is "collapse" or "collapse-with-precedence" for the table the border properties also apply.

Table G-1. Properties (continued)

Element	Properties	Comments
fo:table-row	[7.6 Common Aural Properties], source-document, role, block-progression-dimension, background-attachment, background-color, background-image, background-repeat, background-position-horizontal, background-position-vertical, border-before-color, border-before-style, border-before-width, border-after-color, border-after-style, border-after-width, border-start-color, border-start-style, border-start-width, border-end-color, border-end-style, border-end-width, border-top-color, border-top-style, border-top-width, border-bottom-color, border-bottom-style, border-bottom-width, border-left-color, border-left-style, border-left-width, border-right-color, border-right-style, border-right-width, padding-before, padding-after, padding-start, padding-end, padding-top, padding-bottom, padding-left, padding-right, background-attachment, background-color, background-image, background-repeat, background-position-horizontal, background-position-vertical, relative-position, border-after-precedence, border-before-precedence, border-end-precedence, border-start-precedence, break-after, break-before, id, height, keep-together, keep-with-next, keep-with-previous, visibility	If the value of border-collapse is "collapse" or "collapse-with-precedence" for the table the border properties also apply.
fo:table-cell	[7.6 Common Aural Properties] source-document, role, background-attachment, background-color, background-image, background-repeat, background-position-horizontal, background-position-vertical, border-before-color, border-before-style, border-before-width, border-after-color, border-after-style, border-after-width, border-start-color, border-start-style, border-start-width, border-end-color, border-end-style, border-end-width, border-top-color, border-top-style, border-top-width, border-bottom-color, border-bottom-style, border-bottom-width, border-left-color, border-left-style, border-left-width, border-right-color, border-right-style, border-right-width, padding-before, padding-after, padding-start, padding-end, padding-top, padding-bottom, padding-left, padding-right, relative-position, border-after-precedence, border-before-precedence, border-end-precedence, border-start-precedence, block-progression-dimension, column-number, display-align, relative-align, empty-cells, ends-row, height, id, inline-progression-dimension, number-columns-spanned, number-rows-spanned, starts-row, width,	
fo:list-block	[7.6 Common Aural Properties], source-document, role, background-attachment, background-color, background-image, background-repeat, background-position-horizontal, background-position-vertical, border-before-color, border-before-style, border-before-width, border-after-color, border-after-style, border-after-width, border-start-color, border-start-style, border-start-width, border-end-color, border-end-style, border-end-width, border-top-color, border-top-style, border-top-width, border-bottom-color, border-bottom-style, border-bottom-width, border-left-color, border-left-style, border-left-width, border-right-color, border-right-style, border-right-width, padding-before, padding-after, padding-start, padding-end, padding-top, padding-bottom, padding-left, padding-right, relative-position, margin-top, margin-bottom, margin-left, margin-right, space-before, space-after, start-indent, end-indent, break-after, break-before, id, intrusion-displace, keep-together, keep-with-next, keep-with-previous, provisional-distance-between-starts, provisional-label-separation	

Element	Properties	Comments
fo:list-item	[7.6 Common Aural Properties], source-document, role, background-attachment, background-color, background-image, background-repeat, background-position-horizontal, background-position-vertical, border-before-color, border-before-style, border-before-width, border-after-color, border-after-style, border-after-width, border-start-color, border-start-style, border-start-width, border-end-color, border-end-style, border-end-width, border-top-color, border-top-style, border-top-width, border-bottom-color, border-bottom-style, border-bottom-width, border-left-color, border-left-style, border-left-width, border-right-color, border-right-style, border-right-width, padding-before, padding-after, padding-start, padding-end, padding-top, padding-bottom, padding-left, padding-right, relative-position, margin-top, margin-bottom, margin-left, margin-right, space-before, space-after, start-indent, end-indent, relative-position, break-after, break-before, id, intrusion-displace, keep-together, keep-with-next, keep-with-previous, relative-align	
fo:list-item-body	source-document, role, id, keep-together	
fo:list-item-label	source-document, role, id, keep-together	
fo:basic-link	[7.6 Common Aural Properties], source-document, role, background-attachment, background-color, background-image, background-repeat, background-position-horizontal, background-position-vertical, border-before-color, border-before-style, border-before-width, border-after-color, border-after-style, border-after-width, border-start-color, border-start-style, border-start-width, border-end-color, border-end-style, border-end-width, border-top-color, border-top-style, border-top-width, border-bottom-color, border-bottom-style, border-bottom-width, border-left-color, border-left-style, border-left-width, border-right-color, border-right-style, border-right-width, padding-before, padding-after, padding-start, padding-end, padding-top, padding-bottom, padding-left, padding-right, space-end, space-start, relative-position, alignment-adjust, alignment-baseline, baseline-shift, destination-placement-offset, dominant-baseline, external-destination, id, indicate-destination, internal-destination, keep-together, keep-with-next, keep-with-previous, line-height, show-destination, target-processing-context, target-presentation-context, target-stylesheet	
fo:multi-switch	source-document, role, auto-restore, id	
fo:multi-case	source-document, role, id, starting-state, case-name, case-title	
fo:multi-toggle	source-document, role, id, switch-to	
fo:multi-properties	source-document, role, id,	
fo:multi-property-set	id, active-state	
fo:float	float, clear	
fo:footnote	source-document, role	
fo:footnote-body	source-document, role	
fo:wrapper	id	
fo:marker	marker-class-name	
fo:retrieve-marker	retrieve-class-name, retrieve-position, retrieve-boundary	

Properties and the Elements to Which They Apply

Table G-2. Properties to elements

Property	Applies to
media-usage	fo:root
color-profile-name	fo:color-profile
rendering-intent	fo:color-profile
src	fo:color-profile, fo:external-graphic
country	fo:page-sequence, fo:block, fo:character
force-page-count	fo:page-sequence
format	fo:page-sequence
grouping-separator	fo:page-sequence
grouping-size	fo:page-sequence
id	fo:page-sequence, fo:block, fo:block-container, fo:bidi-override, fo:character, fo:initial-property-set, fo:external-graphic, fo:instream-foreign-object, fo:inline, fo:inline-container, fo:leader, fo:page-number, fo:page-number-citation, fo:table-and-caption, fo:table, fo:table-caption, fo:table-header, fo:table-footer, fo:table-body, fo:table-row, fo:table-cell, fo:list-block, fo:list-item, fo:list-item-body, fo:list-item-label, fo:basic-link, fo:multi-switch, fo:multi-case, fo:multi-toggle, fo:multi-properties, fo:multi-property-set, fo:wrapper
initial-page-number	fo:page-sequence
language	fo:page-sequence, fo:block, fo:character
letter-value	fo:page-sequence
master-reference	fo:page-sequence, fo:single-page-master-reference, fo:repeatable-page-master-reference, fo:conditional-page-master-reference
master-name	fo:page-sequence-master, fo:simple-page-master
maximum-repeats	fo:repeatable-page-master-reference, fo:repeatable-page-master-alternatives
blank-or-not-blank	fo:conditional-page-master-reference
odd-or-even	fo:conditional-page-master-reference
page-position	fo:conditional-page-master-reference
end-indent	fo:simple-page-master, fo:region-body, fo:block, fo:block-container, fo:external-graphic, fo:table-and-caption, fo:table, fo:list-block, fo:list-item
margin-bottom	fo:simple-page-master, fo:region-body, fo:block, fo:block-container, fo:external-graphic, fo:table-and-caption, fo:table, fo:list-block, fo:list-item
margin-left	fo:simple-page-master, fo:region-body, fo:block, fo:block-container, fo:external-graphic, fo:table-and-caption, fo:table, fo:list-block, fo:list-item
margin-right	fo:simple-page-master, fo:region-body, fo:block, fo:block-container, fo:external-graphic, fo:table-and-caption, fo:table, fo:list-block, fo:list-item
margin-top	fo:simple-page-master, fo:block, fo:block-container, fo:external-graphic, fo:table-and-caption, fo:table, fo:list-block, fo:list-item
page-height	fo:simple-page-master

Property	Applies to
page-width	fo:simple-page-master
reference-orientation	fo:simple-page-master, fo:region-body, fo:region-before, fo:region-after, fo:region-start, fo:region-end, fo:block-container, fo:inline-container
space-after	fo:simple-page-master, fo:region-body, fo:block, fo:block-container, fo:external-graphic, fo:table-and-caption, fo:table, fo:list-block, fo:list-item
space-before	fo:simple-page-master, fo:region-body, fo:block, fo:block-container, fo:external-graphic, fo:table-and-caption, fo:table, fo:list-block, fo:list-item
start-indent	fo:simple-page-master, fo:region-body, fo:block, fo:block-container, fo:external-graphic, fo:table-and-caption, fo:table, fo:list-block, fo:list-item
writing-mode	fo:simple-page-master, fo:region-body, fo:region-before, fo:region-after, fo:region-start, fo:region-end, fo:block-container, fo:inline-container, fo:table
background-attachment	fo:region-body, fo:region-before, fo:region-after, fo:region-start, fo:region-end, fo:title, fo:block, fo:block-container, fo:character, fo:initial-property-set, fo:external-graphic, fo:instream-foreign-object, fo:inline, fo:inline-container, fo:leader, fo:page-number, fo:page-number-citation, fo:table-and-caption, fo:table, fo:table-column, fo:table-caption, fo:table-header, fo:table-footer, fo:table-body, fo:table-row, fo:table-cell, fo:list-block, fo:list-item, fo:basic-link
background-color	fo:region-body, fo:region-before, fo:region-after, fo:region-start, fo:region-end, fo:title, fo:block, fo:block-container, fo:character, fo:initial-property-set, fo:external-graphic, fo:instream-foreign-object, fo:inline, fo:inline-container, fo:leader, fo:page-number, fo:page-number-citation, fo:table-and-caption, fo:table, fo:table-column, fo:table-caption, fo:table-header, fo:table-footer, fo:table-body, fo:table-row, fo:table-cell, fo:list-block, fo:list-item, fo:basic-link
background-image	fo:region-body, fo:region-before, fo:region-after, fo:region-start, fo:region-end, fo:title, fo:block, fo:block-container, fo:character, fo:initial-property-set, fo:external-graphic, fo:instream-foreign-object, fo:inline, fo:inline-container, fo:leader, fo:page-number, fo:page-number-citation, fo:table-and-caption, fo:table, fo:table-column, fo:table-caption, fo:table-header, fo:table-footer, fo:table-body, fo:table-row, fo:table-cell, fo:list-block, fo:list-item, fo:basic-link
background-position-horizontal	fo:region-body, fo:region-before, fo:region-after, fo:region-start, fo:region-end, fo:title, fo:block, fo:block-container, fo:character, fo:initial-property-set, fo:external-graphic, fo:instream-foreign-object, fo:inline, fo:inline-container, fo:leader, fo:page-number, fo:page-number-citation, fo:table-and-caption, fo:table, fo:table-column, fo:table-caption, fo:table-header, fo:table-footer, fo:table-body, fo:table-row, fo:table-cell, fo:list-block, fo:list-item, fo:basic-link
background-position-vertical	fo:region-body, fo:region-before, fo:region-after, fo:region-start, fo:region-end, fo:title, fo:block, fo:block-container, fo:character, fo:initial-property-set, fo:external-graphic, fo:instream-foreign-object, fo:inline, fo:inline-container, fo:leader, fo:page-number, fo:page-number-citation, fo:table-and-caption, fo:table, fo:table-column, fo:table-caption, fo:table-header, fo:table-footer, fo:table-body, fo:table-row, fo:table-cell, fo:list-block, fo:list-item, fo:basic-link

Table G-2. Properties to elements (continued)

Property	Applies to
background-repeat	fo:region-body, fo:region-before, fo:region-after, fo:region-start, fo:region-end, fo:title, fo:block, fo:block-container, fo:character, fo:initial-property-set, fo:external-graphic, fo:instream-foreign-object, fo:inline, fo:inline-container, fo:leader, fo:page-number, fo:page-number-citation, fo:table-and-caption, fo:table, fo:table-column, fo:table-caption, fo:table-header, fo:table-footer, fo:table-body, fo:table-row, fo:table-cell, fo:list-block, fo:list-item, fo:basic-link
border-after-color	fo:region-body, fo:region-before, fo:region-after, fo:region-start, fo:region-end, fo:title, fo:block, fo:block-container, fo:character, fo:initial-property-set, fo:external-graphic, fo:instream-foreign-object, fo:inline, fo:inline-container, fo:leader, fo:page-number, fo:page-number-citation, fo:table-and-caption, fo:table, fo:table-caption, fo:table-row, fo:table-cell, fo:list-block, fo:list-item, fo:basic-link
border-after-style	fo:region-body, fo:region-before, fo:region-after, fo:region-start, fo:region-end, fo:title, fo:block, fo:block-container, fo:character, fo:initial-property-set, fo:external-graphic, fo:instream-foreign-object, fo:inline, fo:inline-container, fo:leader, fo:page-number, fo:page-number-citation, fo:table-and-caption, fo:table, fo:table-caption, fo:table-row, fo:table-cell, fo:list-block, fo:list-item, fo:basic-link
border-after-width	fo:region-body, fo:region-before, fo:region-after, fo:region-start, fo:region-end, fo:title, fo:block, fo:block-container, fo:character, fo:initial-property-set, fo:external-graphic, fo:instream-foreign-object, fo:inline, fo:inline-container, fo:leader, fo:page-number, fo:page-number-citation, fo:table-and-caption, fo:table, fo:table-caption, fo:table-row, fo:table-cell, fo:list-block, fo:list-item, fo:basic-link
border-before-color	fo:region-body, fo:region-before, fo:region-after, fo:region-start, fo:region-end, fo:title, fo:block, fo:block-container, fo:character, fo:initial-property-set, fo:external-graphic, fo:instream-foreign-object, fo:inline, fo:inline-container, fo:leader, fo:page-number, fo:page-number-citation, fo:table-and-caption, fo:table, fo:table-caption, fo:table-row, fo:table-cell, fo:list-block, fo:list-item, fo:basic-link
border-before-style	fo:region-body, fo:region-before, fo:region-after, fo:region-start, fo:region-end, fo:title, fo:block, fo:block-container, fo:character, fo:initial-property-set, fo:external-graphic, fo:instream-foreign-object, fo:inline, fo:inline-container, fo:leader, fo:page-number, fo:page-number-citation, fo:table-and-caption, fo:table, fo:table-caption, fo:table-row, fo:table-cell, fo:list-block, fo:list-item, fo:basic-link
border-before-width	fo:region-body, fo:region-before, fo:region-after, fo:region-start, fo:region-end, fo:title, fo:block, fo:block-container, fo:character, fo:initial-property-set, fo:external-graphic, fo:instream-foreign-object, fo:inline, fo:inline-container, fo:leader, fo:page-number, fo:page-number-citation, fo:table-and-caption, fo:table, fo:table-caption, fo:table-row, fo:table-cell, fo:list-block, fo:list-item, fo:basic-link
border-bottom-color	fo:region-body, fo:region-before, fo:region-after, fo:region-start, fo:region-end, fo:title, fo:block, fo:block-container, fo:character, fo:initial-property-set, fo:external-graphic, fo:instream-foreign-object, fo:inline, fo:inline-container, fo:leader, fo:page-number, fo:page-number-citation, fo:table-and-caption, fo:table, fo:table-caption, fo:table-row, fo:table-cell, fo:list-block, fo:list-item, fo:basic-link
border-bottom-style	fo:region-body, fo:region-before, fo:region-after, fo:region-start, fo:region-end, fo:title, fo:block, fo:block-container, fo:character, fo:initial-property-set, fo:external-graphic, fo:instream-foreign-object, fo:inline, fo:inline-container, fo:leader, fo:page-number, fo:page-number-citation, fo:table-and-caption, fo:table, fo:table-caption, fo:table-row, fo:table-cell, fo:list-block, fo:list-item, fo:basic-link

Property	Applies to
border-bottom-width	fo:region-body, fo:region-before, fo:region-after, fo:region-start, fo:region-end, fo:title, fo:block, fo:block-container, fo:character, fo:initial-property-set, fo:external-graphic, fo:instream-foreign-object, fo:inline, fo:inline-container, fo:leader, fo:page-number, fo:page-number-citation, fo:table-and-caption, fo:table, fo:table-caption, fo:table-row, fo:table-cell, fo:list-block, fo:list-item, fo:basic-link
border-end-color	fo:region-body, fo:region-before, fo:region-after, fo:region-start, fo:region-end, fo:title, fo:block, fo:block-container, fo:character, fo:initial-property-set, fo:external-graphic, fo:instream-foreign-object, fo:inline, fo:inline-container, fo:leader, fo:page-number, fo:page-number-citation, fo:table-and-caption, fo:table, fo:table-caption, fo:table-row, fo:table-cell, fo:list-block, fo:list-item, fo:basic-link
border-end-style	fo:region-body, fo:region-before, fo:region-after, fo:region-start, fo:region-end, fo:title, fo:block, fo:block-container, fo:character, fo:initial-property-set, fo:external-graphic, fo:instream-foreign-object, fo:inline, fo:inline-container, fo:leader, fo:page-number, fo:page-number-citation, fo:table-and-caption, fo:table, fo:table-caption, fo:table-row, fo:table-cell, fo:list-block, fo:list-item, fo:basic-link
border-end-width	fo:region-body, fo:region-before, fo:region-after, fo:region-start, fo:region-end, fo:title, fo:block, fo:block-container, fo:character, fo:initial-property-set, fo:external-graphic, fo:instream-foreign-object, fo:inline, fo:inline-container, fo:leader, fo:page-number, fo:page-number-citation, fo:table-and-caption, fo:table, fo:table-caption, fo:table-row, fo:table-cell, fo:list-block, fo:list-item, fo:basic-link
border-left-color	fo:region-body, fo:region-before, fo:region-after, fo:region-start, fo:region-end, fo:title, fo:block, fo:block-container, fo:character, fo:initial-property-set, fo:external-graphic, fo:instream-foreign-object, fo:inline, fo:inline-container, fo:leader, fo:page-number, fo:page-number-citation, fo:table-and-caption, fo:table, fo:table-caption, fo:table-row, fo:table-cell, fo:list-block, fo:list-item, fo:basic-link
border-left-style	fo:region-body, fo:region-before, fo:region-after, fo:region-start, fo:region-end, fo:title, fo:block, fo:block-container, fo:character, fo:initial-property-set, fo:external-graphic, fo:instream-foreign-object, fo:inline, fo:inline-container, fo:leader, fo:page-number, fo:page-number-citation, fo:table-and-caption, fo:table, fo:table-caption, fo:table-row, fo:table-cell, fo:list-block, fo:list-item, fo:basic-link
border-left-width	fo:region-body, fo:region-before, fo:region-after, fo:region-start, fo:region-end, fo:title, fo:block, fo:block-container, fo:character, fo:initial-property-set, fo:external-graphic, fo:instream-foreign-object, fo:inline, fo:inline-container, fo:leader, fo:page-number, fo:page-number-citation, fo:table-and-caption, fo:table, fo:table-caption, fo:table-row, fo:table-cell, fo:list-block, fo:list-item, fo:basic-link
border-right-color	fo:region-body, fo:region-before, fo:region-after, fo:region-start, fo:region-end, fo:title, fo:block, fo:block-container, fo:character, fo:initial-property-set, fo:external-graphic, fo:instream-foreign-object, fo:inline, fo:inline-container, fo:leader, fo:page-number, fo:page-number-citation, fo:table-and-caption, fo:table, fo:table-caption, fo:table-row, fo:table-cell, fo:list-block, fo:list-item, fo:basic-link
border-right-style	fo:region-body, fo:region-before, fo:region-after, fo:region-start, fo:region-end, fo:title, fo:block, fo:block-container, fo:character, fo:initial-property-set, fo:external-graphic, fo:instream-foreign-object, fo:inline, fo:inline-container, fo:leader, fo:page-number, fo:page-number-citation, fo:table-and-caption, fo:table, fo:table-caption, fo:table-row, fo:table-cell, fo:list-block, fo:list-item, fo:basic-link

Table G-2. Properties to elements (continued)

Property	Applies to
border-right-width	fo:region-body, fo:region-before, fo:region-after, fo:region-start, fo:region-end, fo:title, fo:block, fo:block-container, fo:character, fo:initial-property-set, fo:external-graphic, fo:instream-foreign-object, fo:inline, fo:inline-container, fo:leader, fo:page-number, fo:page-number-citation, fo:table-and-caption, fo:table, fo:table-caption, fo:table-row, fo:table-cell, fo:list-block, fo:list-item, fo:basic-link
border-start-color	fo:region-body, fo:region-before, fo:region-after, fo:region-start, fo:region-end, fo:title, fo:block, fo:block-container, fo:character, fo:initial-property-set, fo:external-graphic, fo:instream-foreign-object, fo:inline, fo:inline-container, fo:leader, fo:page-number, fo:page-number-citation, fo:table-and-caption, fo:table, fo:table-caption, fo:table-row, fo:table-cell, fo:list-block, fo:list-item, fo:basic-link
border-start-style	fo:region-body, fo:region-before, fo:region-after, fo:region-start, fo:region-end, fo:title, fo:block, fo:block-container, fo:character, fo:initial-property-set, fo:external-graphic, fo:instream-foreign-object, fo:inline, fo:inline-container, fo:leader, fo:page-number, fo:page-number-citation, fo:table-and-caption, fo:table, fo:table-caption, fo:table-row, fo:table-cell, fo:list-block, fo:list-item, fo:basic-link
border-start-width	fo:region-body, fo:region-before, fo:region-after, fo:region-start, fo:region-end, fo:title, fo:block, fo:block-container, fo:character, fo:initial-property-set, fo:external-graphic, fo:instream-foreign-object, fo:inline, fo:inline-container, fo:leader, fo:page-number, fo:page-number-citation, fo:table-and-caption, fo:table, fo:table-caption, fo:table-row, fo:table-cell, fo:list-block, fo:list-item, fo:basic-link
border-top-color	fo:region-body, fo:region-before, fo:region-after, fo:region-start, fo:region-end, fo:title, fo:block, fo:block-container, fo:character, fo:initial-property-set, fo:external-graphic, fo:instream-foreign-object, fo:inline, fo:inline-container, fo:leader, fo:page-number, fo:page-number-citation, fo:table-and-caption, fo:table, fo:table-caption, fo:table-row, fo:table-cell, fo:list-block, fo:list-item, fo:basic-link
border-top-style	fo:region-body, fo:region-before, fo:region-after, fo:region-start, fo:region-end, fo:title, fo:block, fo:block-container, fo:character, fo:initial-property-set, fo:external-graphic, fo:instream-foreign-object, fo:inline, fo:inline-container, fo:leader, fo:page-number, fo:page-number-citation, fo:table-and-caption, fo:table, fo:table-caption, fo:table-row, fo:table-cell, fo:list-block, fo:list-item, fo:basic-link
border-top-width	fo:region-body, fo:region-before, fo:region-after, fo:region-start, fo:region-end, fo:title, fo:block, fo:block-container, fo:character, fo:initial-property-set, fo:external-graphic, fo:instream-foreign-object, fo:inline, fo:inline-container, fo:leader, fo:page-number, fo:page-number-citation, fo:table-and-caption, fo:table, fo:table-caption, fo:table-row, fo:table-cell, fo:list-block, fo:list-item, fo:basic-link
clip	fo:region-body, fo:block-container, fo:external-graphic, fo:instream-foreign-object, fo:inline-container
column-count	fo:region-body
column-gap	fo:region-body
display-align	fo:region-body, fo:region-before, fo:region-after, fo:region-start, fo:region-end, fo:block-container, fo:external-graphic, fo:instream-foreign-object, fo:inline-container, fo:table-cell
overflow	fo:region-body, fo:region-before, fo:region-after, fo:region-start, fo:region-end, fo:block-container, fo:external-graphic, fo:instream-foreign-object, fo:inline-container

Table G-2. Properties to elements (continued)

Property	Applies to
padding-after	fo:region-body, fo:region-before, fo:region-after, fo:region-start, fo:region-end, fo:title, fo:block, fo:block-container, fo:character, fo:initial-property-set, fo:external-graphic, fo:instream-foreign-object, fo:inline, fo:inline-container, fo:leader, fo:page-number, fo:page-number-citation, fo:table-and-caption, fo:table, fo:table-caption, fo:table-row, fo:table-cell, fo:list-block, fo:list-item, fo:basic-link
padding-before	fo:region-body, fo:region-before, fo:region-after, fo:region-start, fo:region-end, fo:title, fo:block, fo:block-container, fo:character, fo:initial-property-set, fo:external-graphic, fo:instream-foreign-object, fo:inline, fo:inline-container, fo:leader, fo:page-number, fo:page-number-citation, fo:table-and-caption, fo:table, fo:table-caption, fo:table-row, fo:table-cell, fo:list-block, fo:list-item, fo:basic-link
padding-bottom	fo:region-body, fo:region-before, fo:region-after, fo:region-start, fo:region-end, fo:title, fo:block, fo:block-container, fo:character, fo:initial-property-set, fo:external-graphic, fo:instream-foreign-object, fo:inline, fo:inline-container, fo:leader, fo:page-number, fo:page-number-citation, fo:table-and-caption, fo:table, fo:table-caption, fo:table-row, fo:table-cell, fo:list-block, fo:list-item, fo:basic-link
padding-end	fo:region-body, fo:region-before, fo:region-after, fo:region-start, fo:region-end, fo:title, fo:block, fo:block-container, fo:character, fo:initial-property-set, fo:external-graphic, fo:instream-foreign-object, fo:inline, fo:inline-container, fo:leader, fo:page-number, fo:page-number-citation, fo:table-and-caption, fo:table, fo:table-caption, fo:table-row, fo:table-cell, fo:list-block, fo:list-item, fo:basic-link
padding-left	fo:region-body, fo:region-before, fo:region-after, fo:region-start, fo:region-end, fo:title, fo:block, fo:block-container, fo:character, fo:initial-property-set, fo:external-graphic, fo:instream-foreign-object, fo:inline, fo:inline-container, fo:leader, fo:page-number, fo:page-number-citation, fo:table-and-caption, fo:table, fo:table-caption, fo:table-row, fo:table-cell, fo:list-block, fo:list-item, fo:basic-link
padding-right margin-top	fo:region-body
padding-start	fo:region-body, fo:region-before, fo:region-after, fo:region-start, fo:region-end, fo:title, fo:block, fo:block-container, fo:character, fo:initial-property-set, fo:external-graphic, fo:instream-foreign-object, fo:inline, fo:inline-container, fo:leader, fo:page-number, fo:page-number-citation, fo:table-and-caption, fo:table, fo:table-caption, fo:table-row, fo:table-cell, fo:list-block, fo:list-item, fo:basic-link
padding-top	fo:region-body, fo:region-before, fo:region-after, fo:region-start, fo:region-end, fo:title, fo:block, fo:block-container, fo:character, fo:initial-property-set, fo:external-graphic, fo:instream-foreign-object, fo:inline, fo:inline-container, fo:leader, fo:page-number, fo:page-number-citation, fo:table-and-caption, fo:table, fo:table-caption, fo:table-row, fo:table-cell, fo:list-block, fo:list-item, fo:basic-link
region-name	fo:region-body, fo:region-before, fo:region-after, fo:region-start, fo:region-end
extent	fo:region-before, fo:region-after, fo:region-start, fo:region-end
padding-right clip	fo:region-before, fo:region-after, fo:region-start, fo:region-end
precedence	fo:region-before, fo:region-after
flow-name	fo:flow, fo:static-content
[7.6 Common Aural Properties]	fo:title, fo:block, fo:bidi-override, fo:character, fo:initial-property-set, fo:external-graphic, fo:instream-foreign-object, fo:inline, fo:leader, fo:page-number, fo:page-number-citation, fo:table-and-caption, fo:table, fo:table-caption, fo:table-header, fo:table-footer, fo:table-body, fo:table-row, fo:list-block, fo:list-item, fo:basic-link

Property	Applies to
color	fo:title, fo:block, fo:bidi-override, fo:character, fo:initial-property-set, fo:inline, fo:leader
font-family	fo:title, fo:block, fo:bidi-override, fo:character, fo:initial-property-set, fo:inline, fo:leader, fo:page-number, fo:page-number-citation
font-selection-strategy	fo:title, fo:block, fo:bidi-override, fo:character, fo:initial-property-set, fo:inline, fo:leader, fo:page-number, fo:page-number-citation
font-size	fo:title, fo:block, fo:bidi-override, fo:character, fo:initial-property-set, fo:inline, fo:leader, fo:page-number, fo:page-number-citation
font-size-adjust	fo:title, fo:block, fo:bidi-override, fo:character, fo:initial-property-set, fo:inline, fo:leader, fo:page-number, fo:page-number-citation
font-stretch	fo:title, fo:block, fo:bidi-override, fo:character, fo:initial-property-set, fo:inline, fo:leader, fo:page-number, fo:page-number-citation
font-style	fo:title, fo:block, fo:bidi-override, fo:character, fo:initial-property-set, fo:inline, fo:leader, fo:page-number, fo:page-number-citation
font-variant	fo:title, fo:block, fo:bidi-override, fo:character, fo:initial-property-set, fo:inline, fo:leader, fo:page-number, fo:page-number-citation
font-weight	fo:title, fo:block, fo:bidi-override, fo:character, fo:initial-property-set, fo:inline, fo:leader, fo:page-number, fo:page-number-citation
line-height	fo:title, fo:block, fo:bidi-override, fo:initial-property-set, fo:external-graphic, fo:instream-foreign-object, fo:inline, fo:inline-container, fo:leader, fo:page-number, fo:page-number-citation, fo:basic-link
padding-right	fo:title, fo:block, fo:block-container, fo:character, fo:initial-property-set, fo:external-graphic, fo:instream-foreign-object, fo:inline, fo:inline-container, fo:leader, fo:page-number, fo:page-number-citation, fo:table-and-caption, fo:table, fo:table-caption, fo:table-row, fo:table-cell, fo:list-block, fo:list-item, fo:basic-link
role	fo:title, fo:block, fo:initial-property-set, fo:external-graphic, fo:instream-foreign-object, fo:inline, fo:leader, fo:page-number, fo:page-number-citation, fo:table-and-caption, fo:table, fo:table-caption, fo:table-header, fo:table-footer, fo:table-body, fo:table-row, fo:table-cell, fo:list-block, fo:list-item, fo:list-item-body, fo:list-item-label, fo:basic-link, fo:multi-switch, fo:multi-case, fo:multi-toggle, fo:multi-properties, fo:footnote, fo:footnote-body
source-document	fo:title, fo:block, fo:initial-property-set, fo:external-graphic, fo:instream-foreign-object, fo:inline, fo:leader, fo:page-number, fo:page-number-citation, fo:table-and-caption, fo:table, fo:table-caption, fo:table-header, fo:table-footer, fo:table-body, fo:table-row, fo:list-block, fo:list-item, fo:list-item-body, fo:list-item-label, fo:basic-link, fo:multi-switch, fo:multi-case, fo:multi-toggle, fo:multi-properties, fo:footnote, fo:footnote-body
space-end	fo:title, fo:character, fo:instream-foreign-object, fo:inline, fo:inline-container, fo:leader, fo:page-number, fo:page-number-citation, fo:table-and-caption, fo:table, fo:basic-link
space-start	fo:title, fo:character, fo:instream-foreign-object, fo:inline, fo:inline-container, fo:leader, fo:page-number, fo:page-number-citation, fo:table-and-caption, fo:table, fo:basic-link
visibility	fo:title, fo:block, fo:character, fo:inline, fo:leader, fo:page-number, fo:page-number-citation, fo:table-column, fo:table-header, fo:table-footer, fo:table-body, fo:table-row
break-after	fo:block, fo:block-container, fo:table-and-caption, fo:table, fo:table-row, fo:list-block, fo:list-item

Table G-2. Properties to elements (continued)

Property	Applies to
break-before	fo:block, fo:block-container, fo:table-and-caption, fo:table, fo:table-row, fo:list-block, fo:list-item
hyphenate	fo:block, fo:character
hyphenation-character	fo:block, fo:character
hyphenation-keep	fo:block
hyphenation-ladder-count	fo:block
hyphenation-push-character-count	fo:block, fo:character
hyphenation-remain-character-count	fo:block, fo:character
intrusion-displace	fo:block, fo:block-container, fo:table-and-caption, fo:table, fo:table-caption, fo:list-block, fo:list-item
keep-together	fo:block, fo:block-container, fo:inline, fo:inline-container, fo:table-and-caption, fo:table, fo:table-caption, fo:table-row, fo:list-block, fo:list-item, fo:list-item-body, fo:list-item-label, fo:basic-link
keep-with-next	fo:block, fo:block-container, fo:character, fo:external-graphic, fo:instream-foreign-object, fo:inline, fo:inline-container, fo:leader, fo:page-number, fo:page-number-citation, fo:table-and-caption, fo:table, fo:table-row, fo:list-block, fo:list-item, fo:basic-link
keep-with-previous	fo:block, fo:block-container, fo:character, fo:external-graphic, fo:instream-foreign-object, fo:inline, fo:inline-container, fo:leader, fo:page-number, fo:page-number-citation, fo:table-and-caption, fo:table, fo:table-row, fo:list-block, fo:list-item, fo:basic-link
last-line-end-indent	fo:block
line-height-shift-adjustment	fo:block
line-stacking-strategy	fo:block
linefeed-treatment	fo:block
orphans	fo:block
relative-position	fo:block, fo:bidi-override, fo:character, fo:initial-property-set, fo:external-graphic, fo:instream-foreign-object, fo:inline, fo:inline-container, fo:leader, fo:page-number, fo:page-number-citation, fo:table-and-caption, fo:table, fo:table-caption, fo:table-header, fo:table-footer, fo:table-row, fo:table-cell, fo:list-block, fo:list-item, fo:basic-link
script	fo:block, fo:character
span	fo:block, fo:block-container
text-align	fo:block, fo:external-graphic, fo:instream-foreign-object, fo:table-and-caption
text-align-last	fo:block
text-altitude	fo:block, fo:character, fo:leader, fo:page-number, fo:page-number-citation
text-depth	fo:block, fo:character, fo:leader, fo:page-number, fo:page-number-citation
text-indent	fo:block
white-space-collapse	fo:block
white-space-treatment	fo:block
widows	fo:block

Table G-2. Properties to elements (continued)

Property	Applies to
wrap-option	fo:block, fo:inline, fo:page-number, fo:page-number-citation
	fo:block-container, fo:table-cell, fo:multi-properties
absolute-position	fo:block-container
block-progression-dimension	fo:block-container, fo:external-graphic, fo:instream-foreign-object, fo:inline, fo:inline-container, fo:table, fo:table-caption, fo:table-row, fo:table-cell
bottom	fo:block-container
height	fo:block-container, fo:external-graphic, fo:instream-foreign-object, fo:inline, fo:inline-container, fo:table, fo:table-caption, fo:table-row, fo:table-cell
inline-progression-dimension	fo:block-container, fo:external-graphic, fo:instream-foreign-object, fo:inline, fo:inline-container, fo:table, fo:table-caption, fo:table-cell
left	fo:block-container
right	fo:block-container
top	fo:block-container
width	fo:block-container, fo:external-graphic, fo:instream-foreign-object, fo:inline, fo:inline-container, fo:table, fo:table-caption, fo:table-cell
z-index	fo:block-container
direction	fo:bidi-override
letter-spacing	fo:bidi-override, fo:character, fo:initial-property-set, fo:leader, fo:page-number, fo:page-number-citation
score-spaces	fo:bidi-override, fo:initial-property-set, fo:page-number, fo:page-number-citation
unicode-bidi	fo:bidi-override
word-spacing	fo:bidi-override, fo:character, fo:initial-property-set, fo:leader, fo:page-number, fo:page-number-citation
alignment-adjust	fo:character, fo:external-graphic, fo:instream-foreign-object, fo:inline, fo:inline-container, fo:leader, fo:page-number, fo:page-number-citation, fo:basic-link
alignment-baseline	fo:character, fo:external-graphic, fo:instream-foreign-object, fo:inline, fo:inline-container, fo:leader, fo:page-number, fo:page-number-citation, fo:basic-link
baseline-shift	fo:character, fo:external-graphic, fo:instream-foreign-object, fo:inline, fo:inline-container, fo:leader, fo:page-number, fo:page-number-citation, fo:basic-link
character	fo:character
dominant-baseline	fo:character, fo:external-graphic, fo:instream-foreign-object, fo:inline, fo:inline-container, fo:leader, fo:page-number, fo:page-number-citation, fo:basic-link
glyph-orientation-horizontal	fo:character
glyph-orientation-vertical	fo:character
line-height score-spaces	fo:character
suppress-at-line-break	fo:character
text-decoration	fo:character, fo:initial-property-set, fo:inline, fo:page-number, fo:page-number-citation
text-shadow	fo:character, fo:initial-property-set, fo:leader, fo:page-number, fo:page-number-citation
text-transform	fo:character, fo:initial-property-set, fo:page-number, fo:page-number-citation

Property	Applies to
treat-as-word-space	fo:character
content-height	fo:external-graphic, fo:instream-foreign-object
content-type	fo:external-graphic, fo:instream-foreign-object
content-width	fo:external-graphic, fo:instream-foreign-object
scaling	fo:external-graphic, fo:instream-foreign-object
scaling-method	fo:external-graphic, fo:instream-foreign-object
xe	fo:inline-container
leader-alignment	fo:leader
leader-length	fo:leader
leader-pattern	fo:leader
leader-pattern-width	fo:leader
rule-style	fo:leader
rule-thickness	fo:leader
ref-id	fo:page-number-citation
caption-side	fo:table-and-caption
border-after-precedence	fo:table, fo:table-column, fo:table-header, fo:table-footer, fo:table-body, fo:table-row, fo:table-cell
border-before-precedence	fo:table, fo:table-column, fo:table-header, fo:table-footer, fo:table-body, fo:table-row, fo:table-cell
border-collapse	fo:table
border-end-precedence	fo:table, fo:table-column, fo:table-header, fo:table-footer, fo:table-body, fo:table-row, fo:table-cell
border-separation	fo:table
border-start-precedence	fo:table, fo:table-column, fo:table-header, fo:table-footer, fo:table-body, fo:table-row, fo:table-cell
table-layout	fo:table
table-omit-footer-at-break	fo:table
table-omit-header-at-break	fo:table
column-number	fo:table-column, fo:table-cell
column-width	fo:table-column
number-columns-repeated	fo:table-column
number-columns-spanned	fo:table-column, fo:table-cell
[7.6 Common Aural Properties] source-document	fo:table-cell
empty-cells	fo:table-cell
ends-row	fo:table-cell
number-rows-spanned	fo:table-cell

Table G-2. Properties to elements (continued)

Property	Applies to
relative-align	fo:table-cell, fo:list-item
starts-row	fo:table-cell
provisional-distance-between-starts	fo:list-block
provisional-label-separation	fo:list-block
destination-placement-offset	fo:basic-link
external-destination	fo:basic-link
indicate-destination	fo:basic-link
internal-destination	fo:basic-link
show-destination	fo:basic-link
target-presentation-context	fo:basic-link
target-processing-context	fo:basic-link
target-stylesheet	fo:basic-link
auto-restore	fo:multi-switch
case-name	fo:multi-case
case-title	fo:multi-case
starting-state	fo:multi-case
switch-to	fo:multi-toggle
active-state	fo:multi-property-set
clear	fo:float
float	fo:float
marker-class-name	fo:marker
retrieve-boundary	fo:retrieve-marker
retrieve-class-name	fo:retrieve-marker
retrieve-position	fo:retrieve-marker

GNU Free Documentation License (GFDL)

GNU Free Documentation License
Version 1.1, March 2000
Copyright © 2000 Free Software Foundation, Inc.
59 Temple Place, Suite 330, Boston, MA 02111-1307 USA

Preamble

The purpose of this License is to make a manual, textbook, or other written document "free" in the sense of freedom: to assure everyone the effective freedom to copy and redistribute it, with or without modifying it, either commercially or noncommercially. Secondarily, this License preserves for the author and publisher a way to get credit for their work, while not being considered responsible for modifications made by others.

This License is a kind of "copyleft," which means that derivative works of the document must themselves be free in the same sense. It complements the GNU General Public License, which is a copyleft license designed for free software.

We have designed this License in order to use it for manuals for free software, because free software needs free documentation: a free program should come with manuals providing the same freedoms that the software does. But this License is not limited to software manuals; it can be used for any textual work, regardless of subject matter or whether it is published as a printed book. We recommend this License principally for works whose purpose is instruction or reference.

Applicability and Definitions

This License applies to any manual or other work that contains a notice placed by the copyright holder saying it can be distributed under the terms of this License. The "Document", below, refers to any such manual or work. Any member of the public is a licensee, and is addressed as "you."

A "Modified Version" of the Document means any work containing the Document or a portion of it, either copied verbatim, or with modifications and/or translated into another language.

A "Secondary Section" is a named appendix or a front-matter section of the Document that deals exclusively with the relationship of the publishers or authors of the Document to the Document's overall subject (or to related matters) and contains nothing that could fall directly within that overall subject. (For example, if the Document is in part a textbook of mathematics, a Secondary Section may not explain any mathematics.) The relationship could be a matter of historical connection with the subject or with related matters, or of legal, commercial, philosophical, ethical or political position regarding them.

The "Invariant Sections" are certain Secondary Sections whose titles are designated, as being those of Invariant Sections, in the notice that says that the Document is released under this License.

The "Cover Texts" are certain short passages of text that are listed, as Front-Cover Texts or Back-Cover Texts, in the notice that says that the Document is released under this License.

A "Transparent" copy of the Document means a machine-readable copy, represented in a format whose specification is available to the general public, whose contents can be viewed and edited directly and straightforwardly with generic text editors or (for images composed of pixels) generic paint programs or (for drawings) some widely available drawing editor, and that is suitable for input to text formatters or for automatic translation to a variety of formats suitable for input to text formatters. A copy made in an otherwise Transparent file format whose markup has been designed to thwart or discourage subsequent modification by readers is not Transparent. A copy that is not "Transparent" is called "Opaque."

Examples of suitable formats for Transparent copies include plain ASCII without markup, Texinfo input format, LaTeX input format, SGML or XML using a publicly available DTD, and standard-conforming simple HTML designed for human modification. Opaque formats include PostScript, PDF, proprietary formats that can be read and edited only by proprietary word processors, SGML or XML for which the DTD and/or processing tools are not generally available, and the machine-generated HTML produced by some word processors for output purposes only.

The "Title Page" means, for a printed book, the title page itself, plus such following pages as are needed to hold, legibly, the material this License requires to appear in the title page. For works in formats which do not have any title page as such, "Title Page" means the text near the most prominent appearance of the work's title, preceding the beginning of the body of the text.

Verbatim Copying

You may copy and distribute the Document in any medium, either commercially or noncommercially, provided that this License, the copyright notices, and the license notice saying this License applies to the Document are reproduced in all copies, and that you add no other conditions whatsoever to those of this License. You may not use technical measures to obstruct or control the reading or further copying of the copies you make or distribute. However, you may accept compensation in exchange for copies. If you distribute a large enough number of copies you must also follow the conditions in section 3.

You may also lend copies, under the same conditions stated above, and you may publicly display copies.

Copying in Quantity

If you publish printed copies of the Document numbering more than 100, and the Document's license notice requires Cover Texts, you must enclose the copies in covers that carry, clearly and legibly, all these Cover Texts: Front-Cover Texts on the front cover, and Back-Cover Texts on the back cover. Both covers must also clearly and legibly identify you as the publisher of these copies. The front cover must present the full title with all words of the title equally prominent and visible. You may add other material on the covers in addition. Copying with changes limited to the covers, as long as they preserve the title of the Document and satisfy these conditions, can be treated as verbatim copying in other respects.

If the required texts for either cover are too voluminous to fit legibly, you should put the first ones listed (as many as fit reasonably) on the actual cover, and continue the rest onto adjacent pages.

If you publish or distribute Opaque copies of the Document numbering more than 100, you must either include a machine-readable Transparent copy along with each Opaque copy, or state in or with each Opaque copy a publicly-accessible computer-network location containing a complete Transparent copy of the Document, free of added material, which the general network-using public has access to download anonymously at no charge using public-standard network protocols. If you use the latter option, you must take reasonably prudent steps, when you begin distribution of Opaque copies in quantity, to ensure that this Transparent copy will remain thus accessible at the stated location until at least one year after the last time you distribute an Opaque copy (directly or through your agents or retailers) of that edition to the public.

It is requested, but not required, that you contact the authors of the Document well before redistributing any large number of copies, to give them a chance to provide you with an updated version of the Document.

Modifications

You may copy and distribute a Modified Version of the Document under the conditions of sections 2 and 3 above, provided that you release the Modified Version under precisely this License, with the Modified Version filling the role of the Document, thus licensing distribution and modification of the Modified Version to whoever possesses a copy of it. In addition, you must do these things in the Modified Version:

1. Use in the Title Page (and on the covers, if any) a title distinct from that of the Document, and from those of previous versions (which should, if there were any, be listed in the History section of the Document). You may use the same title as a previous version if the original publisher of that version gives permission.

2. List on the Title Page, as authors, one or more persons or entities responsible for authorship of the modifications in the Modified Version, together with at least five of the principal authors of the Document (all of its principal authors, if it has less than five).

3. State on the Title page the name of the publisher of the Modified Version, as the publisher.

4. Preserve all the copyright notices of the Document.

5. Add an appropriate copyright notice for your modifications adjacent to the other copyright notices.

6. Include, immediately after the copyright notices, a license notice giving the public permission to use the Modified Version under the terms of this License, in the form shown in the Addendum below.

7. Preserve in that license notice the full lists of Invariant Sections and required Cover Texts given in the Document's license notice.

8. Include an unaltered copy of this License.

9. Preserve the section entitled "History," and its title, and add to it an item stating at least the title, year, new authors, and publisher of the Modified Version as given on the Title Page. If there is no section entitled "History" in the Document, create one stating the title, year, authors, and publisher of the Document as given on its Title Page, then add an item describing the Modified Version as stated in the previous sentence.

10. Preserve the network location, if any, given in the Document for public access to a Transparent copy of the Document, and likewise the network locations given in the Document for previous versions it was based on. These may be placed in the "History" section. You may omit a network location for a work that was published at least four years before the Document itself, or if the original publisher of the version it refers to gives permission.

11. In any section entitled "Acknowledgements" or "Dedications," preserve the section's title, and preserve in the section all the substance and tone of each of the contributor acknowledgements and/or dedications given therein.

12. Preserve all the Invariant Sections of the Document, unaltered in their text and in their titles. Section numbers or the equivalent are not considered part of the section titles.

13. Delete any section entitled "Endorsements." Such a section may not be included in the Modified Version.

14. Do not retitle any existing section as "Endorsements" or to conflict in title with any Invariant Section.

If the Modified Version includes new front-matter sections or appendices that qualify as Secondary Sections and contain no material copied from the Document, you may at your option designate some or all of these sections as invariant. To do this, add their titles to the list of Invariant Sections in the Modified Version's license notice. These titles must be distinct from any other section titles.

You may add a section entitled "Endorsements," provided it contains nothing but endorsements of your Modified Version by various parties—for example, statements of peer review or that the text has been approved by an organization as the authoritative definition of a standard.

You may add a passage of up to five words as a Front-Cover Text, and a passage of up to 25 words as a Back-Cover Text, to the end of the list of Cover Texts in the Modified Version. Only one passage of Front-Cover Text and one of Back-Cover Text may be added by (or through arrangements made by) any one entity. If the Document already includes a cover text for the same cover, previously added by you or by arrangement made by the same entity you are acting on behalf of, you may not add another; but you may replace the old one, on explicit permission from the previous publisher that added the old one.

The author(s) and publisher(s) of the Document do not by this License give permission to use their names for publicity for or to assert or imply endorsement of any Modified Version.

Combining Documents

You may combine the Document with other documents released under this License, under the terms defined in section 4 above for modified versions, provided that you include in the combination all of the Invariant Sections of all of the original documents, unmodified, and list them all as Invariant Sections of your combined work in its license notice.

The combined work need only contain one copy of this License, and multiple identical Invariant Sections may be replaced with a single copy. If there are multiple Invariant Sections with the same name but different contents, make the title of each such section unique by adding at the end of it, in parentheses, the name of the original author or publisher of that section if known, or else a unique number. Make the same adjustment to the section titles in the list of Invariant Sections in the license notice of the combined work.

In the combination, you must combine any sections entitled "History" in the various original documents, forming one section entitled "History"; likewise combine any sections entitled "Acknowledgements," and any sections entitled "Dedications." You must delete all sections entitled "Endorsements."

Collections of Documents

You may make a collection consisting of the Document and other documents released under this License, and replace the individual copies of this License in the various documents with a single copy that is included in the collection, provided that you follow the rules of this License for verbatim copying of each of the documents in all other respects.

You may extract a single document from such a collection, and distribute it individually under this License, provided you insert a copy of this License into the extracted document, and follow this License in all other respects regarding verbatim copying of that document.

Aggregation with Independent Works

A compilation of the Document or its derivatives with other separate and independent documents or works, in or on a volume of a storage or distribution medium, does not as a whole count as a Modified Version of the Document, provided no compilation copyright is claimed for the compilation. Such a compilation is called an "aggregate," and this License does not apply to the other self-contained works thus compiled with the Document, on account of their being thus compiled, if they are not themselves derivative works of the Document.

If the Cover Text requirement of section 3 is applicable to these copies of the Document, then if the Document is less than one quarter of the entire aggregate, the Document's Cover Texts may be placed on covers that surround only the Document within the aggregate. Otherwise they must appear on covers around the whole aggregate.

Translation

Translation is considered a kind of modification, so you may distribute translations of the Document under the terms of section 4. Replacing Invariant Sections with translations requires special permission from their copyright holders, but you may include translations of some or all Invariant Sections in addition to the original versions of these Invariant Sections. You may include a translation of this License provided that you also include the original English version of this License. In case of a disagreement between the translation and the original English version of this License, the original English version will prevail.

Termination

You may not copy, modify, sublicense, or distribute the Document except as expressly provided for under this License. Any other attempt to copy, modify, sublicense or distribute the Document is void, and will automatically terminate your rights under this License. However, parties who have received copies, or rights, from you under this License will not have their licenses terminated so long as such parties remain in full compliance.

Future Revisions of This License

The Free Software Foundation may publish new, revised versions of the GNU Free Documentation License from time to time. Such new versions will be similar in spirit to the present version, but may differ in detail to address new problems or concerns. See *http://www.gnu.org/copyleft/*.

Each version of the License is given a distinguishing version number. If the Document specifies that a particular numbered version of this License "or any later version" applies to it, you have the option of following the terms and conditions either of that specified version or of any later version that has been published (not as a draft) by the Free Software Foundation. If the Document does not specify a version number of this License, you may choose any version ever published (not as a draft) by the Free Software Foundation.

Addendum: How to Use This License for Your Documents

To use this License in a document you have written, include a copy of the License in the document and put the following copyright and license notices just after the title page:

> Copyright © YEAR YOUR NAME.
>
> Permission is granted to copy, distribute and/or modify this document under the terms of the GNU Free Documentation License, Version 1.1 or any later version published by the Free Software Foundation; with the Invariant Sections being LIST THEIR TITLES, with the Front-Cover Texts being LIST, and with the Back-Cover Texts being LIST. A copy of the license is included in the section entitled "GNU Free Documentation License".

If you have no Invariant Sections, write "with no Invariant Sections" instead of saying which ones are invariant. If you have no Front-Cover Texts, write "no Front-Cover Texts" instead of "Front-Cover Texts being LIST"; likewise for Back-Cover Texts.

If your document contains nontrivial examples of program code, we recommend releasing these examples in parallel under your choice of free software license, such as the GNU General Public License, to permit their use in free software.

Glossary

alignment point

A particular point on each glyph to align any given script.

alphabetic baseline

The alignment point on a Western script used to determine the baseline for other glyphs in similar scripts.

area tree

An ordered tree containing geometric information for the placement of every glyph, shape, and image in the document, together with information embodying spacing constraints and other rendering information.

back-tracking (with regard to refinement)

Re-formatting a page area that has already been formatted.

baseline-tables

A part of the font tables provided to a formatter. Determines the alignment points between different fonts.

block-progression-direction

The direction in which blocks are stacked when building a page. From a Western perspective, this is top to bottom, more specifically, it starts at the before-edge, and ends at the after-edge.

Breaks

Page breaks may occur as determined by the formatter's processing as affected by the widow, orphan, keep-with-next, keep-with-previous, and keep-together properties.

Break conditions are either break-before or break-after. A break-before condition is satisfied if the first area generated and returned by the formatting object is leading within a context-area. A break-after condition depends on the next formatting object in the flow; the condition is satisfied if either there is no such next formatting object, or if the first normal area generated and returned by that formatting object is leading in a context-area.

Break conditions are imposed by the break-before and break-after properties. A refined value of page for these traits imposes a break condition with a context consisting of the page-reference-areas; a value of even-page or odd-page imposes a break condition with a context of even-numbered page-reference-areas or odd-numbered page-reference-areas, respectively; a value of column imposes a break condition with a context of column-areas. A value of auto in a break-before or break-after trait imposes no break condition.

flow map

The assignment of flows to regions on a page-master is determined by a flow-map. The flow-map is an association between the flow children of the fo:page-sequence and regions defined within the page-masters referenced by that fo:page-sequence.

font

A collection of glyphs together with the font tables necessary to use those glyphs to present characters via a formatter.

formatting

The process of turning the result of an XSL transformation into a tangible form for the reader, either on paper or on screen.

formatting objects

Elements in the formatting object tree whose names are from the XSL namespace; a formatting object belongs to a class of formatting objects identified by its element name. Some formatting objects are block-level and others are inline-level. Conceptually, processing a formatting object creates areas and returns them to its parent to be placed in the area tree.

glyph

A recognizable graphic symbol independent of any specific design. The letter A, as seen here, is a glyph with a specific design. The abstract form is the glyph.

ideographic baseline

The alignment point on Far-Eastern scripts, used to determine the baseline for other glyphs in similar scripts.

Indic baseline

The alignment point on Indic scripts, used to determine the baseline for other glyphs in similar scripts. Often aligned to a hanging baseline.

inline-progression-direction

From a Western perspective, left to right, going in the direction of line layout. More generally, following the direction at right angles to the block-progression-direction. Specifically, it leads from the start edge to the end edge of the page.

keeps

Keep conditions are either keep-with-previous, keep-with-next, or keep-together. A keep-with-previous condition on an object is satisfied if the first area generated and returned by the for-matting object is not leading within a context-area, or if there are no preceding areas in a post-order traversal of the area tree. A keep-with-next condition is satisfied if the last area generated and returned by the formatting object is not trailing within a context-area, or if there are no following areas in a pre-order traversal of the area tree. A keep-together condition is satisfied if all areas generated and returned by the formatting object are descendants of a single context-area.

Keep conditions are imposed by the within-page, within-column, and within-line components of the keep-with-previous, keep-with-next, and keep-together properties. The refined value of each component specifies the strength of the keep condition imposed, with higher numbers being stronger than lower numbers and the value always being stronger than all numeric values. A component with a value of auto does not impose a keep condition. A within-page component imposes a keep condition with context consisting of the page-reference-areas; within-column, with context consisting of the column-areas; and within-line with context consisting of the line-areas.

leaders

The idea of a line leading the eye across a page to join two pieces of content.

length-range

The range of values specified by the minimum, maximum, and optimum values.

line-progression-direction

In most Western scripts, the left-to-right direction across the page.

page-level-out-of-line

An area with area-class xsl-footnote, xsl-before-float, or xsl-fixed; placement of these areas is controlled by the fo:page-sequence ancestor of its generating formatting object. A reference-level-out-of-line area is an area with area-class xsl-side-float or xsl-absolute; placement of these areas is controlled by the formatting object generating the relevant reference-area. An anchor area is an area with area-class xsl-anchor; placement of these areas is arbitrary and does not affect stacking. Areas with area-class equal to one of xsl-normal, xsl-footnote, or xsl-before-float are defined to be stackable, indicating that they are supposed to be properly stacked.

page-number-citation

The fo:page-number-citation element is used to reference the page number for the page containing the first normal area returned by the cited formatting object. It may be used to provide the page numbers in the table of contents, cross-references, and index entries.

page-sequence

Pages are generated by the formatter's processing of fo:page-sequence elements. The fo:page-sequence formatting object is used to specify how to create a (sub)sequence of pages within a document; for example, a chapter of a report. The content of these pages comes from flow children of the fo:page-sequence. The children of the fo:page-sequences, which are called flows (contained in fo:flow and fo:static-content), provide the content that is distributed into the pages. Page-sequence-masters have the role of describing the sequence of page-masters that will be used to generate pages during the formatting of an fo:page-sequence.

out-of-line

Formatting object content that is formatted into a separate area of a page where it is available to be read without immediately intruding on the reader.

Refinement

This is a computational process that finalizes the specification of properties based on the attribute values in the XML result tree.

reference areas

The Boolean trait is-reference-area determines whether or not an area establishes a coordinate system for specifying indents. An area for which this trait is true is called a reference-area. Only a reference-area may have a block-progression-direction that is different from that of its parent. A reference-area may be either a block-area or an inline-area.

script.

A collection of glyphs used in one specific language. A Western alphabet is a script.

sub-sequence-specifiers

A sequence of simple-page-master-references specified as the children of a page-sequence-master.

traits

Traits are to areas what properties are to formatting objects and attributes are to XML elements.

writing-mode

The XSL relative frame of reference has four directions (before, after, start, and end), but these are relative to the writing-mode. The writing-mode property is a way of controlling the directions needed by a formatter to correctly place glyphs, words, lines, blocks, etc. on the page or screen. The writing-mode expresses the basic directions noted above. There are writing-modes for left-to-right–top-to-bottom (denoted as lr-tb), right-to-left–top-to-bottom (denoted as rl-tb), top-to-bottom–right-to-left (denoted as tb-rl), and more.

Typically, the writing-mode value specifies two directions: the first is the inline-progression-direction, which determines the direction in which words will be placed, and the second is the block-progression-direction, which determines the direction in which blocks (and lines) are placed.

viewport

The Boolean trait `is-viewport-area` determines whether or not an area establishes an opening through which its descendant areas can be viewed and can be used to present clipped or scrolled material; for example, in printing applications where bleed and trim is desired. An area for which this trait is true is called a viewport-area. For example, `region-body` specifies a viewport/reference pair that is located in the center of the `fo:simple-pagemaster`.

Index

We'd like to hear your suggestions for improving our indexes. Send email to *index@oreilly.com*.

blocks (*continued*)
  importance of identifying/
    understanding, 17
  indented, 85
  last line of, 86
  length specification and, 110
  line-areas and, 66
  positioning of, 73–75
  separating from one another, 88
  side floats and, 74
  special uses of, 91–95
  stacking, 75–78
  types of, 83
  as wrappers, 90
  (see also entries at fo:block)
body element, 22
body of document (see main matter)
body of page, 11
body-start( ) function, 101
bold/bolder font weight, 114
border-before property, 26
border-collapse property, column headings
    and, 106
border properties, 25
  color and, 129
border rectangle, 68
border-{side}-color property, 132
border-start property, 26
borders, 84, 96–98
  section about in XSL specification, 177
br element (HTML), 18
break-after property, 71
  using for special-purpose blocks, 92
break-before property, 70
  using for special-purpose blocks, 92
breaks, 70
  properties for, section about in XSL
    specification, 177
  using blocks as, 87
bricks, 181
bullets, 100
  numbers as, 102

C

C switch block, 52
capitalization, text-transform property
    for, 144
caption-side property, 105
captions
  for images, 94
  for tables, 105

Cascading Style Sheets (see CSS)
case sensitivity, text-transform property
    for, 144
CCW rotations, 37
cells, 109
centimeters (cm), 141
chapters of book, 54
  titles of, including in header/footer, 153,
    173
characters, 133–145
  last on either end of a line, 136
  mapped to glyphs, 139
  non printable, 135
  single, formatting, 134
  styling vs. inline-level styling, 133
  subscript/superscript and, 137, 174
  uppercase/lowercase, 144
  (see also text)
chunks, 46
Clark, James, 13, 14
cm (centimeters), 141
color keyword, 130
color-profile-name property, 131
color property, 129
  formatting objects applied to, 132
colors, 126, 129–132
  background-color property and, 93
  border, 129
  caution with, 129
  decorating blocks and, 96–100
  foreground/background, 129
  names of, 131
  properties for (list), 132
column-areas, 67
column-count property, 45
column headings, 106
columns, 106–109
compliance, 6, 19
  section about in XSL specification, 178
compound datatypes, 28
  section about in XSL specification, 177
.conditionality attribute, 79
conditionality, section about in XSL
    specification, 176
conditions, setting for pages, 51–59
conformance, 25
  section about in XSL specification, 178
constraint relaxation, 72
content
  correcting position of, 172
  derivative, 46
  inline elements and, 112

title page
    included with sample stylesheet, 160, 161
    using blocks for, 91
titles, for images, 94
tools, 5–7, 179–185
trailing areas, 70
traits, 52
treat-as-word-space property, 135
troubleshooting, 171–174

U

UFO formatter, 7, 181
underline option, 114, 143
Unicode
    default writing modes and, 136
    word separators and, 135
Unicorn Formatting Objects formatter, 7,
        181
units, section about in XSL specification, 177
uppercase characters, 144
URLs
    Arbortext, 184
    for this book, xv
    CSS2 specification, 175
    FOA tool, 182
    FOP formatter, 180
    jfor, 182
    Nextsolution, 14
    OpenType specification, 139
    PassiveTeX formatter, 180
    REXP, 182
    UFO formatter, 181
    XFC converter, 183
    XSL specification, 175
U.S. letter page size, 34
utilities, 5–7, 179–185

V

vector graphics, fo:instream-foreign-object
        element for, 116
viewport-area/reference-area pair, 41
viewports, 33

W

WAP messages, 14
white-space-collapse property, 171
white-space property, 171
whitespace, 171
    line-height property and, 117
widows and orphans, 72

width properties, section about in XSL
        specification, 177
WML, 16
word processors, 1
word-spacing property, 116
wrap-option property, 171
wrapping blocks, 90
writing-mode property, 37
    blocks and, 35
    character orientation and, 136
    regions and, 38

X

XEP formatter (RenderX), 179
XFC converter, 183
XML (Extensible Markup Language)
    document processing and, 1–3
    Epic editor for, 184
    id and idref pairings from, 95
    using to document stylesheets, 166
XML source document, 9
XMLmind FO Converter, 183
XPath, 4, 17
XSL (Extensible Stylesheet Language), 16
    indents/margins and, 74
    specification for (see XSL specification)
    pagination and, 33
XSL-FO
    benefits/cautions for print production vs.
            alternatives, 3
    vs. CSS, 14
    vs. DSSSL, 13
    processing steps in, 9
    specification for (see XSL specification)
    terminology evolution of, 16
    tricks and tips/troubleshooting
            for, 171–174
    XPath/XSLT related to, 17
XSL-FO documents, 9, 10
    main parts of, 31–33
    (see also stylesheets)
XSL-FO element set, 12
XSL-FO processors (see formatters)
XSL formatters (see formatters)
xsl namespace (see fo namespace)
xsl:number element (XSLT), 149
    footnotes and, 172
<xsl:preserve-space> (XSLT), 171
xsl-region-after, 12, 42
xsl-region-before, 12, 42
xsl-region-body, 12, 42
xsl-region-end, 42

About the Author

Dave Pawson maintains the XSLT and XSL-FO FAQ site. He got started with XML in 1997, while looking for a means of document reuse for multimedia presentation in print and Braille for the Royal National Institute of the Blind (RNIB). He is the W3C Advisory Committee representative for the RNIB, and he has supported the Web Accessibility Initiative since 1998. His background is in software development in the aerospace industry, followed by five years with RNIB, where he initially worked as a change agent and has more recently been monitoring web standards for accessibility. He has been heavily involved in the digital talking book initiative coordinated by the DAISY consortium (*http://www.daisy.org*).

Colophon

Our look is the result of reader comments, our own experimentation, and feedback from distribution channels. Distinctive covers complement our distinctive approach to technical topics, breathing personality and life into potentially dry subjects.

The animal on the cover of *XSL-FO* is a pennant-winged nightjar. Pennant-winged nightjars (*Macrodipteryx vexillarius*) are night-flying birds native to southern parts of Africa. Nightjars are also known in some areas as goatsuckers, because they were once thought to drink the milk of goats. However, they are actually insectivores and were probably common near goats because of the insects the animals attract.

Pennant-winged nightjars have long, pointed wings; weak feet; and small, wide bills. Fluffy feathers make them almost noiseless fliers. Males are known for their long, black-and-white, pennant-like feathers that flutter like streamers to attract mates. When a male finds a mate, his long feathers fall off.

Linley Dolby was the production editor and proofreader, and Tatiana Apandi Diaz was the copyeditor for *XSL-FO*. Darren Kelly, Rachel Wheeler, and Claire Cloutier provided quality control. Derek Di Matteo and Phil Dangler provided production support. Brenda Miller wrote the index.

Hanna Dyer designed the cover of this book, based on a series design by Edie Freedman. The cover image is a 19th-century engraving from the Dover Pictorial Archive. Emma Colby produced the cover layout with QuarkXPress 4.1 using Adobe's ITC Garamond font.

David Futato designed the interior layout. This book was converted to FrameMaker 5.5.6 with a format conversion tool created by Erik Ray, Jason McIntosh, Neil Walls, and Mike Sierra that uses Perl and XML technologies. The text font is Linotype Birka; the heading font is Adobe Myriad Condensed; and the code font is Lucas-Font's TheSans Mono Condensed. The illustrations that appear in the book were produced by Robert Romano and Jessamyn Read using Macromedia FreeHand 9 and Adobe Photoshop 6. The tip and warning icons were drawn by Christopher Bing. This colophon was written by Linley Dolby.

More Titles from O'Reilly

XML

XML in a Nutshell

By Elliotte Rusty Harold & W. Scott Means
1st Edition December 2000
400 pages, ISBN 0-596-00058-8

XML in a Nutshell is just what serious XML developers need in order to take full advantage of XML's incredible potential: a comprehensive, easy-to-access desktop reference to the fundamental rules that all XML documents and authors must adhere to. This book details the grammar that specifies where tags may be placed, what they must look like, which element names are legal, how attributes attach to elements, and much more.

Java and XSLT

By Eric M. Burke
1st Edition September 2001
528 pages, ISBN 0-596-00143-6

Learn how to use XSL transformations in Java programs ranging from stand-alone applications to servlets. *Java and XSLT* introduces XSLT and then shows you how to apply transformations in real-world situations, such as developing a discussion forum, transforming documents from one form to another, and generating content for wireless devices.

Learning XML

By Erik T. Ray with Christopher R. Maden
1st Edition January 2001
368 pages, ISBN 0-596-00046-4

XML (Extensible Markup Language) is a flexible way to create "self-describing data"—and to share both the format and the data on the World Wide Web, intranets, and elsewhere. In *Learning XML*, the authors explain XML and its capabilities succinctly and professionally, with references to real-life projects and other cogent examples. *Learning XML* shows the purpose of XML markup itself, the CSS and XSL styling languages, and the XLink and XPointer specifications for creating rich link structures.

XSLT

By Doug Tidwell
1st Edition August 2001
473 pages, ISBN 0-596-00053-7

XSLT (Extensible Stylesheet Language Transformations) is a critical bridge between XML processing and more familiar HTML, and dominates the market for conversions between XML vocabularies. Useful as XSLT is, its complexities can be daunting. Doug Tidwell, a developer with years of XSLT experience, eases the pain by building from the basics to the more complex and powerful possibilities of XSLT, so you can jump in at your own level of expertise.

Java & XML, 2nd Edition

By Brett McLaughlin
2nd Edition September 2001
528 pages, ISBN 0-596-00197-5

New chapters on Advanced SAX, Advanced DOM, SOAP, and data binding, as well as new examples throughout, bring the second edition of *Java & XML* thoroughly up to date. Except for a concise introduction to XML basics, the book focuses entirely on using XML from Java applications. It's a worthy companion for Java developers working with XML or involved in messaging, web services, or the new peer-to-peer movement.

XML Pocket Reference, 2nd Edition

By Robert Eckstein with Michel Casabianca
2nd Edition April 2001
102 pages, ISBN 0-596-00133-9

The *XML Pocket Reference* is both a handy introduction to XML terminology and syntax, and a quick reference to XML instructions, attributes, entities, and datatypes. Although XML itself is complex, its basic concepts are simple. This small book combines a perfect tutorial for learning the basics of XML with a reference to the XML and XSL specifications. The new edition introduces information on XSLT (Extensible Stylesheet Language Transformations) and Xpath.

XML

SAX2

By David Brownell
1st Edition January 2002
240 pages, ISBN 0-596-00237-8

This concise book gives you information you need to effectively use the Simple API for XML (SAX2), the dominant API for efficient XML processing with Java. With SAX2, developers have access to information in XML documents as they are read without imposing major memory constraints or a large code footprint. SAX2 gives you the detail and examples required to use SAX2 to its full potential.

SVG Essentials

By J. David Eisenberg
1st Edition, February 2002
368 pages, ISBN 0-596-00223-8

SVG Essentials shows developers how to take advantage of SVG's open text-based format. Although SVG is much more approachable than the binary or PostScript files that have dominated graphics formats so far, developers need a roadmap to get started creating and processing SVG files. This book provides an introduction and reference to the foundations developers need to use SVG, and demonstrates techniques for generating SVG from other XML formats.

Programming Jabber

By DJ Adams
1st Edition January 2002
480 pages, ISBN 0-596-00202-5

This book will offer programmers a chance to learn and understand the Jabber technology and protocol from an implementer's point of view. Every detail of every part of the Jabber client protocol is introduced, explained, discussed, and covered in the form of recipes, mini-projects or simple and extended examples in Perl, Python, and Java. *Programming Jabber* provides a walk-through of the foundation elements that are common to any messaging solution, including a detailed overview of the Jabber server architecture.

Web Services Essentials

By Ethan Cerami
1st Edition February 2002
304 pages, ISBN 0-596-00224-6

This concise book gives programmers both a concrete introduction and handy reference to XML web services. It explains the foundations of this new breed of distributed services, demonstrates quick ways to create services with open-source Java tools, and explores four key emerging technologies: XML-RPC, SOAP, UDDI, and WSDL. If you want to break through the Web Services hype and find useful information on these evolving technologies, look no further.

Programming Web Services with XML-RPC

By Simon St.Laurent, Joe Johnston & Edd Dumbill
Foreword by Dave Winer
1st Edition June 2001
230 pages, ISBN 0-596-00119-3

XML-RPC, a simple yet powerful system built on XML and HTTP, lets developers connect programs running on different computers with a minimum of fuss. Java programs can talk to Perl scripts, which can talk to ASP applications, and so on. With XML-RPC, developers can provide access to functionality without having to worry about the system on the other end, so it's easy to create web services.

Programming Web Services with SOAP

By James Snell, Doug Tidwell & Pavel Kulchenko
1st Edition December 2001
264 pages, ISBN 0-596-00095-2

In typical O'Reilly fashion this book moves beyond the theoretical and explains how to build and implement SOAP web services. The book begins with a solid introduction to SOAP, detailing its history and structure, followed by an introduction to the three major types of SOAP applications: SOAP-RPC, SOAP-Messaging, and SOAP-Intermediaries. Each SOAP application is illustrated with an in-depth implementation.

O'REILLY®

TO ORDER: *800-998-9938* • *order@oreilly.com* • *www.oreilly.com*
ONLINE EDITIONS OF MOST O'REILLY TITLES ARE AVAILABLE BY SUBSCRIPTION AT *safari.oreilly.com*
ALSO AVAILABLE AT MOST RETAIL AND ONLINE BOOKSTORES

XML

Perl & XML

By Erik T. Ray, Jason McIntosh
1st Edition April 2002
224 pages, ISBN 0-596-00205-X

Perl & XML is aimed at Perl programmers who need to work with XML documents and data. This book gives a complete, comprehensive tour of the landscape of Perl and XML, making sense of the myriad of modules, terminology, and techniques. The last two chapters of Perl and XML give complete examples of XML applications, pulling together all the tools at your disposal.

Python & XML

By Christopher A. Jones & Fred Drake
1st Edition December 2001
378 pages, ISBN 0-596-00128-2

This book has two objectives: to provide a comprehensive reference on using XML with Python and to illustrate the practical applications of these technologies (often coupled with cross-platform tools) in an enterprise environment. Loaded with practical examples, it also shows how to use Python to create scalable XML connections between popular distributed applications such as databases and web servers. Covers XML flow analysis and details ways to transport XML through a network.

O'REILLY®

TO ORDER: **800-998-9938** • **order@oreilly.com** • **www.oreilly.com**
ONLINE EDITIONS OF MOST O'REILLY TITLES ARE AVAILABLE BY SUBSCRIPTION AT **safari.oreilly.com**
ALSO AVAILABLE AT MOST RETAIL AND ONLINE BOOKSTORES

How to stay in touch with O'Reilly

1. Visit our award-winning web site

http://www.oreilly.com/

★ "Top 100 Sites on the Web"—PC Magazine
★ CIO Magazine's Web Business 50 Awards

Our web site contains a library of comprehensive product information (including book excerpts and tables of contents), downloadable software, background articles, interviews with technology leaders, links to relevant sites, book cover art, and more. File us in your bookmarks or favorites!

2. Join our email mailing lists

Sign up to get email announcements of new books and conferences, special offers, and O'Reilly Network technology newsletters at:

http://www.elists.oreilly.com

It's easy to customize your free elists subscription so you'll get exactly the O'Reilly news you want.

3. Get examples from our books

To find example files for a book, go to:

http://www.oreilly.com/catalog

select the book, and follow the "Examples" link.

4. Work with us

Check out our web site for current employment opportunites:

http://jobs.oreilly.com/

5. Register your book

Register your book at:
http://register.oreilly.com

6. Contact us

O'Reilly & Associates, Inc.
1005 Gravenstein Hwy North
Sebastopol, CA 95472 USA
TEL: 707-827-7000 or 800-998-9938
          (6am to 5pm PST)
FAX: 707-829-0104

order@oreilly.com
For answers to problems regarding your order or our products. To place a book order online visit:

http://www.oreilly.com/order_new/

catalog@oreilly.com
To request a copy of our latest catalog.

booktech@oreilly.com
For book content technical questions or corrections.

proposals@oreilly.com
To submit new book proposals to our editors and product managers.

international@oreilly.com
For information about our international distributors or translation queries. For a list of our distributors outside of North America check out:

http://international.oreilly.com/distributors.html

O'REILLY®

TO ORDER: **800-998-9938** • **order@oreilly.com** • **www.oreilly.com**
ONLINE EDITIONS OF MOST O'REILLY TITLES ARE AVAILABLE BY SUBSCRIPTION AT **safari.oreilly.com**
ALSO AVAILABLE AT MOST RETAIL AND ONLINE BOOKSTORES

Notes